The Southern Swamp Explorer

written and illustrated by **Irene Brady**

The Explorer Library

Nature Works Press

Acknowledgements

Creating this book has been a work of love. To me, a swamp is a thing of profound beauty and deep mystery. I have sketched and photographed in many of them now, and immersed myself in the amazing croaks, creaks, yelps, and roars of herons, fish crows, frogs, crickets, cicadas, alligators, bitterns, hawks, and barred owls, to name a few. I have chased fireflies and armadillos in the steamy, ebony darkness of a swampy verge, and gone nose-to-nose with a massive cottonmouth snake. I've watched alligator mothers guard their young, night-herons build their nests, banners of pink ibises stream overhead, and golden-silk spiders recreate their webs after my passing. I've smelled the rich scents of heron rookeries and yellow jessamine. If I could, I would live there forever.

But since I don't live in or near any swamps, I have approached these mysteries with a clean slate and deep curiosity. Spending time whenever I could in swamps, bogs, marshes, bayous, and bottomlands, I have wandered into fantastic vistas and secret nooks, and met a whole raft of wonderful people who love their wetlands deeply. Some of them welcomed me into their lives for a brief time to show me the dark reaches of their swamps, the innumerable water plants and the shy animals they know and love. They gave me lodging, took me swamping, identified and provided skulls and seeds and flowers for sketching, offered advice, and helped me in many other ways both tangible and intangible. To those tireless protectors of the magical swamps, this book is dedicated.

Many swamps and wet environs I visited throughout the Southeast added to my store of knowlege, including Acadiana Park Nature Trail & Station, Andrews Wildlife Management Area, Bayou Segnette State Park, Big Thicket National Preserve, Blackwater River State Forest, Cecil Webb Wildlife Management Area, Charlotte Harbor Environmental Center, Congaree National Park, Corkscrew Swamp Sanctuary, Cypress Island Preserve, Davis Bayou, Ding Darling National Wildlife Refuge, Everglades National Park, Francis Beidler Forest in Four-Holes Swamp, Fakahatchee Strand, Homosassa Springs, Honey Island Nature Trail, Honey Island Swamp, Jay B. Starkey Wilderness Area, Jean Lafitte National Historical Park Nature Trail, Myakka State Park, Ochlokonee State Park, Okeefenokee National Wildlife Refuge, Okeefenokee Swamp Park, Six-mile Cypress Slough, Stephen C. Foster State Park, Washoe Preserve, White Kitchen Preserve, and little pullouts alongside the road.

The sights, insights, and sounds I encountered, and the observations I made during my sojourns, are in this book as I experienced them. Further sketches and notes were made at the Charleston Museum, Cypress Gardens Aquarium, and at the Biophilia Nature Center where Carol Lovell-Saas is recreating a swamp from a long-abused acreage, and shared with me her knowledge and her collection of native plants and insects.

For assistance in preparing the Swamp Highlight pages, I thank Wanda Lee Dickey, Claire Coco, John Grego, Jason Lauritsen, Regina Mahoney, Carol Lovell-Saas, Bob Thomas, Matt Fagan, Norman Brunswig, Andrew Blascovich, and Eric Brunden.

I sketched and photographed the animals in several wildlife rehabilitation centers. I'd like to thank Michael Ruggieri at Flamingo Gardens, Dr. Deb Anderson at The Wildlife Care Center, and Gail Straight at Wildlife Inc. who allowed me to draw their wood ducklings, baby opossums and gray squirrels, white-tailed kites, black vultures, moorhens, and other creatures.

Some of my research was done in the Francis Beidler Forest in Four Holes Swamp, an Audubon Sanctuary where I was given free run of the environs for ten days. Daytimes, I wandered everywhere with my camera and sketchpad, then I soaked up owl calls and firefly sparkles at the end of the boardwalk after dark. I was put up in the researcher's cabin and looked after and shepherded by Barb Thomas and Millie Chaplin from the Visitor Center; Mike Dawson, the Assistant Sanctuary Manager; Ann Shahid, the Naturalist; and the two internists, Barbara & Chuck, whose last names I never learned. Most importantly, I was given a personal tour through the sanctuary – replete with alligators, ibises, and turtles – by the Sanctuary Director, Norm Brunswig, who knows his swamp like the back of his hand. John, who lived nearby, identified local wildflowers and showed me a bog filled with pitcher plants and sundews.

Dr. Bob Thomas, who holds the Loyola Chair in Environmental Communications, took me on an illuminating bayou tour, and was always available via email to answer swampy questions – and found the time to do a critical final edit of the scientific details and write the foreword. Dr. Paul Wagner showed me his famous Honey Island Swamp, and undertook a crucial edit. Ann Shahid and Norm Brunswig of Francis Beidler Forest, and Fran Rametta of Congaree Swamp, examined the manuscript for accuracy. Kelley Weitzel gave invaluable advice and guidance on ancient Southeastern Native Americans and their cultures. Daniel Bish, David Brady, Diane Harris, Laura O'Brady, Marcia Way-Brady, Ben Brady, Darby Morrell, Cathy Egelston, Jackie Clay, Abe Karam, Martin David Harris, Sharon Heisel, and the late Dave Luman also edited and annotated the book's content, grammar and flow. Stephanie Sue Collison joined me for swamping in Florida and South Carolina.

The following people gave generously of their help in various other ways, both in person and on the web: Amanda Brooks, Sidney W. Dunkle, Eric R. Eaton, Nick Fensler, Martin Golden, Walter Gould, Mac Kobza, Bill Loftus, Deb & Vin Lula, Andrew Moldenke, Sue Perry, Zachary Prusak, Amanda Brooks Queen, Brad Robinson, Steve Robinson, Sue Shearouse, Petra Sierwald, Roberta Silfen, Derek Sikes, Sarah Singleton, Charles Storrs, Joel Trexler, Sue Williams, and Doug Yanega.

I sincerely apologise to anyone for whose efforts I have neglected to express appreciation – it has taken nearly seven years to complete this book, and I may have lost your name in the process.

I take full reponsibility for any errors found in this book. There's no way to create a book of this scope without extensive help, and I have had the best there is. I thank you all.

Published and distributed by:

Nature Works Press

For reviews of this book
and ordering information visit
www.natureworkspress.com
info@natureworkspress.com

PO Box 469
Talent, OR 97540

Table of Contents

Foreword by Bob Thomas

The word "swamp" elicits a variety of images. Some people picture a swamp as a scary, dank place with danger lurking behind every tree. Others think of it as a curious place that is distantly enchanting. Many of us, however, look upon a swamp as an intriguing ecosystem full of wonders and endless discoveries that we simply must investigate. This excellent book will nudge more people into the latter category.

My first memory of swamps is from my childhood in the early 1950s, when my family passed through Louisiana on a trek across the Gulf Coast. I remember looking out the car window as we passed bayous and swamps, and wondering about the alligators, turtles, snakes, and people who lived in those forbidding wooded wetlands.

In the late 1950s, my family relocated to central Louisiana, and we lived beside Rapides Bayou, which teemed with snakes, frogs, turtles, egrets, wood ducks, and an occasional alligator. That bayou, its adjacent swamps, and the friends with whom I enjoyed many adventures, turned me into an avid naturalist.

Life has never been the same since!

Swamps are complex ecosystems. Though certain plants and animals are found in most swamps, there is variation throughout the Southeast. Even in adjacent swamps, some species will replace others because of slight differences in the swamp's makeup. Nevertheless, there is an encompassing image of swamps which makes them a magnet to their admirers. We find it difficult to drive by a beautiful swamp without stopping to see what lurks along the edge and wonder what is watching from the inky depths.

Not only are swamps home to an amazing number of interesting creatures, they are intertwined with the ecosystems around them. Swamps depend on nearby natural levees and bottomland hardwoods for many of their nutrients, and they, in turn, feed neighboring freshwater marshes. Some creatures move freely between adjacent habitats, while others stay in one place. As a teen, I learned, for example, that if I wanted to find chicken turtles and southern painted turtles, I had to wade into the swamps and move stealthily with net in hand. My chances of finding beautiful red-and-black mud snakes were better if I worked the edges of the swamps at night. And the best place to hear bird-voiced tree frogs was in swamps, not open wetlands.

The Southern Swamp Explorer* is a book I would have loved to possess in my youth. In fact, in my seasoned age, I am absolutely captivated with the natural history information contained in this book. Its unique presentation style adds to the enjoyment.

Irene Brady has masterfully woven a profusion of interesting facts into a story of sequential events in an imaginary (yet very possible) swamp. Thus, she introduces the reader to the interconnected lives of swamp denizens and their habitats, brilliantly demonstrating the very meaning of the word *ecosystem*.

This creative, intriguing guide will forever change your opinion of swamps. I will definitely give one to each of my grandchildren, and will highly recommend it to friends and colleagues of all ages!

Robert A. (Bob) Thomas. Ph.D
Center for Environmental Communication
Loyola University New Orleans

*WARNING: This book will give you a serious case of *swampatitis*. Symptoms include a great yearning to know more about swamps, an uncontrollable desire to hike around and through swamps, an irresistable urge to collect supplemental field guides, and a gradual webbing of the toes!

Have You Ever Gone Swamping?

It's interesting to read a book like this about wet swampy places and the fascinating lives of the animals and plants that live there. But it's even more interesting to visit such a place and see it with your own eyes. The real adventure comes when you wander down a boardwalk out into the heart of a swamp, marsh or bog, and feel and hear and experience it for yourself.

There are thousands of wetlands all over the United States which you can visit. Some have trails and boardwalks to help you get up close to these fascinating habitats without getting soaked. It may be possible to take a boat, kayak or canoe out into some swamps.

Other swamps and bogs can only be seen from roads or hiking trails around their edges. Several swamps and a pitcher plant bog are described in the Swamp Highlights section, beginning on page 110. Websites are listed at the bottom of each page to help you find more information about them.

In addition to boardwalks and trails some wetlands have visitor centers with interesting exhibits that will answer questions you might have. Sometimes there is even a bookstore where you can get books full of information about swamps and their denizens.

Any time you are near wetlands (especially near dawn or dusk) be sure to smear on mosquito repellent. Take along binoculars, your camera and a field guide to whatever you're most interested in, and take this book to help you look for and understand the neat stuff you are sure to see, hear, smell, feel, taste and discover. If you go out at dusk, don't forget your flashlight. Find out more about swamp safety on pages 106 and 107.

When you visit a swamp, wear old clothes and shoes so you won't worry about getting wet, and just have FUN!

5

Hardwood Forests

A hardwood forest is made up of broadleaf trees and a whole community of shrubs, wildflowers, ferns, grasses, lichens and mushrooms. *Hardwood* is an old logging term used to describe tough-wooded trees like oaks and maples. Hardwood trees are generally "broadleafed," with wide, flat leaves. *Conifers* (KAH-nih-furz) – the pines, firs, spruces and cypresses, etc. – have narrow, needle-like leaves.

Hardwoods are usually *deciduous* (dih-SID-yew-us = losing their leaves each year). Some hardwoods, like holly and magnolia, don't stand around with bare limbs all winter. Instead, they keep the old leaves until their fresh new ones emerge in the spring. Then they drop the old ones and the summertime forest floor is covered with crunchy leaves – which makes it harder for *predators* (PREH-duh-turz = meat-eating hunters) to sneak around quietly as they hunt.

Forests in the East and Southeast are mostly hardwoods, while forests in the West are mostly conifers.

Bottomland Hardwood Forests

Growing in rich soils along rivers and around swamps, bottomland hardwood forests are sometimes flooded with several feet of water. But they aren't **usually** underwater and the plants and animals that live there survive occasional flooding of their habitat.

The floods deposit fresh soil, replacing nutrients which were used up by plants in the previous season, and producing healthy habitat and wildlife food.

Look carefully around a bottomland hardwood forest of elm, red maple, sweetgum, hickory, tulip tree, overcup oak, swamp chestnut oak, river birch, sycamore, bald cypress, red buckeye, blue beech and swamp ash.

You will probably be able to see signs of how high the water rises on the tree trunks when it floods. Look way up. Such forests may be easy to walk through because there are fewer shrubs – although you may see swamp dogwood, red mulberry, hawthorn, giant cane (actually a huge grass), holly, wax myrtle, pokeweed and dwarf palmetto. Most shrubs won't survive unless their tops can grow quickly above the flood line. Spiderworts, ferns and smartweed may also be present. And lots of vines: poison ivy, greenbrier, rattan vine, peppervine, and trumpet vine climb up the trees.

overcup oak
Quercus lyrata
The nut of this lowland acorn is almost covered by its cap.

acorn is ½" to 1" wide

hawthorn
Crataegus species
The fruits of these long-spined shrubs hang on the stem all winter. They're important in wildlife diets when food is scarce. The blossoms yield good honey. The 1 - 1½" long thorns protect nesting birds from predators.

Upland Hardwood Forests

Above the flood line, the upland hardwood forest has sandier soil and its own unique plant community. The soil here is not as fertile since it isn't enriched regularly during flooding, but the forest is thicker with shrubs and plants that would be washed away or killed by floods, or need good drainage. Many kinds of oaks are found in these forests.

Other trees include hackberry, beech, southern magnolia, hickory, tupelo, ash, basswood, mulberry, holly, hornbeam, dogwood, black cherry, sweetgum and elm. Cabbage palm and red cedar may be there too, although they aren't hardwoods.

acorn is ½" long

southern red oak
Quercus falcata
The bitter acorns of this tall oak are important wildlife food.

Also look for shrubs and vines such as witch hazel, fetterbush, Virginia creeper, wax myrtle, fox grape, buttonbush, viburnum, chinaberry, and beautyberry.

Some forest dwellers eat mushrooms that sprout up on the forest floor. Look on the ground and in trees for lichens (which have little wildlife food value) all year round.

fruiting bodies

beard lichen
Usnea strigosa
Greenish white with bristly stems and "fruiting bodies" (the flat disks), these lichens grow on twigs. Birds use them as nesting material.

actual size

tiny white berries

poison ivy
Toxicodendron radicans
Memorize this plant: three shiny leaves (the fresh, new ones often reddish) with tiny white flowers or round white berries. It may be a hairy rootlike climbing vine, or a shrub, or it may trail along the ground. Old vines can be up to 2" thick and covered with hairy rootlets. Unless you want to itch and scratch, don't touch!

The main stem may have a mat-like covering of rootlets.

The Hardwood Forests

There is an old saying that before Europeans settled on the North American continent, a squirrel living in a forest on the Atlantic shore could have jumped from branch to branch on the gigantic ancient hardwood trees all the way to the Mississippi River without ever touching the ground.

The hardwood forests of ancient times were open and parklike. Their old-growth trees had trunks four to six feet in diameter and their crowns towered high above.

Most of those ancient forests were logged off more than once, but many have grown back, at least partially. It is hard to imagine how grand those huge trees must have been, but since we never *personally* saw them, most of us don't really know what we lost. Hardwood forests grow in the rich soils that surround our Southeastern swamps, marshes, and bogs. They anchor the soil to hold in the water and provide *habitat* (a place to live) for wildlife and plants. Some of these forests flood to a depth of several feet nearly every year. Others flood less often or not at all.

But how did this pattern of swamps and forests begin in the first place? It all began underwater.

Much of Florida was once an ocean floor covered with fossil coral reefs that formed about six million years ago. During the Ice Age, water evaporating from the oceans fell to land as snow, and much of the world's water became stored in glaciers and icebergs. Sea levels dropped and the reefs became dry land and were eventually covered with plants. The hard limestone of Florida's ancient coral reefs now holds water like a tilted bathtub, keeping the waters that flow south and west out of Lake Okeechobee from sinking into the ground. The water flows slowly through the Everglades to the Gulf of Mexico.

The rest of the Southeastern United States is also low and fairly flat. It tilts down toward the Atlantic Ocean on the east and toward the Gulf of Mexico on the south. Rivers and streams run down from the hills and mountains to the ocean. Where these waterways run through flat or saucer-like areas, the water collects to form swamps, marshes and bogs.

Water action leaves ridges of soil at the edges of rivers, making natural dams and levees that hold the water inside. Many swamps, some of them now far from present rivers, are enclosed by these ridges of soil which mark where rivers flowed long ago.

No two hardwood forests are exactly the same. The hardwood forests surrounding swamps may be dense or open, dark or airy. The kind of soil, the amount of rainfall, the frequency of wildfires and floods, the depth of floodwaters, and many other conditions make a forest what it is.

Many animals, such as herons, wood storks, egrets, owls, gray squirrels, fox squirrels, frogs, opossums, fish, crows, snakes, wood ducks, cardinals, bears, deer, otters, mink and raccoons (to name a few), range the hardwood forests. They depend on nearby swamps for much or all of their food, their safety, or their living quarters.

All of the plants and animals are connected to weather, soil, water, wildfire and each other to make this amazing web of swamp, hardwood forest and pinelands work.

Pinelands, Pine Flatwoods & Scrub

Pinelands, pine flatwoods and scrub ecosystems are always changing. A fire caused by a lightning strike may burn an ancient hardwood forest to the ground. A black wasteland at first, the burnt ground will become a nursery for tiny plant seedlings that may have been waiting in the forest for many decades for enough sunshine to let them to grow.

In a remarkably short time, the bare earth will transform into a grassland, a pine forest, a palmetto prairie, or even a low, open scrub oak forest. Perhaps all these things will happen at the same time in a great crazy-quilt pattern. It all depends on the soil type, what seeds are in the ground when the dark forest disappears, and the weather that follows the fire – wet, dry, flooding or whatever.

These pinelands, pine flatwoods and various scrub habitats may exist for awhile. Eventually the hardwoods will poke up through the cover of the palmettos and shrubs, reach up past the pines, and finally shade them out.

Until another fire comes along.

Pinelands

Pinelands are flat, dry and sandy, studded with long-leaf and slash pines.

Wiregrass, other grasses and sedges, wildflowers and some small shrubs grow beneath them, as well. They don't get flooded, although they may become moist or even temporarily soggy during wet weather. Pinelands are maintained by lightning-caused fires which burn off shrubs and any hardwood seedlings that get started.

The plants that make up pinelands vary throughout the Southeast, but all pinelands look very similar.

wiregrass
Aristida oligantha
This 1' - 2' bristly grass, (different from salt marsh wiregrass) is also called whitegrass. It grows on dry, poor soil. When it dries out, it is white and highly flammable.

longleaf pine
Pinus palustris
The needles are 8-18" long and grouped in threes. They cluster in pom-poms at the ends of the branches. Cones are 6-10" long.

Pine Flatwoods

Pine flatwoods are open woods growing in low-lying areas that sometimes get flooded. The land is flat, so the water drains off poorly.

Palmettos and evergreen shrubs like wax myrtle, gallberry, staggerbush, fetterbush, dwarf huckleberry, and tarflower grow beneath the pines, producing berries and fruits eaten by wildlife. Grasses and herbs grow between the shrubs. If fires don't burn off the shrubs, a pine flatwoods becomes a crowded "scrubby flatwoods."

fetterbush
Lyonia lucida
This evergreen shrub grows up to 13' tall, with 1"- 3" oval leaves and tiny, pinkish flowers.

actual size

Atamasco lily
Zephyranthes atamasco
Growing to 12," the lovely 3" blooms of this lily change from white to pink as they age.

wax myrtle
Myrica cerifera
The waxy white ⅛" berries grow along the stem and are important late-winter songbird food. They've been used to make candles since colonial times.

actual size

jester cladonia lichen
Cladonia leporina
This green-white lichen looks like a tiny shrub, with little red balls on the branch tips (like balls on a jester's hat)

Scrub

Scrub is a community of low-growing shrubs or stunted trees on poor, sandy soil. A scrub may even include cactus and other desert-like plants.

Pine scrub has stunted pines mixed with shrubs and wiregrass. *Oak scrub* has small, gnarly oaks (see below) mixed with shrubs. On wetter sites, palmettos may take over.

Some shrubs found in scrub are gallberry (a holly), blueberry, rosemary, wax myrtle, and fetterbush. If hot fires don't burn the scrub off every twenty to eighty years, forest trees will sprout beneath the shrubs and the scrub will become a forest. The oaks shown below grow in dry, sandy soil.

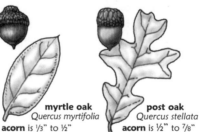

myrtle oak
Quercus myrtifolia
acorn is ⅓" to ½"

post oak
Quercus stellata
acorn is ½" to ⅞"

turkey oak
Quercus laevis
acorn is 1" long

dwarf palmetto
Sabal minor
This is actually a miniature palm. Its 3'-5' leaves split into segments. Palmetto thatch made water-tight dwellings and woven baskets for Native Americans. Palmettos are important food and shelter plants for wildlife.

The Pinelands, Pine Flatwoods and Scrub

The hardwood forests around swamps and other wetlands often blend into other types of habitat, such as pinelands, pine flatwoods and scrub. Fire sweeping through a hardwood bottomland will clear it for fast-growing conifers and palmettos which crowd out the slower-growing hardwoods. Many animals depend on pine flatwoods and the rustling cover of the palmettos, which look like midget "palm bushes." If wildfires aren't allowed to burn and remove the hardwood trees, the flatwood habitat disappears and those animals won't survive.

Pine flatwoods are fairly level, sandy lowlands with poor drainage. They may be flooded occasionally, but most of the time they are dry. They don't have the variety of plants and wildlife found in the hardwood forests, but the habitat they *do* offer to wildlife is a necessary part of the healthy ecosystem.

Nature is never finished. Just as a hardwood forest will replace a pine flatwood over time, a fire can start the whole process over again with palmettos and seedling pines. If the fire is spotty or not very hot, some of the hardwoods may survive. That produces a mixed hardwood-pine forest. A very hot fire may kill *all* the trees, leaving only grasses. The grasses may later be joined or overgrown by shrubs or scrub. Scrub may make way for trees, or return to grassland in another fire.

Sometimes you can look at a scene and know right away what it is. But where two or more habitats meet, they may mix or blend so that it is hard to say "that is a pineland," or "that is scrub."

And always, all habitats are changing from one type to another, depending on fire, rain, drought, flood, and wildlife or human activities.

What makes a habitat change naturally?
- frequent flooding
- few floods or NO floods
- major floods that wash plants and animals away
- floods that remain, drowning plants and animals
- long droughts
- frequent wildfires
- few wildfires or NO wildfires
- hurricanes
- plant or animal extinction through natural causes
- arrival of a new plant or animal through gradual natural patterns of migration

Human activities cause changes, too – mostly ones that affect the ecosystem in a harsh or unfortunate way:
- draining, destroying or leveling wetlands
- farming or building houses on wild lands
- logging and removing woody materials and nutrients
- putting out every lightning-caused fire
- introducing invasive non-native plants or animals

- eliminating native wildlife or plants
- damming streams stops fish migration/reproduction
- building reservoirs which change water temperatures and drown original river habitats
- straightening and lining rivers with stone or concrete, which stops water from sinking back into soil to refill *aquifers* (underground water supplies from which we pump much of our water)
- asphalting roads and parking lots, which drain rain water away into creeks so that it can't refill aquifers
- erecting dikes and levees which keep floods from depositing fresh, rich soil in low areas and creating barrier islands which protect inland habitats
- using pesticides and herbicides which destroy wildlife food and insect predators
- allowing human sewage to pollute ecosystems during major floods or through carelessness.
- increasing CO_2, which increases global warming – threatening everything on earth, including humans.

Warm Wetlands

A wetland is any low place that has standing water on or near the surface for part of the year, and supports wetland plants. In the Southeast, that covers a *lot* of territory. To keep things simple, in this book let's say that **warm wetlands** include swamps, bayous, marshes, bogs, ponds and lakes. Florida's waterlogged "wet prairies" are also included.

Although animals such as raccoons and crows do well in a variety of habitats, many creatures of the wetlands, such as alligators or bullfrogs, can't survive if their special habitat dries out. Some water dwellers, such as crawfish and turtles, are adjusted to seasonal wet and dry – but if a drought happens at the wrong time or continues for too long, it may be fatal. Some plants have similar limits. Many water plants collapse and die if their water habitat disappears.

But the situation may also work in reverse – some plants, and trees like bald cypress, *must* have an occasional drought in order to sprout seedlings for the next generation. We are learning that this delicate balance can be very fragile.

Marshes

close-up of seed cluster

A **marsh** is a dished area holding open water (as does a swamp) but with mostly soft vegetation (cattails, rushes, grasses and waterlilies) instead of trees.

Marshes near the ocean may be saltwater or *brackish* (mixed salt and fresh water). Marshes are named for the plants that rule them, so there are sawgrass, cattail, sedge, waterlily and other kinds of marshes. The marsh in this book's story is a freshwater cattail marsh.

Other marsh plants are pickerel weed, ferns, cane, arrowhead, flag, spike rush, and bulrush, to name a few.

A marsh is usually treeless and shallow, and may border a lake, swamp, bog or pond.

spike rush
Eleocharis species
Each leafless spike is 1"- 12" tall, with a seed cluster at the tip. It is really a sedge, not a rush.

Swamps and Bayous

leafy mistletoe
Phoradendron flavescens
This parasite feeds off the tree it grows on. The sticky seeds are carried to new sites on the feet of birds.

actual size

A **swamp** is a low-lying area holding fresh water. The water may be shallow or deep, and some plants, such as waterlilies, duckweed and pondweed, may grow in its sunnier parts.

The water is usually full of tannin (see p. 24) which darkens the water, limiting how much *photosynthesis* (foh-toh-SIN-thuh-sis = turning sunlight into plant growth) can take place below the surface. Some water-loving shrubs and trees – such as bald and pond cypress, tupelo, black-gum, red maple, black willow, sweetbay, ashes, water elm, water locust and Virginia willow – grow right in the swamp water or on the swamp's saturated edges. Trumpetvine, poison ivy, and greenbrier climb into the trees. Buttonbush, palmetto, lizard's-tail and ferns grow below the trees. *Epiphytes* (EP-ih-fights = air plants) such as Spanish moss and orchids, and parasites like mistletoe decorate the branches. Ferns sprout on mossy limbs.

A swamp may be called a **bayou** (BY-yooh) in parts of the South, and a very slow-running river may also be called a bayou.

sweetbay magnolia
Magnolia virginiana
This big tree's 2"-3" creamy flowers have an incredibly sweet scent.

trumpet vine
Camsis radicans
This vine climbs high into trees using aerial roots. Its 3" long, red flowers are visited by hummingbirds, bees and hawkmoths.

water oak
Quercus nigra
A large oak, often growing in soggy soil, it rots quickly, making good cavities for wildlife nests and shelters.

the acorn is about ½" long

Bogs and Wet Prairies

A **bog** is a waterlogged area usually kept wet by rain. Bogs support special collections of plants like sedges, pitcher plants, sundews, heaths and mosses that can grow in waterlogged *peat*.

Peat is made of *sphagnum* (SFAG-num) moss, which grows out into ponds in big mats. Sphagnum moss produces acid that slows down decay. In time, deep deposits build up, compacting into peat which can hold as much as twenty times its weight in water. Peat may completely fill in a wetland.

A bog may border a marsh, pond, lake or swamp.

A **wet prairie** is a meadow whose plants can survive an occasional flood.

peat moss
Sphagnum species

actual size

Sphagnum moss leaves are only one cell thick but can survive long droughts.

Ponds and Lakes

A **pond** or **lake**, under normal conditions, is a permanent pool of fresh water. It resembles a swamp but no trees grow in it. Unlike a marsh, its central parts are too deep for plants to take root. It features floating plants such as waterlilies, spatterdock, duckweed, bladderwort, water hyacinths, and various pondweeds. A pond or lake may be surrounded or bordered by a marsh, bog or swamp.

The Cypress Swamps

The Southeastern United States is special for several reasons. Compared to the rest of the country, its mountains are lower. It is extremely humid, and has warmer, wetter weather for most of the year because rain falls more often. Much of its soil is made up of *impervious* (im-PER-vee-us = watertight) clay that doesn't let water drain away.

But while one wetland may be always covered with water, another may be dry at times – or wet for only a short time each year. The length of time water covers the ground determines the kinds of plants that can grow there.

Soil types are important, too. Many plants – bog plants, for instance – can't grow in the limestone soil found in much of Florida. Bog plants must grow in acidic soil where many other plants can't survive. Some plants require rich organic soil, or fast-draining sand. Some plants can survive being flooded occasionally. Others can't.

In a wetland, the water's temperature, depth, movement and purity also affect which plants and animals can live and flourish there. For example, some fish and plants need warm water, others require cool water.

Southern Florida has many tropical plants: mangroves, native palms, strangler figs, Key lime trees, papayas, butterfly orchids and lots of "air plants" that grow on trees. The rest of the Southeast, from Louisiana to the Carolinas, has many plants that wouldn't survive in hot, humid, southern Florida.

No two wetlands are exactly the same. But nearly **all** of the southeastern swamps are dim and mysterious, echo with bird and frog songs, and have maze-like watery corridors that wind and twine through buttressed cypress trees festooned with Spanish moss.

They all have much of the same vegetation and many of the same animals (opossums, snapping turtles, dragonflies, little blue herons, bluegill fish, jumping spiders, treefrogs, crawfish, and snakes) to name a few.

In fact, this book is meant to be a book about ANY Southeastern swamp – with plants and animals you'd find anywhere in the southeastern part of the U.S.

Imagine you've been taken blindfolded to a swamp somewhere in the southeastern United States. Now take off the blindfold. Standing knee-deep in cool, tea-colored water, you inhale warm, moist magnolia-scented air and look carefully around. Can you tell whether you are in Florida, the Carolinas, Louisiana, Georgia, Alabama, Mississippi or even Delaware, Arkansas, Tennessee or eastern Texas?

That dragonfly over there – wouldn't you see one like her in any swamp? And look at this strange, brown thing crawling out of the water and up a pickerelweed stem. What is it doing? What IS it? Does it bite?

Wouldn't you like to find out? Just turn the page →

Green Darner Dragonfly

Anax junius (AN-ax JOO-nee-us)
Anax = "ruler of" ***junius*** = "June"

Why on earth would anybody want to call a shiny green dragonfly *"Anax junius"* (ruler of June)? Well, it's one way to help people figure out which dragonfly it is.

There are many different kinds of dragonflies. In one part of the country people call a certain kind of dragonfly a "snake doctor" (in southern folk tales, dragonflies nurse dead snakes back to life), but elsewhere the very same dragonfly may be called a "devil's darning needle," "darner," "eye sticker," "mule killer" or "mosquitohawk."

A scientific name, like *Anax junius*, more properly called the *specific name*, is the same worldwide. It is usually Latin or Greek, and often describes something about the organism. **Your** "darner" may be **my** "mosquitohawk," but we both can agree it's *Anax junius*. Scientific names are fun to learn and use. You'll be amazed at what they can tell you.

Flying Dragons

A dragonfly looks fierce and scary. It's big, it flies fast, it grabs other insects in a basket formed by its curved legs (then eats them), and it WATCHES you with those huge, wrap-around eyes. Even its name, **dragon**fly, makes it seem spooky. But it doesn't have a sting and although it *can* bite you, it NEVER attacks people. It is too busy flying as fast as it can – as far away from you as possible.

Jaws
The way a dragonfly nymph catches food underwater is really amazing. The *labium* (LAY-bee-um), a kind of lower lip like an arm with a clawed hand, flips out, snags the prey, and jerks it back to the nymph's mouth.

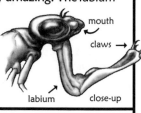
mouth
claws →
labium   close-up

1 Insect Fossil

Dragonflies were among the first insects to appear as fossils – about 300 million years ago, long before dinosaurs. They were BIG. Their wingspreads could be 30" from tip to tip, and they had 12" bodies. Imagine the wing clatter!

While they're a lot smaller now, dragonflies are still among the fastest flying insects, speeding around at 35 mph. They can lift prey twice their own weight, fly backward and stop instantly in midair to hover. They're hard to surprise, too. They see and react to things as much as 100 feet away.

Morphing Nymphs
Dragonflies start life as *nymphs* (NIMFS), which look more like "dragons" than adult dragonflies do. A dragonfly nymph sheds its skin about twelve times as it grows (over a period of 1 - 5 years) and at the final shedding (molt) it emerges with its adult shape. This series of changes is called metamorphosis (met-uh-MOR-fuh-sis). An adult dragonfly can be seen on page 13.

a damselfly goes through changes similar to a dragonfly's.

damselfly nymph and adult

Above is a **dragonfly** egg and three nymph stages – the adult comes next.

Screamin' Rock Band

If you've spent a hot southern afternoon outside, you've probably heard the shrill whine of cicadas. The larvae live underground, sucking on plant rootlets. When the scary-looking larvae finally dig their way to the surface, sometimes in the tens of thousands, the females molt into sleek screaming rock stars while the metamorphosed males tap or click.

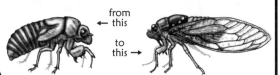
from ← this
to this →

Bald Cypress *Taxodium distichum*

Bald cypress trees give swamps their special look – with "knees" which rise from the water (see p. 50), buttresses (wide, flaring bases) to prop them up in soft mud, and weird draperies of silvery Spanish moss. Some cypress trees become quite large with age.

Although the trees prefer "wet feet," cypress seedlings can take root only in dry soil, so bald cypress trees sprout only during droughts – one reason a drought isn't totally bad news in the cypress swamps.

Bald cypresses "go bald' when they lose their needles each fall.

knees
buttress
underwater

1. The Green Darner Dragonfly

Mist rose wispily from the smooth tea-brown swamp water, passing up through hanging veils of Spanish moss that dangled like uncombed gray hair from the cypress branches above. Cypress trees rose tall and straight from the water on their massive, flared buttresses. Lichens plastered their trunks, and ferns sprouted from the mud around their moist, knobby knees.

The creamy blossoms of a nearby magnolia tree filled the air with heavy, sweet perfume. The scent blended with the lemony fragrance of sweetbay and the rich, rank odor of wet swamp ooze.

The cheery **"jubilee, jubilee, jubilee"** of a Carolina wren echoed down watery avenues as a shaft of early sunshine lit up a patch of pickerelweed at the edge of the open pond. The heart-shaped leaves and purple flower spikes of the pickerelweed were mirrored in the water.

In the cool silence, a small "dragon" climbed out of the water and halfway up a pickerelweed stem. She stopped and clutched the stem, gathering her strength.

Inside the inch-long body, things were changing swiftly. Within her abdomen, inside her thorax, legs and head, this dragon, actually a dragonfly nymph, was morphing into something new and very, very different. She began to breathe deeply, and her body swelled larger with each breath. With a faint *snikk* the skin down her back split and the pale new creature that had formed inside began to bulge out, backward and down.

A head with giant eyes. Soft wing buds on a large thorax. And at last, six thin, wiry legs. Morphing was hard work. She hung upside down for awhile, exhausted, as her legs dried and hardened. Finally, she reached up and hooked her claws into the split skin, arching her upper body until her abdomen popped out.

Now she hung head-up as her wings uncrinkled to their full size and her abdomen lengthened into a slim stick. In just three hours the "ugly duckling" dragonfly nymph

had become a gleaming dragonfly. She was tan now, but she'd be bright green when mature. Below her now empty nymph skin, still anchored to the stem, another dragonfly was emerging from its skin just as she had done a short while before. She spread her shimmering wings and looked around alertly. This was an awesome world. All on her own, she must now learn to fly, catch food, reproduce and avoid predators.

A damselfly fluttered past, and the dragonfly leaped into the air on her first flight. After a swift chase, she snatched the damselfly from midair and lit on a pickerelweed leaf to eat. She launched into flight again, searching for more prey. Her appetite was huge as she cruised the swamp.

Three weeks later she mated, and was ready to lay her eggs. Zooming swiftly just above the water, the dragonfly dipped the tip of her abdomen into the clear brown water every few feet, releasing a tiny egg which sank slowly to the mud on the bottom of the swamp. Most of the eggs would hatch into nymphs. Many would morph into adults. Concentrating on her task, the dragonfly didn't notice the two large, round eyes gleaming in the duckweed directly ahead.

Bullfrog

Rana catesbeiana (RAY-nuh kayts-bee-AY-nuh)
Rana = "frog"   ***catesby*** = a person's name   ***ana*** = "belonging to"

Bullfrogs are an essential part of the southern swamp ecosystem. As eggs and tadpoles, they are important food for many other swamp dwellers. As frogs, they eat thousands of aquatic and flying insects, small snakes, other frogs, and even birds. And they definitely improve the swamp chorus.

Bullfrogs start to croak after dusk, and build up to a midnight roar as they try to attract females. They usually mate around three a.m. But a swamp is a dangerous place to make a racket because predators are attracted to the noise. Snapping turtles and other predators feed well on bullfrogs in the summer.

Up to seven inches long and weighing as much as a pound, the bullfrog is our biggest American frog. It is native to the southeastern U.S., but it has been released other places where it kills off native *aquatic* (uh-KWAH-tik = water-living) animals who have no natural defenses against this large alien invader.

Ye Olde Pollywog

In Old English, "tadpole" meant "*toad's head*" and "pollywog" meant "*wiggling head.*" They should have called it "*wiggling stomach*," because a tadpole is really mostly just mouth, stomach and tail.

Bullfrogs are late bloomers. Tadpoles don't *metamorphose* (met-uh-MOR-fohz = transform) until their second year. Most other frogs go from egg to adult in just a few weeks. Here's a typical bullfrog schedule:

YEAR 1 – **Spring:** up to 20,000 eggs are laid amongst swamp plants (about half get eaten).

Summer: surviving eggs hatch into tadpoles which graze on rotting vegetation. Most are eaten by predators.

Autumn: surviving tadpoles burrow into the mud. Many don't survive until spring.

YEAR 2 – **Spring:** surviving tadpoles emerge, eat and grow until they're 6" from nose to tail. Most will be eaten. *THEN*

Midsummer, within a space of two weeks:
1. Back legs pop out.
2. Lungs develop, gills shrink and vanish, and the digestive system matures.
3. Front legs emerge.
4. Mouth widens, tail absorbs into the body, and the eyes enlarge.
5. A 2"-3" bullfrog hops out onto land.*
6. Living up to 30 years, it may reach seven inches in length.

*Only about one out of 10,000 bullfrog eggs make it to the adult stage.

tracks of a sitting bullfrog

Frogs 'n Toads (a poem)
Frogs can jump, a toad just hops.
Toads taste bad, but frogs are tops.
Frog-egg jelly sticks to things.
Toads release their eggs in strings.
Frogs eat other frogs a lot.
Toads are bumpy, frogs are not.
Frogs are slippery, toads are dry.
Both of them are very shy.
Each sings loudly as it courts.
But neither one will give you warts.

(Actually, **some** frogs are bumpy. Bullfrogs **may** be.)

If It Fits, It's FOOD!

A bullfrog will eat almost any moving thing it can get in its mouth. Flattening its eyes down and closing its see-through eyelids to protect them, a big frog can leap up to twenty-four inches out of the water to catch its prey.

The sticky tongue flips out, gloms onto the victim, then jerks the food in. The frog crams large food down its throat with its fingers as it drops back into the water. YUM!

The Hydra
Hydra species
Named for a Greek goddess with tangled hair, this creature lives in ponds, grabbing prey with its tentacles. New babies bud from its side.
buds
actual size is ¼"-½"

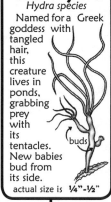

Guess Who?

Whose voice sounds like a bow being dragged across the bottom string of a bass fiddle – or like the words "jug o' rum" or "better go 'round" – or like a bull clearing its throat – ***"UH-UH-UH-RUHHNN"?***

Who sounds like an alligator bellowing out in the swamp? It's the bullfrog, natch. And an unexpected bellow can scare you out of your wits!

If you spook a bullfrog, it will yelp like a stepped-on chihuahua puppy or yowl like a cat.

Bullfrogs give a shocking scream when caught, which often startles predators into dropping them. Wouldn't you?

You might mistake a pig frog for a bullfrog, especially where pig frogs are common. But even though they look very similar, one "oink" from a pig frog should set you straight.

2. The Bullfrog

Only the bullfrog's eyes poked up above the layer of floating duckweed plants and water spangles. The rest of the bullfrog hung in the warm water, motionless. He saw the green darner dragonfly dip the tip of her abdomen into the water a few feet away as she released an egg then swooped up through the steamy evening air right in front of his nose.

The bullfrog was middle-aged as bullfrogs go. Each spring for nineteen years he had bellowed out his deep bass **"UH-UH-UH-RUHHNN, UH-UH-UH-RUHHNN"** to attract a mate. During mating, he had released his sperm over the emerging jelly-covered eggs — sometimes as many as twenty thousand eggs at once – to fertilize them. Many of his offspring lived in the swamp, and many more had become "fast food" for other carnivores. In fact, he had eaten some of them himself.

As a tadpole, the bullfrog had almost been gobbled up by a fierce brown dragonfly nymph. The nymph had actually gotten a grip on his tail, but the soft flesh had torn and the young tadpole had been lucky to escape with only a tattered tail.

Now a chorus frog was croaking an occasional **"cre-e-e-e-e-eek"** from beneath a greenbrier leaf hanging from its thorny, twisting vine looped over a shrub at the edge of the water. The small frog stopped in mid croak as the bullfrog leaped into the air, flipped out his gooey tongue and zapped the dragonfly. The dragonfly's tough clackety wings sawed at the bullfrog's soft mouth and her springy legs clawed at his tongue as he plopped back into the water.

The frog crammed the dragonfly deeper into his mouth with his long fingers. He pulled his tongue back to drag the dragonfly further down his throat, then he gulped. He closed his big eyes, pulling them down so that they bulged into the inside of his mouth, pressing against the dragonfly to flatten the oversize bite. This was not the bullfrog's first dragonfly dinner. He knew just what to do.

A barred owl drifting by on silent feathers had heard the clattering wings and now saw the big, juicy bullfrog trying to swallow the dragonfly.

A bullfrog is usually hard to catch. Its strong hind legs can launch it into a three-foot sideways leap in an instant – but only if its eyes are open to see the danger. This time they weren't open. The owl dived.

Barred Owl

Strix varia (STRICKS VAIR-ee-uh)
Strix = "night bird" ***varia*** = "variable" (referring to markings)

You're passing a forest, or maybe camping out and just about asleep when somebody starts hollering **"WHO COOKS FOR YOU?! WHO COOKS FOR YOU-ALL? !"** No, it's not somebody looking for a job as a chef – it's a barred owl.

It's also called a hoot owl, swamp owl, and eight-hooter (**"YOU-ALL"** is one word, right?). Barred owl conversations can get really wild, with cackles, cat-like screams, laughing, and whooping yodels. In fact, the barred owl may be responsible for many reports of panther screams (panthers do yowl, but don't scream).

Barred owls are big, nearly two feet from beak to tail tip, and their wings stretch out well over three feet. They're an important part of the ecosystem, eating mice, rats, birds, crawfish, frogs and even fish. But they have to watch out for great horned owls, which eat **them**. In the Southeast, only **barred** and **barn** owls have dark eyes. Other owls have yellow eyes.

Skull Secrets

If you could push forward the feathers beside an owl's face, you would see the ear openings. The shape, size or position of the opening on one side may be different from shape, size or position on the other side. Varying shapes and positions detect sounds differently, so this probably helps the owl pinpoint where its prey is before it dives.

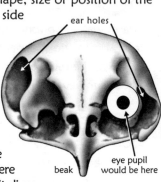

ear holes

beak

eye pupil would be here

On the owl skull above, the eyes look straight ahead (like a human's). Most birds have eyes on the sides to watch for danger sideways, behind and above. But an owl needs binocular (two-eyed) vision to judge its prey's location during dives. That leaves it blind toward the rear, but since owls seldom get chased, that's okay.

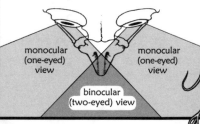

monocular (one-eyed) view

monocular (one-eyed) view

binocular (two-eyed) view

Light Flight

Barred owls are big, and you'd think they'd be heavy and flap loudly in pursuit of prey. Actually, bird bones are light – they are mostly hollow and full of air, which makes even big owls lightweight.

Airplane wings are built hollow, with inner braces for the same reason.

Mouse Trap
Most owl victims never know what hit them – the razor-sharp *talons* (TAL-unz = claws) usually kill instantly. The barred owl is a calm and friendly sort of bird – if you don't look like lunch. Just don't mess with its nest or chicks!

fringe

enlarged

braces

bird bone cross-section

Owl flight feathers are fuzzy and have fringed edges so that air can pass over them silently. This helps an owl fly along very quietly.

Using Spanish Moss *Tillandsia usneoides*

Barred owls and other wildlife use the silvery Spanish moss (early settlers called it "French wig" and "Spanish beard") for nests or shelter. This *epiphyte* grows on trees but doesn't hurt them since it feeds by absorbing rain, fog and dust, which is full of nutrients, from the air.

Native Americans, starting about 2000 years ago, added Spanish moss to their pottery clay to strengthen it. During warm weather, some women wore Spanish moss skirts.

seed capsule

When Birds Eat Bones...

Bones, feathers, and things like beetle wings are a problem for a toothless bird. They have no food value and they could puncture a bird's *intestines* (in-TESS-tinz = the bowels). So after eating, the bird burps up a pellet of things it can't digest.

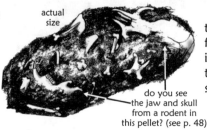

actual size

do you see the jaw and skull from a rodent in this pellet? (see p. 48)

All owls, hawks, and songbirds that eat tough insects upchuck pellets full of spare parts. Cleaned by acids in the gizzard, the parts are quite sanitary. Scientists and students in school science and biology classes often *dissect* (dih- SEKT = tear apart) pellets to find out what the bird ate.

3. The Barred Owl

Awhile before, as the sun began sliding toward the horizon and the green treefrogs began their bell-like *"wahnk.......wahnk......wahnk,"* the barred owl had blinked and yawned, slowly awakening on his daytime roost. Hidden behind a swag of Spanish moss on a cypress branch, the owl greeted the evening with deep hoots:

"WHOO-WHO-HU-WHOOO!
WHOO-WHO-HU-WHO-AAAHHH!"

The faint hoot of another barred owl in a distant territory answered his call. The barred owl's mate, sitting on the nest in a nearby tree with their two hungry owlets, remained silent. Hooting might attract crows or other predators to her nest. The barred owl male leaned far forward through the curtain of Spanish moss and hooted again, drawing out the final *"AHHHhhh...."*

Dropping silently from his perch, the barred owl began his evening hunt. The fringed feathers on his wings made no sound as he drifted through the trees, his large, dark eyes searching the dim shadows. His huge ears, hidden under feathers, heard the slightest rustle. Later, when darkness fell, he would depend much more on his ears. For even the keenest owl eyes can't see in inky darkness.

Swooping out from the bald cypress trees into brighter light at the edge of open swamp water, the owl suddenly heard the rasp of dragonfly wings, and saw the huge bullfrog, eyes closed, tamping the insect into its smouth. YES! He dived, talons spread wide, gaffing the frog from the water with one sharp-clawed foot. Pierced through the heart, the bullfrog perished instantly.

The owl, still drowsy from his hot afternoon nap, pulled out of the dive clumsily. As he rose into the trees with the heavy frog, the tip of one wing hit a wax myrtle branch. Caught off balance, he nose-dived and his frog-clutching talons flew open. Dinner arched through the air and hurtled into a buttonbush draped with wild grapevines. Inside the bush, four startled grackle chicks ducked deep down into their nest as the frog tumbled down past them.

Crash-landing in a nearby clump of ferns, the owl scrambled out hastily and made several long leaps toward his last sight of the bullfrog. He bobbed his head up and down under the screen of vines and buttonbush leaves, clicking his beak angrily. But the frog had hit the ground deep inside the tangle, well out of sight, and the frustrated owl was finally forced to fly off to find other prey.

His little owlets were waiting for their evening meal and he must find them something soon.

17

Burying Beetle

Nicrophorus orbicollis (ny-KRAW-fer-us or-bih-KALL-us)
Nicrophorus = "death carrier" *orbi* = "round" *collis* = "neck"

What would happen if nothing ever got moldy or rotten or crumbled away? What if everything that died just lay there forever? What a horrible mess we would be walking around on – a thick layer of dinosaurs and trees and dead insects. If nutrients weren't recycled, there would be no soil – so there'd be no plants because nothing could grow. **We wouldn't be here at all.** Bacteria, vultures, burying beetles, and other organisms which eat and recycle dead things are **very** necessary.

The burying beetles, also known as sexton beetles (church sextons used to be responsible for getting graves dug), are important members of the ecosystem – although your first reaction on seeing one at work might be "Eeeuuuw! Yuk!"

Their job is to recycle dead bodies so that the nutrients can return to the soil to nourish more life. They help everything else live. What could be more important than that?

Insect Body Plan

All insects have three pairs of legs, a body divided into three parts: head, *thorax* (THOR-ax = chest area) and abdomen, and usually two **pairs** of wings (but not always – see the cranefly on page 20). A beetle's front wings cover and protect the hind wings, the ones it flies with.

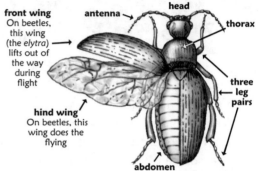

front wing
On beetles, this wing (the *elytra*) lifts out of the way during flight

antenna

head

thorax

three leg pairs

hind wing
On beetles, this wing does the flying

abdomen

Is it an insect? Count the legs – insects have 6.

Seriously Weird

Insect "feelers" or antennae (an-TEN-ee) may be oddly shaped, depending on their use. Here are some cool ones seen from above.

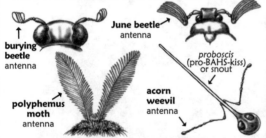

burying beetle antenna

June beetle antenna

proboscis (pro-BAHS-kiss) or snout

acorn weevil antenna

polyphemus moth antenna

Entomologist's Delight

Entomologists (en-tuh-MOLL-uh-jists) study insects. When entomologists talk about burying beetles, they use words like "amazing" and "strange" and "unusual."

For instance, very few female insects look after their young – they lay the eggs and leave. But a burying beetle not only sticks around, she also prepares the food, feeds her larvae, and guards them until they can make it on their own.

Even more rare is a male insect that helps care for the young. A male burying beetle will feed and care for the larvae even if the female disappears. As far as we know, no other male insect does this.

"Pssst! Over Here!"

Pheromones (FAIR-oh-mohnz) are chemical signals that male and female organisms, from ants to humans, release from their bodies – a kind of natural perfume. For instance, many female moths release pheromones that male moths detect from far away with their feathery antennae.

A female burying beetle uses her antennae knobs to "smell" pheromones released by a male burying beetle. She follows the scent, and when she finds him, they start a family.

What purpose do you suppose human pheromones might have?

Buttonbush
Cephalanthus occidentalis

The heavily leafed buttonbush, with inch-wide frothy-looking white flower globes, is common in swamps because it can survive flooding. Its dense leaves may hide all kinds of nests.

Big Brains?

An entomologist once hung a dead mouse at the end of a string and was astonished when burying beetles cut the string and buried the body as usual. At first, people thought the beetles were really S*M*A*R*T. Then they realized that the beetles must often chew through things to move prey. They chew fur or feathers off a body so that they can smear it with antibiotic juices so it won't rot before the young can eat it. They bury a carcass to keep others from eating or using it.

They even move a body to softer soil if the soil where it died is too hard to bury it in.

If burying beetles aren't "smart," at least they're amazing!

4. The Burying Beetle

The unlucky bullfrog had been dead only a few hours when a shiny black-and-orange burying beetle smelled it and raced up to claim the body. He nudged it to see whether it weighed enough to bother with. Finding it properly heavy, he raised his tail to release pheromones into the air. Their scent drifted through the darkness.

A female arrived soon, eagerly following the inviting perfume to the male burying beetle and his frog prize. Together, they began to burrow beneath the body, digging, kicking, and bulldozing the soil up and out from under it. Slowly, the frog sank into the deepening pit. When it had sunk below the surface of the ground, they carefully covered it with the soil they had dug away.

Underground, the beetles worked steadily. Pressing the rotting frog into a solid ball, they covered it with spittle and anal droppings (beetle poop) to slow its decay. They mated then, and the female laid eggs in the soil beside the frog. Both beetles snuggled down to wait for the eggs to *incubate* (IN-kew-bayt = mature). Three days later, they hatched.

Now the female chirped to the larvae from a hollow she had dug in the top of the carcass, calling them to dinner. She chewed bits of the frog and dribbled soft globs into the mouths of her tiny larvae. Within a few days, they could feed themselves, growing larger each day while the father beetle guarded them.

Within a week, the larvae tunneled out into the soil to *pupate* (PEW-payt = mature into the final insect stage). After two weeks they were full-size adults, and they dug up to the surface, ready to seek their own carcasses to claim and bury. The adults left too, to find another carcass and start another family.

The remains of the bullfrog and the droppings from the beetles fertilized and enriched the soil, starting a chain of events much like one that had begun nearby with a dead mole many years earlier.

That mole had first nourished a family of burying beetles, then it had fertilized the buttonbush and grapevine now holding the nest of grackle chicks. Many insects prowled the buttonbush flowers for nectar. The grapevine's grapes were food for many birds and mammals. And both plants created shelter for birds, mammals, insects – and a jumping spider just now prowling along a looped grapevine stem near the ground.

Royal Jumping Spider

Phidippus regius (FID-ih-pus REE-jus)
Phidippus= (physician to an ancient Greek King) **regius**="royal"

A jumping spider is gentle, alert, and very nosy – it will watch you curiously with its huge black eyes and wave its palps at you, trying to figure you out. Invite one onto your sleeve – it won't bite. Just be sure it's a jumping spider.

Here's how to identify jumping spiders: 1) they are diurnal (daytime) spiders and may be very colorful – with iridescent green mouthparts called *chelicerae* (chel-ISS-ur-ee); 2) they have large eyes on the front of the face to give them binocular vision, while the remaining eyes are small and on top; and 3) instead of waiting in a web they build, they chase their prey with immense leaps several times their body length. They catch bugs, flies, adult and larval butterflies, and grasshoppers. The body of *Phidippus regius* is about 5/8" long. ┝━━━━┥

Jumping spiders hunt in the underbrush. The best way to find them is to spend some time around shrubby foliage.

Spider Body Plan

Arachnids (uh-RAK-nidz: spiders, scorpions, mites and ticks) have four pairs of legs, usually eight eyes, a pair of *palps* (feelers), and a body divided into two parts: a *cephalothorax* (sef-ul-uh-THOR-aks = head and thorax combined), and an *abdomen* (AB-doh-men).

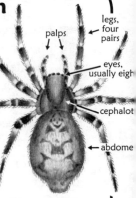

legs, four pairs

palps

eyes, usually eigh

cephalot

abdome

Spider Love Poem

A male jumping spider
Courts *his* "lady fair"
By waving his
Brightly-marked
Legs in the air.
(Hey, whatever works.)

Phidippus regius
2X actual size

Aerial Broad Jump

Imagine you are perched on a branch about two hundred feet above the ground. You are hungry and you see something yummy in the top of a tree seventy feet away (that's about the width of two city streets, and fourteen times your body length). What are you gonna do? Why, just take one flying leap, grab it, pump it full of tenderizer, and eat it, of course! But first, tie a safety rope from your waist to a branch just in case you miss and plunge to the ground.

Uhhh, yeah....!

burger and fries

Jumping spiders notice prey as far away as fourteen times their body length, and they leap to attack from there, too. The *Phidippus regius* in our story is ¾" long, making its striking range about ten inches. It dabs its spinnerets (see p. 82) against a twig before leaping, to fasten a safety line (a "dragline") in case it misses and falls.

Spider Food
Flies are major spider food. But flies are interesting in other ways, too. Some have tongues that soak up juices like a sponge.

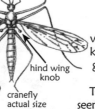

sponge tongue

A fly's hind wings are only tiny knobs, which act as gyroscopes to help it keep its balance. The knobs are easily seen on big craneflies.

hind wing knob

cranefly actual size

Boy

male palps are bulbed and contain sperm

meets

female palps are not bulbed

Girl

Fox Grapes
Vitis rotundifolia

The fox grapes in swamp country provide food for foxes, squirrels, birds and many other animals.

The leaves hide small wildlife, and the vines make great insect and spider roads, connecting trees and shrubs.

Looking Good

Spiders that sit and wait for their food don't need good vision, so their eyes are tiny, and sometimes they have only six of them.

Two of a jumping spider's eyes are big, and especially designed and

a jumping spider's face

a typical web sitter's face

placed to help it track and catch moving prey.

Spiders are fascinating, but they haven't been studied as well as many other creatures. We don't know a lot about them. More research is needed to discover more of their secrets.

5. The Royal Jumping Spider

The beautifully-marked jumping spider crept along the grapevine tendril watching carefully for something to catch and eat. His huge black eyes saw everything. He moved quickly in small, jerky leaps.

In the deep shade beneath the buttonbush, he spotted a green-bottle fly licking the soil that covered the rotting bullfrog. The stout, hairy fly could smell the dead frog, but it couldn't find the deeply buried body. It tested the soil in several places, but no rotten juices wet the spongy surface of its tongue.

Leaping squarely onto the fly, the spider grappled with it, folding the fly's wings and legs tightly back against its struggling body. His glittery green fangs injected quick-acting *toxin* (venom) into his prey to paralyze it. Holding the fly firmly, the spider waited.

As soon as the green-bottle fly stopped moving, the spider chewed a hole in it and squirted an *enzyme* (a kind of meat tenderizer) into its body. The insides of the fly began to turn to liquid. In a few moments, the hungry spider would be able to suck up the insides like slurping a milkshake through a straw. He fidgeted, waving his legs impatiently.

A mother grackle, returning to her nest with a beakful of craneflies and a bright green caterpillar, spotted the jumping spider's movements. She dived down through the buttonbush branches, planning to add the fat spider to the menu in her beak.

But the jumping spider's super vision gave him plenty of warning. Dropping the paralyzed fly onto the grape leaf, he leaped swiftly to one side, landing out of sight in a cluster of leaves. The grackle didn't waste time searching for the spider. She grabbed the limp fly and scrambled up into the shrub to feed her mouthful of goodies to her hungry nestlings.

Common Grackle

Quiscalus quiscula (KWIS-kuh-lus KWIS-kew-luh)
Quiscalus = "quail" *quiscula* (from the same Latin word) = "quail"

Grackles are also known as china-eyed blackbirds (their eyes are whitish) or crow blackbirds. But they aren't crows or blackbirds, although they're related. Oddly, their *specific name* (above) means "quail." In colonial times, they were called "Maize Thieves," (maize is corn or grain) and young men living near Cape Cod, Massachusetts, couldn't marry until they had delivered their quota of grackle heads to the town clerk. Soon grackles became rare, and locusts, cutworms and other insects they had been eating multiplied and wiped out the crops. Ooops! After that, the quotas were ended and grackles were protected, even though they **do** eat some corn, fruits and vegetables.

Sunlit grackle feathers are *iridescent* (eer-ih-DEH-sent – showing rainbow colors from different angles) blue, purple, green, copper or bronze. But in shade or on cloudy days a grackle actually looks a lot like a blackbird. Is it a grackle? Look at its tail.

Oil Those Hinges !!!
Here are some descriptions of grackle songs: "a wheelbarrow chorus," "iron gates swinging, creaking and clanging on rusty, un-oiled hinges," and "a split rasping note that is both husky and squeaky." Still, when a lot of them sing together, as they do at their *roosts* (places they hang out), it's a marvelous jangling chorus.

Could YOU sing like a grackle? Groan these sounds in a high squeaky squeal: ***"REE-duh'LEEK!" "ch-GASSSS-kweek!" "SKOO-duh'LEEK!"*** and ***"SEEeeeEEE."***

So. How did it sound? Maybe all your friends would join in so you could sound like a whole flock (just kidding)!

a courting grackle does its "RuffOut" display as it sings

Swamp Tupelo (TOO-puh-loh)
Nyssa aquatica
(Nyssa was a Greek water nymph)

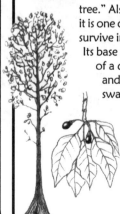

Tupelo is a Creek Indian word that means "swamp tree." Also called "tupelo gum," it is one of the few trees that can survive in a permanent swamp. Its base swells up like the trunk of a cypress to help support and prop up the tree in soft swamp mud.

Tupelos are good wildlife trees, with cavities and knotholes that make great nest sites. The shiny, black, edible, citrus-flavored fruit is eaten by birds and mammals.

Nursery Tales
Grackles make nests on branches, and they also use tree cavities. The female incubates four to five dark-blotched pale-green eggs for about two weeks.

Both parents feed the hatchlings for another two weeks, then the young birds are ready to fledge and fly.

actual size

What's a Keel?
A grackle has a *keel-shaped tail*. But what's a keel? The keel is the part of a boat that pokes down into the water like an upside-down roof. A grackle displays its keeled tail during courtship to ← impress females and discourage other males. Both **boat-tailed** and **great-tailed grackles** are larger than the **common grackle**, with even bigger and deeper keels.

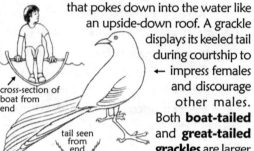

cross-section of boat from end

tail seen from end

Black Birds
Several birds that live around cypress swamps could be mistaken for common grackles. Boat-tailed and great-tailed grackles look very similar. A boat-tailed grackle is shown below. The great-tailed grackle reaches 18" and has bright golden eyes.

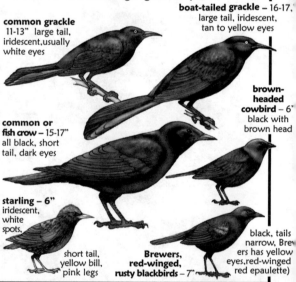

common grackle 11-13" large tail, iridescent, usually white eyes

boat-tailed grackle – 16-17, large tail, iridescent, tan to yellow eyes

brown-headed cowbird – 6" black with brown head

common or fish crow – 15-17" all black, short tail, dark eyes

starling – 6" iridescent, white spots,

short tail, yellow bill, pink legs

Brewers, red-winged, rusty blackbirds – 7"

black, tails narrow, Brewers has yellow eyes, red-winged red epaulette)

Seedcracker
A grackle isn't a picky eater. It wolfs down insects, fish, spiders, snakes, crawfish, lizards, birds, mice, nuts, seeds, fruits and berries.

It even tries to catch insects in the air, although that heavy tail makes flying clumsy.

a grackle cracks a nut

It presses seeds against a ridge in the roof of its mouth to crack them open (see above).

6. The Common Grackle

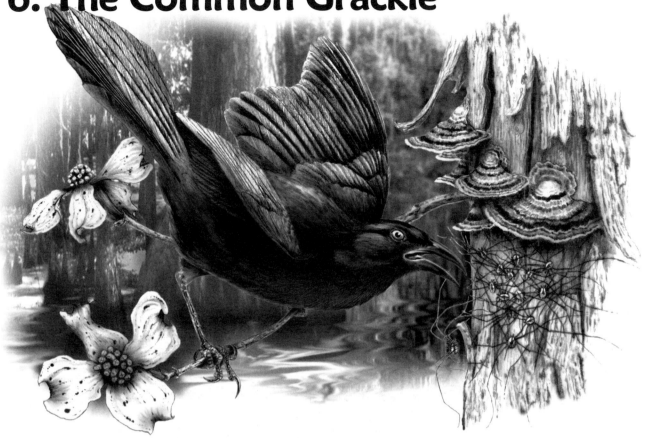

Grackles are sociable birds. They greatly enjoy one another's company, especially during nesting and other activities. At dusk, they gather together in night-roosts and make a tremendous racket of squeaks, squeals, and metallic grating noises. **"Koo-ko-cha-WEEE-kee!"** they sing. **"Ko-goo-bah-LEEK!"** **"SKOO-duh'LEEK!"** When upset, they explode with **"CHAK! CHAK!"** cries.

The nest in the grapevine/buttonbush was one of several grackle nests in the tupelo and bald cypress grove at the edge of the swamp. Most had an outer structure of sticks and cattail blades from the marsh, an inner cup made of dry grass and pine needles, and a lining of silvery Spanish moss.

Arriving at her nest with her beakful of goodies, the mother grackle stuffed the entire wad into the mouth of the noisiest rusty-grey chick, then immediately left the nest again to search for more food.

The unfed nestlings squawked with disappointment for a while, then fell silent to wait for the next delivery. All day long, this scene played out again and again in several of the grackle nests. In one of the nests, a parent grackle sat quietly on eggs, waiting for them to hatch.

Finding enough food for the growing nestlings was an enormous task, one that kept both grackle parents busy from dawn to dusk. They plucked caterpillars off leaves, beetles from the forest floor, and snatched insects fluttering around the dogwood blossoms. They were clumsy at such mid-air captures – their large up-folded tails made quick twists and turns difficult.

Late in the afternoon, the male noticed a clump of harvestmen (daddy-longlegs) clustered beneath a colony of bracket fungi on an ancient, half-dead water hickory which grew out over the water at the edge of the swamp. Landing on a nearby dogwood twig, he leaned forward to grab a beakful. But the branch dipped as he lunged, and his off-balance peck knocked the entire squirming knot of harvestmen into the brown swamp water below.

As he fluttered above the water in frustration, a large black horsefly buzzed past, and he forgot about the harvestmen as he chased after it at top speed.

Longnose Gar

Lepisosteus osseus (leh-pis-OSS-tee-us   OSS-ee-us)
Lepis = "scale"   **osteus** = "bony" (Greek)   **osseus** = "of bone" (Latin)

The gars in southern swamps are so extremely successful that the design hasn't changed for millions of years. Gar fossils from the *Mesozoic* (mess-uh-ZOH-ik) period (70 to 220 million years ago) look a lot like gars do now (but a bit chunkier). *Tyrannosaurus rex* would feel right at home with today's gars.

a gar fossil

The longnose gar, also known as garpike, garfish and billfish is our most common gar (see at right). The snout of this "living fossil" is very l-o-n-n-n-g, narrow and full of sharp teeth. The snout is *twice* as long as the rest of its head.

All gars have long, slim bodies with dorsal and anal fins set far back toward the tail. They are covered with an armor of heavy, diamond-shaped scales. Baby gars (fry) eat tiny fish and water insects like mosquito larvae. The adult longnose gar eats small fish and crawfish. It may reach six feet in length and weigh 35lbs.

The Five Gars

Depending on where you are in the southern swamps you can find at least one of the five gars shown below. You are most likely to see a gar from above, so look carefully at the shape, markings, and length/width of its nose (from eye to nose-tip).

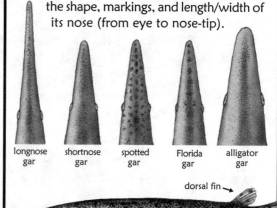

longnose gar   shortnose gar   spotted gar   Florida gar   alligator gar

dorsal fin →

longnose gar   anal fin →

Armored Fish

Tough scales protect gars from nearly all predators except alligators – and Native American peoples of long ago – who killed and ate gars, and shaped their heavy scales into stout arrowheads. Caribbean Indians used the scale-covered skins of gars as armor against the arrows of their enemies.

Early colonial settlers in the Southeast sometimes lined the front edges of their wooden plow blades with the tough scales.

gar scale, actual size

Why Is Swamp Water Brown?

Gars are likely to be swimming in water the color of clear brown breakfast tea. In fact, swamp water is similar to the "sun tea" people brew in jars (except it has fish, snails, and other yummy stuff in it). When leaves and bark drop into warm swamp water, the brown *tannin* in them colors the water, just as it colors ordinary "tea." Such water is called "blackwater" because where it is deep it looks black. And, like tea, it is usually a bit *acidic* (ass-ID-ik = tart or acid). You'd think warm swamp water would be chock full of plants. But it isn't – because plants need sunshine to grow, and sunlight can't get to them through the dark water.

Gars Are Survivors

Fish take in oxygen with their gills. But in warm or polluted water, there may not be much oxygen. Most fish and other water dwellers can't live in such poor conditions.

But the gar, in addition to its gills, has a special air sac or bladder. When oxygen levels in the water are low, it just goes to the surface for a gulp of fresh air. This helps it live comfortably where other animals can't survive. That's one reason the gar is still hanging around after all these eons.

Daddy-Longlegs

A harvestman is also called a "daddy-longlegs."

This arachnid is not a spider although it is closely related to spiders.

harvestman actual size

craneflies (on page 20) may also be called daddy-longlegs.

Jaws (from an artist's sketchpad)

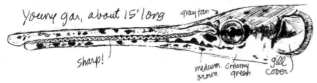

Young gar, about 15" long   gray tan
sharp!   medium brown   creamy green   gill cover

Gars can't chew – their teeth don't actually meet each other. The tiny, needle-sharp teeth of the upper jaw fit into the hollows between teeth in the lower jaw, creating a perfect gripper for catching and holding slippery prey until it can be swallowed whole.

7. The Longnose Gar

Under the water's smooth surface swam a school of fingerling gars. They looked more like floating grass or twigs than fish.

They basked lazily in the shallow water, absorbing the dappled sunlight, using very little energy. Baby gars normally eat mosquito and other insect larvae, and since there were plenty of mosquito larvae developing in the swamp, the little fish were well fed. They cruised along slowly in a loose group, each one eating whatever it discovered on the way.

A gar's mouth is long, slim, and toothy. To catch prey, a gar drifts until its mouth is beside an aquatic insect or smaller fish. A swift sideways jerk of open jaws studded with needle-sharp teeth, a snap, and the larva, insect or fish is history.

By the end of the year, the tiny garfish fry would be about eighteen inches long – if they weren't first eaten by larger fish and other predators such as bullfrogs, alligators, herons and snapping turtles. At eighteen inches, they would be eating other fish, frogs, worms, and anything else that they could get down their narrow throats.

Now, dislodged by the grackle, the long-legged harvestmen hit the water, breaking the surface into a froth of dimples and waving legs near the school of baby gars. Startled at first, the fish scattered, hiding under a raft-like mat of floating hearts plants. Then, seeing that the harvestmen were food-size, they circled them hungrily, flashing in for the kill like mini-sharks.

Jerk! Snap! The harvestmen were almost too large for the baby garfish mouths, but that barely slowed them. Wiry harvestman legs drifted off in all directions as the gars stuffed themselves greedily.

A little blue heron flying past noticed the frantic activity and landed in the water nearby. Her gliding approach was hidden by the floating hearts leaves, and the little gars, busy with dinner, didn't see her. She crouched silently, fixing her eyes on the swirl. As the last of the harvestmen disappeared down tiny fishy throats, the little garfish slowed and regrouped into a drifting school.

Little Blue Heron

Egretta caerulea (ee-GRET-uh see-ROO-lee-uh)
Egretta = "small heron" *caerulea* = "blue"

You can hear a heron rookery (nursery) from quite a long way off – croaks, squawks, quacks, grunts, bleats, hoots, yaps and squeals. Little blue herons make a low, clucking note when feeding and ***"tell you what, tell you what!"*** calls between rookery nests.

Several bird species may share the same rookery. Where you see little blue herons you often see tricolored (Louisiana) herons, snowy egrets and cattle egrets. Other water birds like anhingas, white ibises, night herons, wood storks and great blue herons may also nest there. In rookeries near the ocean, you may see roseate spoonbills.

Most rookeries are surrounded by water. Little blue herons usually nest in buttonbush, wax myrtle and holly shrubs, or in low willow trees two to fifteen feet above the water at the *perimeter* (per-IM-uh-ter = edge) of a colony. The nests of little blue herons, tricolor herons and snowy egrets look very similar, and so do their three to five pale-green eggs.

Hunting Techniques

Little Blue Heron: When hunting, this heron stalks slowly through water. Spotting prey, it sneaks up and strikes with its beak. In a school of fish, it runs around snatching up one fish after another.

a **little blue heron** sneaks along

Tricolored Heron: The tricolored heron hunts much like a little blue heron. It may also hold its wings out to shade the water so it can see better.

a **tricolored heron** makes shade

Snowy Egret: The snowy egret runs around in shallow water, wings up, nabbing small fish, crawfish and water insects. There are several white wading birds, but you can identify the snowy egret by its "golden slippers." No other small white wader has black legs/yellow feet.

Cattle Egret: White, with tan on its head, neck and chest during mating season, the cattle egret came from Africa to South America (blown in by a hurricane?) in the 1930's and spread to Florida by the 50's. Other herons and egrets hang out around water, but the cattle egret prefers to follow cows, catching insects scared up by their hooves.

a **snowy egret** in its "golden slippers"

Singin' the Little Blues (a poem)

This untidy clump's
a li'l blue heron nest.
You'll have to admit
that it isn't the best.
It's made by the mother
with sticks brought by dad,
    but the nest isn't great –
    its construction is **BAD**.
Although the top's hollow, it's not very deep
So eggs may roll out of the untidy heap.
The little blue parents both sit on the eggs
    (although this is awkward with long, skinny legs).
And some poor chicks fall from the nest to the ground,
where crows, snakes and vultures are hanging around.
....But the chicks that remain will get lots more to eat
when their unlucky siblings aren't there to compete.

The "Calico" Heron

A nestling blue heron chick is covered with white *down* (fluffy feathers – see page 74) when it hatches. Then white feathers grow out, making it look like a snowy egret (see above). But while snowy egrets have "golden slippers" a little blue heron's feet are gray.

Its white feathers are gradually replaced by the bluish-gray feathers of an adult, but in the meantime, a young little blue heron looks like it's wearing a blue-and-white calico shawl.

Duck Potato *Sagittaria latifolia*

Water plants like arrowhead (also called "duck potato") hide crawfish, insects, tadpoles, fish and other water creatures from hungry hunters. Their shade cools the water. Turtles and insects eat stems and leaves. The starchy root (the "potato") was once an important food plant for Southeastern Native Americans. Ducks and muskrats eat it, too.

(What snack food could you make from duck potatoes? "Quackers"?)

KWAWK!
"Kwawk" is a local name for night herons, since that's one of their calls. They also cry ***"roop?"*** and ***"ayoke!"*** and make various other shrieks and squawks.
Immature youngsters of both these herons are striped brown-and-white.

black-crowned night heron (male)

yellow-crowned night heron (male)

Watch for heron tracks in muddy places.

8. The Little Blue Heron

The little blue heron lived in an island rookery deep in the swamp. Tall pines and cypresses draped with Spanish moss were surrounded by sweet gum and tupelo trees and a fringe of willows. Many of the trees were bony white snags. A colony of little blue herons and anhingas had built their nests just a few feet above the water in the willows. Higher up, in the sweet gum and tupelo trees, the nests of yellow-crowned and black-crowned night herons and white ibises were jumbled together. The tall trees held the nests of the largest wading birds – the gleaming white great egrets, wood storks, and great blue herons.

In the different nests were eggs and chicks of all ages – some freshly hatched, and others nearly ready to leave the nest. They clattered, shrieked, squawked, honked, squealed, crooned, croaked and clucked in an ear-splitting chorus. The frequent, rustling flutter of birds taking off and landing blended with the occasional *CRA-A-A-CK* of breaking twigs and branches.

The little blue heron could faintly hear the rookery from where she stood watching the tiny garfish. Creeping up on the shadowy forms of the little gars, she pecked rapidly into the school, gulping them down quickly. She splashed back and forth catching as many as she could as the frightened fry tried to hide under the banana-shaped storage tubers of the floating heart plants and the large, arrowhead-shaped leaves of the duck potatoes. Finally, she stopped, staring intently into the dark water around her feet. Nothing moved.

She crouched down, launched into the air and flew back to the rookery.

As she landed on her small nest, her two chicks sprang up screaming. The chicks grabbed her bill crosswise and began to jerk at it, sliding their small bills lower toward the tip with each jerk. When one nestling's bill reached the end of the mother heron's bill, she opened her bill slightly, and disgorged all the things she had spent the last hour gathering – minnows, grasshoppers, partly-digested crawfish, and twelve tiny gars – into the chick's bill.

On the next trip she might bring frogs, caterpillars, crickets or a lizard, feeding the other nestling in the same way. The anhinga chicks in the next nest watched the feeding herons hungrily. They hadn't been fed in a long time.

Anhinga

Anhinga anhinga (an-HING-guh an-HING-guh)
Anhinga = the name used by Amazonian Indians for this bird

The anhinga (also called "snakebird" or "water turkey") is an amazing water bird. For one thing, it **spears** large prey – very unusual in the bird world. Most birds just peck and **grab**.

The anhinga cruises underwater like a skinny black submarine, with wings folded and head and neck stretched out ahead. It thrusts powerfully with its webbed feet as it searches for fish, frogs, crawfish, or water insects. It seizes small fish up to 7" long, but stabs bigger ones with snake-like speed.

It's called a "snakebird" because it may paddle along with just its long, snaky head and neck above the surface.

Its feathers are odd, too. The main tail feathers are crimped like crinkly potato chips. And to keep out water, the body feathers grow so close together they look like fur.

These crimps are on only half of the feather. Their purpose is unknown.

Funny Feet

How does a bird live its life? Look at its feet!

A woodpecker has two toes forward and ← two toes backward to help it go **up and down trees.**

An anhinga can **swim well** because its big feet are webbed and very stretchy.

A common moorhen (see pages 70 - 71) needs long toes to help it **walk on floating plants and mud.**

Largemouth Bass

This big-mouthed fish is a native of the southeastern U.S. It may live in water that is shallow or deep, warm or cool, moving or still – it's not picky.

Largemouth bass can reach twenty-five pounds and three feet in length. With its enormous mouth, it's no problem for this fish to OPEN WIDE!

As a small minnow, it eats insects. As an adult, it will suck in ducklings, young muskrats, fish, crawfish and frogs (see above).

Flying Kites

Swamps have lots of insects in summer, making them ideal habitat for kites (which eat mainly flying insects, frogs, snakes and snails). The kites shown below patrol the swamps. Males are shown here. Females have different coloration.

swallow-tailed kite
A summer resident all over the Southeast, this big kite, with up to 50" wingspread, is common only in Florida. Its forked tail makes it easy to identify. ↓

Mississippi kite
Throughout much of the Southeast, the Mississippi kite catches and eats mostly insects in the air, but also mice, toads and small snakes on the ground. It is a graceful flyer.

snail kite
Resident (but rare and threatened) in the Everglades, this kite eats only the meat of water snails which it grabs, in flight, from marsh grass and pulls from the shell with its long, sharp, hooked beak (see close-up at left).

hooked beak

Kinky Bird

The neck of the anhinga is kinked for lightning-fast underwater stabs.

A bone-and-muscle hinge at the eighth and ninth vertebrae (see C below) snaps the anhinga's head forward to help it spear fish.

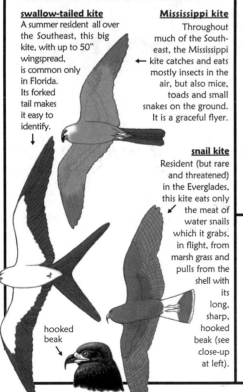

Do you suppose this gave the Paleo-Indians from prehistoric times the idea for the spear-thrower or **atlatl** (at-LAH-tul)? Compare points **A, B,** and **C.**

B
anhinga
C

A
using the atlatl
C

Notice how alike they are. But one thing **is** different – the anhinga doesn't throw its head away!

Anhinga or Cormorant?

That's easy. Anhingas have straight, sharp bills which help them spear their prey, and no exterior (outside) nostrils. The closely related cormorants have hooked bills which keep prey from sliding out, and exterior nostrils.

hooked bill, nostril here

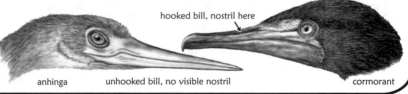

anhinga   unhooked bill, no visible nostril   cormorant

9. The Anhinga

The noise level in the rookery rose to a roar as several Mississippi kites appeared overhead. But these kites were interested only in the insects flying around the rookery, so they circled awhile, snapping up flies, before gliding away.

As the rookery racket subsided, the two anhinga chicks groomed their peach-colored fuzz and watched the sky for their father. It had been a long time since the last food delivery. The week before, their mother had dived into a tangle of discarded fishing line and drowned. Now their father was struggling to raise his nestlings alone.

Several miles away, the male anhinga rose up through the water to the surface of a pond, a six-inch largemouth bass skewered on his dagger-sharp bill.

He paused, inhaling to draw air into special air-sacs within his body to help him float higher. Then he paddled through cypress knees and arrow arum plants and clambered up onto a willow branch that dipped into the water. Curling his soft, webbed feet around a branch, and pointing his head skyward, he spread his wings and tail to drain off the water and let the morning sun bake his dark feathers.

Dry at last, he returned to the rookery. With a great flapping of wings and excited jumping up and down, the chicks greeted their father with wheezy squawks.

The anhinga brought up the partly digested bass from his crop for one chick, then left, returning almost immediately with a lucky find for the second hungry chick – several tadpoles he had found in a drying pool. After grooming awhile, the chicks climbed to the edge of the nest to eject soupy white guano (see page 30) over the edge into the water below.

Jerking his head up sharply, he flipped the bass off his bill and into the air. As it came down, he caught it cross-ways in his bill and banged it against a floating branch until it stopped flopping. Flinging it into the air again, he caught its head in his bill and swallowed. The anhinga now had enough food in his crop (see page 86) for one chick, but his feathers were too soaked with water to fly.

All over the rookery, birds were eating, grooming, and guarding their territories with stabs, squawks and beating wings. Chicks and adult birds were digesting their food and shooting excrement over the sides of the nests. The guano "whitewash" spotted the leaves, spattered the branches, and either enriched the water below or covered the ground beneath the trees with a smelly white blanket.

Red-bellied Woodpecker

Melanerpes carolinus (mel-un-ER-peez cair-oh-LIE-nus)
Melanos = "black" ***herpes*** = "creeper" ***carolinus*** = "of Carolina"

To the Cherokees, the red-bellied woodpecker, whom they called *Dalala*, symbolized war – perhaps because of its red head and neck which made it seem to be wearing a headdress, or maybe because it appeared to be scalped.

These charming birds are common in open woods around swamps. They're fairly tame and easy to find and watch, although if you're looking for a "red belly" you may not see one – the lower belly is sort of a blushing pink, but the real red is on the head.

That fire-engine red cap is hard to miss. If you see a mostly-black-and-white bird swooping from tree to tree calling **"*churrrrr, churrrrr,*"** it is probably a red-bellied woodpecker.

pattern of wingbeats

Guano - The Real Poop

Bird poop is called *guano* (GWAH-no). It makes great fertilizer because it is rich in nitrogen, phosphate and other nutrients. Rookeries produce LOTS of guano.

Rookery trees grow greener and larger from the birds' guano at first, but soon the guano acids begin to kill them. The weakened trees may be invaded by woodboring beetles – great woodpecker food.

Diseases may enter the tree through beetle tunnels. When the trees die, their trunks, branches and roots are recycled into the soil, enriching it for new plants and animals, continuing the endless circle of life.

These patterns on wood are the tunnels of small woodboring beetles.

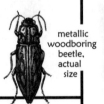

metallic woodboring beetle, actual size

To Make an Egg

An egg yolk is released into a bird's oviduct from a cluster of eggs in the ovary (if it is fertilized, a chick will hatch out later – if it's not fertilized, it won't hatch). Here's what happens next:

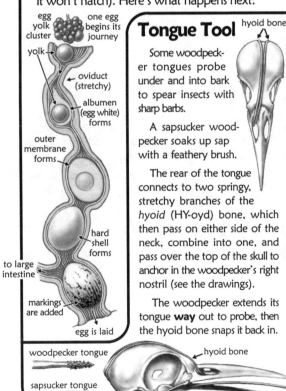

egg yolk cluster

one egg begins its journey

yolk

oviduct (stretchy)

albumen (egg white) forms

outer membrane forms

hard shell forms

to large intestine

markings are added

egg is laid

woodpecker tongue

sapsucker tongue

hyoid bone

Tongue Tool

hyoid bone

Some woodpecker tongues probe under and into bark to spear insects with sharp barbs.

A sapsucker woodpecker soaks up sap with a feathery brush.

The rear of the tongue connects to two springy, stretchy branches of the *hyoid* (HY-oyd) bone, which then pass on either side of the neck, combine into one, and pass over the top of the skull to anchor in the woodpecker's right nostril (see the drawings).

The woodpecker extends its tongue **way** out to probe, then the hyoid bone snaps it back in.

Woodpecker Woodworkings

Who's that beating on a drum out in the swamp – a gentle rolling drum tattoo? It might be a **red-bellied woodpecker.**

So, what's it doing? It might be advertising its territory to other males, drilling a dead or dying tree for insects, or excavating a nest hole. The round hole of a red-bellied woodpecker is about two inches across.

Pileated (PY-lee-ay-tid) and **ivory-billed woodpeckers** make big rectangular holes while drilling for burrowing insects. Occasional reports of ivorybills indicate they may not be extinct as once thought.

The **red-cockaded woodpecker** drills only into living pines

inside view of a red-bellied woodpecker nest

flicker

pileated woodpecker

red-cockaded woodpecker at hole

yellow-bellied sapsucker sucking sap

tongue

with heartwood disease. This makes the injured tree drip gooey pitch all around the hole, which keeps snakes from crawling inside to eat the chicks.

A **yellow-bellied sapsucker** drills holes in living trees. The holes fill with sap, which it licks up with its feathery tongue (see at lower left). It also returns frequently to eat any insects that have become trapped in the sap. Wasps and other birds also feed at the holes.

The round entrance hole of a **flicker** is about 2¾" wide, and is usually drilled into a dead tree or stump.

10. The Red-bellied Woodpecker

The stinky guano and the noise advertised the rookery's location to any creature with ears or a nose. But the rookery was protected from predators – most wouldn't swim out to the island through the alligator-patrolled swamp. The swamp made a perfect moat or water barrier around the rookery

Some of the trees were dying. This didn't make them any less usable as homes for the herons and other wading birds. In fact, it actually made them simpler to land in, and it was easier for the birds to see danger and give a warning, or launch into flight to chase a hawk or crow. On the downside, the trees didn't offer much protection to the chicks from the hot sunshine, and chicks were more exposed to attack from the air by crows, vultures and grackles who sometimes robbed unprotected nests of eggs and small chicks.

But for some of the rookery dwellers, those things weren't a problem – because they lived safely *inside* the dead trees.

A courting pair of red-bellied woodpeckers were inspecting decaying rookery trees. Red crowns flashing in the sunshine, they swooped from tree to tree, landing and inspecting each one, tapping loudly, calling **"CHAR-r-r-r! CHAR-r-r-r! CHAR-r-r-r!"** to each other as they searched.

They decided on a location near the center of the rookery, and the male began to excavate a hole about fifteen feet above the ground in one of the trees. The female soon joined him and they both worked on the hole, taking turns pecking and excavating. They tossed the bits of wood out the opening. It took the two woodpeckers nearly a week to carve out a nest about twelve inches deep and five inches in diameter. Exhausted by the difficult job, they rested – eating, sleeping and gathering their strength for a day or two.

Then the female laid four white eggs in the clean, new nest. The big job was about to begin, the raising of their family.

There were several other holes in their home tree. For many seasons, pileated woodpeckers had been drilling for wood-boring beetles in the decaying tree. And just below the red-bellied woodpeckers' nest, a level branch jutting out from the silvery trunk like an apartment balcony was a daytime roost for a chuck-will's-widow.

Chuck-will's-widow

Caprimulgus carolinensis (cap-rih-MUL-gus   cair-oh-lih-NEN-sis)
Caper = "goat"   ***mulgeo*** = "to suck"   ***carolinensis*** = "of Carolina"

The chuck-will's-widow has many peculiar names, starting with its family name, which means goatsucker (see at right). But rather than sucking on goats, the chuck-will's-widow is busy eating all kinds of insects and loudly calling ***"CHUCK-WIDDLES-WIDOW"*** during late afternoons and on moonlit summer nights. Its call has a bubbly sound like water running over rocks into a pool. It closely resembles a whip-poor-will.

It's also called "chicka-willa," "chuck," "mosquito-hawk" and "nightjar." Nightjar refers to the jarring, sleep-wrecking cries it makes after dark. One moonlit night, a chuck-will's-widow was heard [by the author] to make 840 calls without stopping.

It may sit on warm roads after dark, darting into the air for insects. If you drive down a country road at night and see two red lights rise into the air and disappear, it may be a chuck-will's-widow – one of the few birds with red eyeshine.

Hiding In Plain Sight
Imagine walking through the woods, watching the ground carefully for wildflowers or whatever, when a pile of leaves which ***you are looking straight at*** suddenly sprouts wings, flits silently up off the ground and disappears into the woods like a gigantic twelve-inch-long moth with a two-foot wingspread. WHAT WAS THAT?!

A chuck-will's-widow had been on the leaves almost at your feet and you didn't see it even though you looked right at it!

Rictal Bristles

Rictal (RIK-tull) bristles around the chuck-will's-widow's open mouth may help scoop up insects. They may also sense insect wing vibrations and improve the bird's aim. We aren't sure.

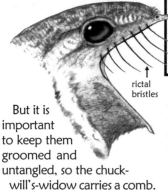

But it is important to keep them groomed and untangled, so the chuck-will's-widow carries a comb.

rictal bristles

You have just experienced *cryptic* (KRIP-tik = concealing) *coloration*. A chuck-will's-widow is almost invisible if it doesn't move. In trees, it perches parallel on branches, blending into the outline of the limb. Even if you often hear them call, you may never see one.

Herons and barn owls have similar combs – little teeth on the claw of each middle toe, used to scratch and groom their feathers.

toe comb

Goatsuckers
A chuck-will's-widow is in a family of birds called goatsuckers. This strange name supposedly got started when people long ago noticed birds that are related to chuck-will's-widows hanging around goats, where they may have been catching flies that buzz around livestock.

Their huge mouths were about the right size to fit around a goat's teat. So a whole group of birds, which also includes whip-poor-wills, nighthawks and others, got named **goatsuckers!**   (But they *don't* suck goats.)

PEENT!
Chuck-will's-widows look a lot like the closely related nighthawks (also called nightjars). But flying nighthawks show big white bands on their pointy wings, and their cry is a high ***"peeent!"*** or ***"jeeep."***

nighthawk

The Great Egg Escape
A chuck-will's-widow doesn't make a real nest – the eggs are just laid on dry leaves. If danger threatens, the parent may carry the eggs away in its bill to a safer place. Sometimes they drop eggs, so to avoid causing a catastrophe, keep well away from any nest you find!

Night Lights
Swamps are habitat for many species of firefly or lightning bug. These beetles flash glowing areas on their abdomens on and off to attract mates. Each species blinks a different pattern of flashes.

Fireflies taste terrible so they have few enemies. Here are two blinking patterns:

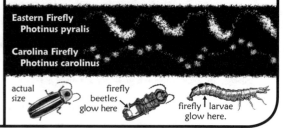

Eastern Firefly
Photinus pyralis

Carolina Firefly
Photinus carolinus

actual size   firefly beetles glow here   firefly larvae glow here.

11. The Chuck-will's-widow

A chuck-will's-widow usually builds its nest on the ground, generally in plain sight, right on the leaves and twigs. Actually, it **isn't** in plain sight, because a chuck-will's-widow is so well camouflaged that most predators

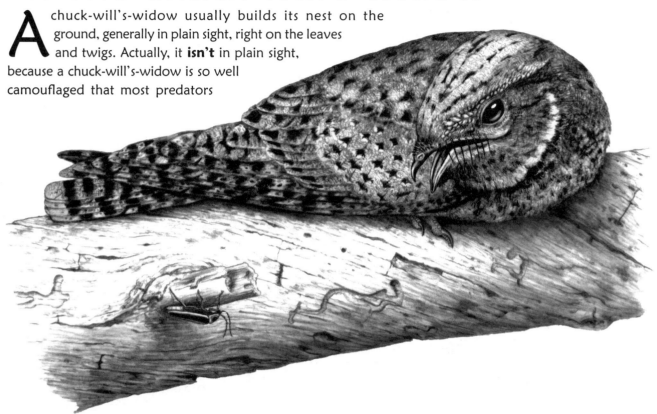

wouldn't notice it unless they stepped on it. When not on the nest, the chuck-will's widow may roost in a spot further above the ground.

This chuck-will's-widow had chosen to roost on a large level branch so close to the red-bellied wood-peckers' hole that the breeze from the woodpeckers' wings fanned his mottled feathers as they came and went from their entrance.

He rested parallel to the branch instead of cross-wise as most birds do. His brown/grey/black speckled feathers were colored like bark, so he blended with the tree, disguised as a broken-off branch. He blinked lazily as he watched a firefly beetle moving along the branch, then went back to sleep. Chuck-wills are night birds and don't move about much during daylight – and they prefer to catch their food in the air.

As the evening shadows turned blue beneath the great cypresses, and the roar of the rookery quieted to the occasional creaking of a nest and the yelps of chicks being pecked by their nestmates, the firefly launched into the air. It disappeared then reappeared, tracing a dotted line through the darkness as the light in its abdomen flared on and off like a tiny flashlight.

The chuck-will's-widow opened his large, black eyes wide, and looked around. Then he yawned. Until then, his bill had seemed tiny – just a small black point on the front of his face. But as the two halves opened, the crack grew wider and wider, opening into a huge, gaping two-inch hole, big enough to gulp down a small bird. Stiff, curving whiskers, called rictal bristles, framed the opening, ready to rake in any moth, beetle, fly, wasp or little bird that might escape his open beak.

The chuck-will's-widow closed his bill with a tiny snap and peered around. Below him, many fireflies were now flying, twinkling like miniature Christmas tree lights, winking in and out of the darkness.

"CHUCK-WIDDLES-WIDOW," he burbled loudly. *"CHUCK-WIDDLES-WIDOW, CHUCK-WIDDLES-WIDOW."* Then he was gone, a flickering shadow in the dark.

He cruised through the air like a bat, gulping down whatever he came upon: beetles, fluttery moths, and swarms of mosquitos hatching from the dark, quiet backwaters of the swamp.

Anopheles Mosquito

Anopheles quadrimaculatus (an-OFF-ul-eez kwa-drih-mack-yew-LAY-tus)
Anopheles = "troublesome" **quadri** = "four" **maculatus** = "spotted"

It's really hard to think ANY good thoughts about mosquitoes. But if there weren't any mosquitoes, the swamp would be an entirely different place. And maybe not a better place – because the many different species of mosquitoes are actually the "bread and butter" of a lot of swamp animals.

The lives of many fish, insects and their larvae, crawfish, frogs, and others *depend* on eating mosquito babies ("wigglers") that hatch from eggs laid in the calm swamp waters.

But eggs laid in rain-filled pails or old tires don't get eaten. You may have been bitten by mosquitoes hatching from these "pools." (What could you do to help solve that problem?)

How can you avoid getting bitten? Use insect repellent, stay behind mosquito netting or screens, don't wear dark clothes, and **don't breathe** – mosquitoes will follow the trail of the carbon dioxide (CO_2) you breathe out, right back to yummy you!

a *Culex* mosquito egg raft on water

Egg Raft Styles

single floating *Anopheles* egg, enlarged

Mosquito *larvae* (LAR-vee= more than one larva) must mature in water. Some mosquito species lay hundreds of eggs which they glue together into floating rafts. The *Anopheles* mosquito lays single eggs, each kept afloat with an "inner tube" collar. Others lay their eggs on land which will flood later. Most mosquitoes lay eggs in calm water – rough or moving water could injure a larva or *pupa* (PEW-puh). Eating small organisms and liquid nutrients, a larva grows and molts four times, maturing into a pupa, then hatching into an adult.

larva "wiggler"

pupa

a mosquito begins to emerge from its pupal skin

a female mosquito hatches from the water surface (compare her with the male below)

A Swamp Food Chain

Swamps depend on mosquito and other insect larvae to eat algae, decayed plant parts and animal microorganisms; then *they* are eaten by small carnivores like dragonfly nymphs, and by gambusia. Nymphs and gambusia are eaten by frogs, fish, turtles and other creatures; then *they* are gobbled by alligators, herons, otters, and so on. Excrement (poop) plus plants and animals which die in the water, decay and enrich the water. This causes algae to grow faster for insect larvae to eat. . . . around and around it goes.

Poisons used to kill mosquitoes also kill many other organisms which the swamp ecosystem depends upon. Alien plant and animal invaders can mess things up, too.* If any link in the chain of life is broken, it upsets the balance of life in the swamp.

Gambusia
Gambusia affinis

The gambusia (gam-BOO-zee-uh) is a mosquitofish native to our Southeastern swamps.

It eats mostly mosquito wigglers.

½ - ⅔ actual size

Spatterdock
Nuphar advena

The spatterdock or yellow pond lily is common in most cypress swamps. Every autumn it dies back and decays, adding its nutrients to the water. Many of the swamp creatures use it for shelter and food.

Blood Suckers *Macrobdella decora*

The prey of the freshwater leech is turtles, frogs, fish and other swamp visitors (maybe you). It holds on with toothy suckers, injects a numbing fluid, and drinks up to five times its own weight in blood. Then it lets go and swims away, rippling like a ribbon in the water.

head end

The site bleeds for awhile because an enzyme is added to keep the blood flowing. But the sucking doesn't hurt and the wound doesn't get infected, so relax – no big deal.

Mosquitoes Really Suck!

A mosquito pierces the skin with tiny blades, then sucks blood up one tube and drips saliva (filled with disease microbes and "blood thinner") down another to keep the blood flowing. If a mosquito sucks up blood from a sick person, it can pass on that disease in its saliva to the next person it bites.

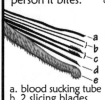

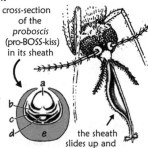

cross-section of the *proboscis* (pro-BOSS-kiss) in its sheath

a. blood sucking tube
b. 2 slicing blades
c. 2 sawing blades
d. saliva drip tube
e. proboscis sheath surrounds a-d

the sheath slides up and loops out when the mosquito inserts its proboscis into the victim

The *Anopheles* mosquito, also called the malaria mosquito, can spread the terrible disease malaria. But since few people in the U.S. have malaria, mosquitoes don't often spread it in the continental U.S.

Male mosquitoes (the ones with feathery antennae)→ suck plant juices, not blood.

Mosquito History

From mosquitoes preserved in amber, and fossils from forty million years ago, we know ancient mosquitoes looked almost the same as today's mosquitoes. There are currently more than 2000 mosquito species in the world; 121 species are in the US.

*Note: Sometimes **drastic** steps are needed to control **aliens** (non-native plants or animals). See pp 104-105.

12. The Anopheles Mosquito

The female mosquito was flying low over the water, the whine of her wings wavering up and down as she dropped her eggs one by one into the water. Then... snap! She was engulfed in a cavernous mouth.

She had laid only eleven eggs before she became the chuck-will's-widow's snack. But those eggs would become mosquitos to take her place – if they were lucky.

In the warm water several days later, the little eggs developed into larvae "wigglers." Eating algae, tiny water creatures and decayed plant parts, they grew and shed their skins several times until they were ready to morph into pupae after about seven days. Only six of them made it this far. Two of the original eleven had been eaten by larger mosquito wigglers, and three had become lunch for dragonfly and damselfly nymphs.

The remaining wigglers curled and stiffened into dormant pupae. They floated just under the water's surface, breathing through tiny snorkel tubes on their backs but doing little else as they changed inside. If danger threatened, they could dive, but in a short while they would rise again through the murky water to the surface. This, and breathing, seemed to be their only activities. Five more potential mosquitoes were lost at this point. One became stuck to a stinkpot turtle shell as the turtle climbed out on a rock to bask, and it fried in the hot sunshine, unable to wiggle hard enough to squirm off the turtle's shell. The other four were eaten by mosquitofish.

About two weeks after being dropped into the swamp water as eggs, a single surviving mosquito pupa hatched. As it floated on the surface of the water, the skin slowly split down the length of its back, and a female mosquito rose up through the split like an inflating balloon. Resting on the raft of the shed skin, she waited for her wings to dry, then she flew off to search for a mate. Later that night she found one.

Once she had mated, she needed a feast of blood in order for her eggs to grow. The late afternoon air of the swamp sang with the whine of her flight as she detected and followed a carbon dioxide trail of exhaled air. It led straight to a family of raccoons exploring the mud in a shallow bed of spatterdock pond lilies at the edge of the marsh.

Raccoon

Procyon lotor (PRO-see-on LOH-tor)
Pro = "before" ***cyon*** = "dog" ***lotor*** = "a washer"

The name "raccoon" is a remodeled Algonquin (Native American) name, "a-ra-kun-em," meaning "one who scratches with his hands." Sometimes we even shorten its name to "coon."

A raccoon feels right at home just about anywhere. In fact, it is found in every state in the continental U.S. It prefers to live around water, so a cypress swamp is Raccoon Paradise.

Tree cavities and hollows under fallen trees are perfect for shelter from storms, quiet naps, and maternity (muh-TUR-nuh-tee) dens (places to raise young). The shallow waters are full of crawfish, frogs and other goodies that are high in protein and easy to catch. Turtles bury their delicious eggs on nearby slopes. Persimmons, pawpaws, berries, fox grapes and nuts are found there; so are water birds and their eggs.

By the way, pet food left outside for your dog or cat is also a favorite raccoon feast.

Prettier Every Day!

newborn kit

five weeks

You'd think a newborn raccoon baby would be especially adorable. After all, look how charming its parents are.

NOT! A raccoon kit is dull black, scrawny, and, well, kinda ugly. But soon its markings show up, its eyes open, and it is cuter than a kitten! Don't try to make one into a pet, though. A raccoon is curious, noisy and nocturnal – up all night and into everything. It'd drive you nuts. Besides, it's against the law in most states to keep **any** kind of wildlife as a pet. Raccoons may also spread rabies (see page 106).

Cinnamon Fern
Osmunda cinnomomea
The first fronds this fern sends up in spring look as though they were dipped in cinnamon powder.

Stone Croaker

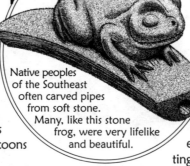

Native peoples of the Southeast often carved pipes from soft stone. Many, like this stone frog, were very lifelike and beautiful.

Scrub-a-Dub

Raccoons wash their food if water is nearby to rinse away mud or sand. The urge is *instinctive* (in-STINK-tiv) – the raccoon is born with it. But if no water is around, it skips washing and eats anyway.

A raccoon's long-fingered front paws are almost like human hands (but without clasping thumbs), and allow the raccoon to do many things quite skillfully. People who raise chickens may learn how easily raccoons can open a gate latch in order to snitch hen eggs (and hens)!

right front foot

Skull Styles

muskrat 2½"
HERBIVORE

house cat 3½"
CARNIVORE

raccoon 4¾"
OMNIVORE

(Also see **Skullduggery** on page 88.)

0 1" 2" 3" 4" 5"

Herbivores (ER-bih-vorz) such as muskrats and deer, eat plants. Their *incisors* (IN-sy-zerz = front nippers) bite off greenery, and their grinding *molars* (MO-lurz = rear teeth) crush it to mush.

Carnivores (CAR-nih-vorz) eat meat. Wolves, minks (and our pet cats and dogs) are carnivores. Carnivores grab prey with sharp teeth and bite off chunks, which they swallow whole. Carnivores may eat veggies, too. Have you seen your kitty eat grass?

Omnivores (AHM-nih-vorz) like raccoons, bears and people eat almost *anything* edible. They have sharp grabbing and cutting teeth PLUS flattish grinding molars.

raccoon track & scat (poop)

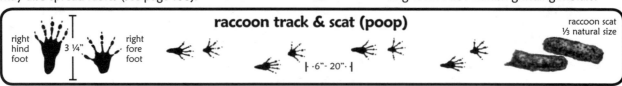

right hind foot 3¼"
right fore foot
|·6"- 20"·|
raccoon scat ⅓ natural size

13. The Raccoon

The mother raccoon was teaching her kits how to find food at the muddy edge of the swamp. They were still small – old enough to keep up with their mother on a hunting trip, but still uncertain about how to catch dinner.

Feeling around in the squishy mud was fun, and the little raccoons were splashing and paddling about playfully until one of them felt something nip its toe. With a yip, eyes round with surprise, the young raccoon grabbed with the other paw and plunged its head into the water to see what it had found. It reared right back out, snorting and sneezing – that *couldn't* be the right way to take a look! The other raccoon kits crowded close, trying to see what was going on and the mother spashed over to them, pushing into the group and feeling expertly with her sensitive hand-like front paws.

There! A big crawfish, with furiously snapping claws, was squirming under her fingers. She grabbed it just as the roving mosquito plunged its tiny daggers into her sensitive eyelid. Squinting and shaking her head, she jerked her paw from the water to brush the mosquito off. But it dodged her paw and flew away, uninjured, to look for another victim.

The crawfish, suddenly free, whipped her tail forward underneath her body like a swim fin and shot backward into a cavity beneath a stone.

The stone wasn't just any old stone. It was a pipe carved from soapstone – then lost by its owner in the far distant past. It had fallen into deep mud, and later it had become overgrown by tree and shrub roots. Now it was entangled with the roots of a bayberry at the edge of the swamp. The crawfish didn't notice the frog shape. She only appreciated the safe, dark hiding place the ancient pipe now created. Settling into the shadows, she waited for the raccoons to go away.

The mother raccoon soon caught another crawfish. One of the raccoon kits grabbed it and leaped out onto the bank, chased by the others. For awhile they tugged and chewed, flattening a patch of cinnamon ferns and a young wax-myrtle shrub to a leafy carpet as they learned the crawfish's taste and scent.

Back into the water, squealing from nipped toes but full of excitement, the kits began to learn the art of "crawdadding" in the tea-brown waters of the swamp.

Red Swamp Crawfish

Procambarus clarkii (pro-KAM-bur-us KLAR-kee-eye)
Pro = "before" *cambarus* = "sea crab" *clarkii* = a person's name

People living in the Southeast may call them "mudbugs," "ditchbugs," "crawfish" or "crawdads." Others say "crayfish." But they're not fish or bugs, and lots of them are moms, not dads. These freshwater *crustaceans* (krus-TAY-shunz) are related to shrimps, lobsters and crabs.

An adult red swamp crawfish may be five inches long and colored red, gray or brown. It's the edible tail of this crawfish that most often ends up on Southern menus. Although there are about 330 native crawfish species in the U.S., 90% of commercially sold crawfish are red swamp crawfish. Most crawfish found in markets and restaurants are grown on crawfish farms.

Like mosquitoes, the crawfish is an important member of the food chain. It eats algae, snails, insects, worms, mussels, and **lots** of *detritus* (dih-TRY-tis = floating plant and animal bits). Grackles, herons, egrets, ibis and other birds eat crawfish. Turtles, alligators, otters, raccoons and fish also gobble them eagerly.

Gnome Chimney

In seasons when the edges of swamps go dry, you might find a strange little "gnome chimney" up to ten inches high, and two or three inches across, rising from the mud where water once stood. What on earth made it? A moisture-seeking crawfish!

When a swampy pool dries up, the crawfish tunnels down to find water, which is sinking lower each day. It brings up blobs of mud and sets them down at empty spots on the rim of the hole. With every blob, the rim rises higher and higher on the crawfish's smokeless chimney!

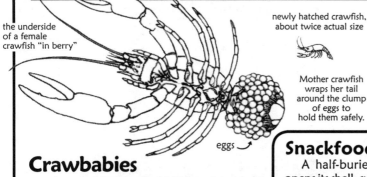

the underside of a female crawfish "in berry"

newly hatched crawfish, about twice actual size

Mother crawfish wraps her tail around the clump of eggs to hold them safely.

eggs →

Crawbabies

A crawfish female with eggs is said to be "in berry" because of the berry-like eggs which adhere to small, sticky bristles on her underbelly. The eggs change from blue or purple to transparent as they mature. A tiny crawfish is visible inside each one. Two to ten weeks later, they hatch (sooner in warm water) and cling to her swimmerets until they're too big to fit beneath her.

Snackfood?

A half-buried mussel opens its shell, sucks water in, and filters out edible things to digest. A hungry crawfish pokes a claw inside, and grabs the mussel before it can snap shut. YUM!

water goes in here
out here

Flue Fishing

How can a white ibis catch its main prey, crawfish, when the swamp dries up and the crawfish are as far as 24" below the surface?

Easy! It drops little bits of the crawfish's chimney down the hole. When the crawfish climbs out of the chimney to clean up the mess, the ibis grabs it. Now, how did the ibis ever learn THAT trick?

Dumping Bait

Some native crawfish are in big trouble. Anglers often dump their leftover live crawfish (used as fish-bait) into the swamp at the end of a day of fishing.

The aggressive rusty crawfish from the Ohio River Basin is often used as fish-bait. Dumped into a new habitat, this alien is a big bully, taking over native crawfish hiding places, eating their food, and causing them to become *extinct* (die out). Read more about aliens on pages 104 and 105.

Mudbug's New Clothes (a poem)

As a crawfish gets bigger, its shell doesn't fit,
So it finds a dark spot where a crawfish can sit,
dissolving the calcium that hardens its skin.
Then it ditches the old shell it used to fit in.

It swells one size larger (as soft as a worm,
and easy to eat since its shell isn't firm).
Then calcium enters and hardens the shell.
The crawfish is safe now, and bigger, as well.

14. The Red Swamp Crawfish

The crawfish that escaped the mother raccoon was a female – a mother with a cluster of about two hundred tiny crawfish babies clinging to the bristles of the swimmerets under her tail. The raccoons had knocked some of the babies off, but most were still attached as she whisked her tail forward beneath her body to propel herself backward under the long-lost frog pipe.

She waited, cramped and ready with upraised claws, to defend herself and her young from another attack of the giant paws. But the raccoons moved on without discovering her hiding place, and the water became quiet again. She moved out into the shallow water to hunt for food.

The young crawfish babies attached to her underside were about a third of an inch long and nearly transparent. Only a few days before, they had hatched from eggs attached to bristles on her feathery swimmerets, splitting their eggs' thin shells to emerge and cling to their mother's underside.

This squirmy burden slowed the mother crawfish down considerably, but carrying them around was part of her job. Tucked out of sight beneath their fierce,

protective mother, they were safer than most little snacks their size. Few dragonfly larvae, bullhead catfish or frogs would try to snatch a baby crawfish out from under those snapping claws.

The swamp water, still shallow because the rains were late, was warmer than usual. That meant the tiny crawfish would grow faster and need to *molt* (emerge from their old skins) into larger skins quite soon. The molting would take about six hours for each tiny crawfish, and during that time the youngster would be soft and very fragile. The same was true for adults – crawfish retreat to safe dark nooks to molt, because even the biggest crawfish becomes a soft, tender morsel until more tough calcium hardens its new shell.

Some of the tiny crawfish that had been brushed off in the encounter with the raccoon found their mother again. They would cling to her swimmerets until after their second molt, finally leaving when there was no longer enough room for them to hang on.

Early Peoples of the Southeast

Many early Native Americans of the Southeast felt very close to the animals they lived with in the forests and swamps. Ancient clans (family groups) claimed kinship with the animals whose name they bore. There were deer, raccoon and bear clans. There were panther, bird, mole, toad, snake and earth clans, to name just a few. Strict laws about marriages, wars and status ruled the people of the clans. Each clan had its own symbols and customs.

Some Native Americans thought a moon eclipse was a huge frog eating the moon, and they made loud noises to frighten it off (medieval Europeans held similar beliefs). To some, turkey vultures, able to eat rotten things without getting sick, symbolized healing. Owls were thought by many to bring bad luck. Rabbits were viewed by some as tricksters. And snakes were considered by many to be powerful, associated with lightning, thunder and rain.

Each of the numerous clans scattered across the vast expanse of the Southeast had its own customs, beliefs, and habits, which changed and shifted as the centuries passed.

Women's Roles, Men's Roles

In some native groups of the Southeast (in historic times), women and men had different roles. Women often owned houses and fields, and their husbands came to live with them.

Women and girls usually gathered firewood and cooked. Animal fur, plant and bark fibers, and feathers were used to weave, sew, dye and twine into clothing, blankets, baskets, nets, mats, cords and ropes. It was usually women who worked their fields and harvested crops. They gathered wild foods in the forest and swamps.

Men and boys generally hunted, made tools and buildings, took care of politics, wars and ceremonies, and cleared fields for crops. They usually skinned the animals they killed, then women made the skins into leather. But not always.

In some groups, women held office in tribal councils, but in others they didn't. In some instances, women even sat differently from men, with their feet tucked beneath them, while the men sat cross-legged (see at left).

Notice the carved pipe, pierced-ear ornaments and the woman's Spanish moss skirt.

The Glorious Gourd

Used by Native Americans for three thousand years, the bottle gourd, *Lagenaria siceraria*, is a globe 3" to 14" in diameter. Light but very tough, it was made into water jugs (see next page), dippers, cups, bowls, rattles, masks, etc.

Gourds were hung from poles around fields as nests for purple martins, swifts, and wrens, to encourage them to eat insects and chase crows and blackbirds away from the crops. See page 109.

The First Americans

The native peoples living in the vast Southeast before Europeans arrived had rich and varied lives. Cherokee, Catawba, Creek, Timucua, Chocktaw, Chickasaw, Caddo, Ocale, Calusa, Natchez, and many, many more native groups lived on the coastal plains. Although they shared some social and cultural customs, each tribe had its own ways, and many different languages were spoken. Some, such as Muskogee (the Creek language), are still in use today. Simple words and signs called *trade jargon* were used for trading between tribes.

In 1819 a wise Cherokee statesman, Sequoyah, invented an alphabet with 85 letters. Thousands of Cherokees learned to read and write it. Here's how Sequoyah signed his name:

Even though these native groups had highly-developed cultures, the slaughter and diseases brought by Europeans reduced their numbers drastically.

While some of these native cultures survive today, most disappeared with barely a trace, along with their distinctive languages, customs and skills.

Swamp Living

Life in the warm, humid swamps was hard in some ways. Mosquitoes were fierce and food spoiled quickly. But the climate was mostly warm, and food and materials for tools and homemaking were available throughout the year. Clay was collected for pottery. Cane lengths made fine tool shafts and handles, and cane strips made durable mats and baskets. Dugout canoes were carved from tulip trees, pines or bald cypress trees. In this dugout canoe are a pottery jar, split-cane basket and mat, and a cane blowgun.

dugout canoe →

woven mat and basket

blowgun and darts

pottery jug

15. The Early Peoples of the Southeast

Once, long ago, on a muggy autumn day, as the high buzz of cicadas throbbed in the air, the owner of the frog pipe hunted for crawfish in the swamp near his camp. While placing a net trap for the crawfish, the man's foot slipped on a muddy stick, pitching him into the swamp. The deerskin lacing that fastened the pouch to his belt caught on a branch and jerked the bag open, dumping his beautifully carved pipe into the water.

The man didn't notice his pipe was missing until after he returned to camp with the net trap full of crawfish. Returning to the crawfish pool, he searched for the pipe in the dark water for a long time but returned home with empty hands.

The camp, a favorite summer location, hummed with activity. Children raced between the small, palmetto-roofed shelters in a pickup game of *chungke (CHUNG-kee)*, rolling the stone *chungke* disk ahead of them with long cane sticks. They nearly collided with a grandmother who was cracking and grinding hickory nuts to add to her family's next meal.

A woman sorted through her fresh squashes and gourd containers full of dried beans, berries, corn, ragweed, goosefoot and other seeds. Her husband sat down near the cooking fire on a mat woven from cane strips. In his hand was a piece of soapstone he had received in trade for a spear he had made. He must carve a new pipe to replace the one he had lost.

He studied the stone, searching for its spirit. What did it want to look like?

The woman began to make some pumpkin bread, cutting up a pumpkin into the boiling water of a clay pot nestled in the coals of the cooking fire. She dribbled a little water into some corn flour, then mashed in hot pumpkin pieces until it made a stiff batter.

She added a handful of dried berries, sunflower seeds and hazelnuts to make a treat for her family, then folded the dough into small loaves. Oiling a shallow pot with bear grease, she placed the loaves inside, covered them with an upside-down pot, and buried them under hot coals. Then she dumped the crawfish into the still-hot water in the pot the pumpkin had cooked in.

As the cicadas whined in the trees, the rich scents of baking bread and simmering crawfish filled the air, blending with the aroma of bean stews, browning catfish, roasting raccoon and hominy from other cooking fires. The man shifted to a more comfortable position on the woven mat and smiled up at his wife with pleasure. The old pipe had been good, but this new one would be even better. He could tell already.

Yellow Bullhead

Ameiurus natalis (ah-MY-ur-us nuh-TAL-us)
A = "not" *mei* = "smaller" *urus* = "tail" *natalis* = "big buttocks"

This catfish may also be called a white-whiskered bullhead, Mississippi bullhead, mudcat, butterball, buttercat, yellow cat, creek cat, greaser, paper-skin, chucklehead cat or polliwog. It is found in warmish vegetated swamps, shallow ponds and slow-moving Southeastern streams.

The yellow bullhead has a light-yellow to mottled olive-green back and a yellowish belly. Its tail is rounded, not notched. Eight white, pink or yellow *barbels* (tentacles) decorate its face.

Catfish can be immediately recognized by those eight barbels, scale-less skin, and the spines in their *dorsal* (back) and *pectoral* (side) fins. A yellow bullhead averages about 10".

Bullheads, catfish and madtoms (a madtom is a small catfish, not an angry dude) are all members of the catfish family, *Ictaluridae* (ik-tuh-LUR-ih-dee). So a bullhead might be a catfish, but a catfish might *not* be a bullhead. Got it?

Fish World

When they forage for food, catfish sweep their barbels, which are covered with taste buds, across the mud, into holes and under rocks to taste for edibles. Their skins are sprinkled all over with sensory cells, too – so a catfish is like a big swimming tongue, tasting everything it passes. This is useful for night feeding.

But that's not all. Like other fish, it inhales water into its nostrils, smells the watery scent, and heads straight for possible food items.

Finally, it "hears" movements and sounds by picking up vibrations along its *lateral line*, a tube of *mucus* (MEW-kus) running under the skin along each side. It can detect passing pawsteps and sounds such as bird alarms above the water. It also senses water temperature, and changes in water pressure caused by creatures swimming past.

Labels on illustration: anal fin, dorsal fin, lateral line, pectoral fin, nostrils, barbels

"Moo" or "Mew"?

See the whiskers? That's how the **cat**fish got its name. As for **bull** head, well, the two upper barbels ARE where bull horns would be, and its eyes DO look like beady little bull eyes.

Labels on illustration: bull, cat, **bullhead catfish**

OWWWW!

The yellow bullhead looks soft and harmless, but don't grab one with bare hands! Inside its dorsal and pectoral fins are wicked spines, and the pectoral spines have sharp, saw-like teeth. The spines can lock into an erect position and jab a nasty hole in you. Wounds made by the spines may sting painfully from the catfish's slightly toxic slime.

pectoral spine, actual size

Bladderwort *Utricularia species*

Bladder sacs line the stems of these underwater carnivorous plants. When small organisms like mosquito larvae touch the bladder's trigger hairs, the bladder pops open, sucking in the prey. After enzymes digest it, the trap resets.

actual size

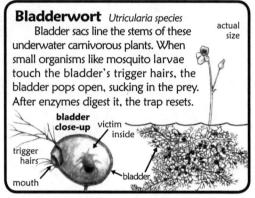

Labels on illustration: **bladder close-up**, victim inside, trigger hairs, mouth, bladder

Southern Water Snake *Nerodia fasciata*

The southern water snake finds prey, escapes danger, and keeps cool or warm in the water. You might mistake one for a venomous cottonmouth snake, which has a white mouth interior and may vibrate its tail rapidly (see p. 95). Water snakes don't have white mouths, and don't shake their tails.

southern water snake no white cheeks

cottonmouth snake See the white cheek? The mouth is white inside, too.

Scatter!

Catfish are omnivorous, eating living and dead plant and animal material – insects; rotten stuff; bits of water plants; aquatic larvae; snails; crawfish; and small, minnow-sized fishes. And yellow bullhead parents guard their babies. Wait a minute. If yellow bullheads eat little fish, is there a problem here? There sure is! When the fry reach a certain size, their guardian parents suddenly don't see "my babies" anymore. They see "dinner."
uh-oh....
SCATTER, KIDS!

16. The Yellow Bullhead

In the shallow arm of the swamp where the water had warmed to nearly seventy degrees, a yellow bullhead catfish nosed a flickering baseball-sized mass that floated in the water.

Earlier that spring, the bullhead and his mate had hollowed out a nest on the muddy swamp bottom. The female bullhead had laid her eggs in the warm muck, then the male had spurted silvery *milt* (fish sperm) over them to fertilize them.

Later, when the tiny fish fry hatched, they crowded together in a compact floating ball, eating bits of plants and algae and any dead flesh they came across.

Guarding the young, the yellow bullhead circled the spherical school of fingerlings, waving whiskery white barbels in all directions to taste the water. Nearby, his mate nibbled a snail off a pond lily stem.

A shaft of sunlight glinted off a southern water snake zigzagging past. The bullhead dashed at it to frighten it off, but the snake wasn't hungry. It slipped smoothly away into the shadows of the warm, dark water.

As the family of raccoons foraged in the shallows for crawdads, the yellow bullhead and his mate shooed the school of babies to shelter in a mass of floating bladderwort plants. Bladders popped and sucked all around the tiny fry as the small fish brushed against their trigger hairs, but the fry were too big for the bladders to suck in.

For a moment, the yellow flowers thrusting above the water waggled furiously. Then all was still as the fry waited, safely hidden within the floating plants.

When the raccoons finally left, the bullheads herded the fry to the raccoons' feasting area. The mud they had stirred up was afloat with yummy tidbits.

As the swamp shrank during the hot spring weather, the bullhead parents would escort the fast-growing young fish into deeper water, protecting them until they were about an inch long. Then each small fish would be on its own.

Only a few fingerlings would survive long enough to *spawn* (lay eggs), because bullhead fry are lunch for many swamp dwellers – including fish crows.

Fish Crow

Corvus ossifragus (KOR-vus oss-IF-ruh-gus)
Corvus = "raven" **ossifragus** = "bone-breaking"

There's an old saying that if a person can name only three birds, the crow will be one of them (what do you think the other most familiar birds might be? Robin? Eagle? Pigeon? Owl? Bluebird? Sparrow? Try asking someone to name three birds.)

The fish crow is slightly smaller than the common crow, but the main differences are in its habitat, voice, and behavior.

The fish crow is found mostly on beaches from Rhode Island to Texas, and along nearby rivers and streambanks. It usually roosts and nests in trees next to water. The common crow's call is "*CAAAAW, CAAAAW*" while the fish crow makes a higher nasal barking "*CARR! CARR!*" or "*CA-AH.*" It flies differently, too. Other crows flap along steadily, but the fish crow flaps and soars, flaps and soars, and sometimes it hunts insects by fluttering in the air like a kestrel (sparrow hawk) and diving on prey below.

The Fish Crow's Song

Rotten turtle makes me drool.
I snatch fishies from their school,
Crawfish, nestlings, these are cool.
I eat dead things from the pool.
CA-AH! CARR! CARR! CARR!

Berries, insects – can't be beat!
Heron eggs are rich and sweet!
Other birds just can't compete!
Give me ANYTHING to eat!
CA-AH! CARR! CARR! CARR!

a fish crow carries off a heron chick

A fish crow cleans up a lot of smelly garbage. It may also raid the rookeries of herons and other wading birds. It waits for the parents to leave, then carries off an egg or newly hatched nestling to its own chicks. Crows eject pellets of undigested bones and insect parts (see page 16).

Brainy Birds

Crows, ravens, magpies and jays are all in the *Corvid* family, and are among the smartest birds in the world. They can learn by watching other animals (or people), and they even figure out puzzles that we used to think could be solved only by humans or monkeys. Crows may live up to twenty years, so they have lots of time to experience, learn, and figure things out. And they do.

Unique throat muscles allow crows to make a great variety of sounds – more than any other kind of bird. At least twenty different calls express everything from "Hi, honey," to "Help! I'm in danger! Save me!"

hawk

If one of their kind is in trouble, *corvids* attack or "mob" the predator.

Swamp Lawn

duckweed
Lemna minor
actual size

Duckweed (a favorite food of ducks) often carpets quiet waters. Each plant has one or two tiny oval leaves and a hanging root, plus another leaf/plant budding off on one side. It grows swiftly in warm water, budding off new plants which float away to bud off new plants, which float away to... well, you get the idea. Duckweed forms a smooth lawnlike surface on the water. But don't try walking on it – you'll plunge right through.

Water spangles also reproduces quickly in warm, shallow water. It makes a lumpier carpet since its leaves are larger and covered with stiff bristles. Its hairy roots are actually remodeled fronds. Unlike the duckweed, it's not native.

water spangles
Salvinia minima
actual size

enlarged bristles show the tiny "baskets" on each tip which trap air to help keep the plant afloat

These and other floating plants "roof over" parts of the swamp water, making refuges in which insects, fish and other small creatures feed and grow, safe from predators like raptors, egrets and fish crows which hunt from above.

The Crow's Nest

Fish crows usually nest high in trees near water. The barklined, 14" to 18" nest will contain up to five brown-blotched, blue-green eggs.

You probably wouldn't call the nestlings "cute."

Getting A Drink

To drink, a fish crow sometimes skims over the water with its beak open like a swift or a bat.

17. The Fish Crow

"**CA-AH CA-AH......CARR.....CARR......CARRR!!!**" The high barking cries rang eerily through the early morning mist rising off the dark waters of the swamp. Two fish crows perched in the crown of a tall magnolia tree, grooming their shiny black feathers and gabbling to each other. "**Maah....maah....maah,**" he commented. "**Waak, waak,**" she replied. They groomed and carried on an animated conversation until the sun had burned the fog away.

Up into the sky the parent crows looped and circled, wing to wing, waiting for the swamp to warm and the fish to come to the surface to bask and feed.

With one last "**CA-AH,**" the couple flew down to hover over an open area of swamp surrounded by ancient moss-draped tupelo and bald cypress trees with bony cypress knees. A carpet of duckweed and *Salvinia* water spangles covered the water like a smooth, flat lawn. Almost, but not quite. A long black trail of open water coiled along the edges of the trees, then into deeper swamp, then ended abruptly. An alligator had passed by a few moments before, plowing an open lane through the duckweed as it followed a gar into deeper water. There the 'gator had sunk under the duckweed to continue the chase. Now, mosquito wigglers and tiny yellow bullhead fry rose into the open water trail to bask in the thin layer of warm swamp water heated by the sun. No, this was definitely not a lawn.

The fish crows swooped low over the water, hovering with quick wingbeats and darting bills to snap up bullhead fry. Instantly, the school of fingerlings, minus several classmates, scooted beneath the duckweed.

The female fish crow flew off toward the nest, her pouch bulging with bullhead fry for the chicks. *Corvids* (crows and their relatives) have special pouches in their throat in which to carry food. Her mate, who had caught only two fry, headed for the heron rookery to steal an unguarded egg or small nestling to take home for breakfast.

Out in the pine flatwoods, their four chicks perched impatiently on the edge of the large stick nest, waiting for breakfast. The nest, lined with Spanish moss and cedar bark, was only one of several fish crow nests crammed into a small grove of slash pines near an arm of the swamp. One chick flapped its wings so actively that it rose several inches into the air. Startled by the novel sensation, it dropped anxiously back into the nest.

But soon they were all experimenting with this new skill. Today the five-week-old fish crow chicks, nearly full-size, would fledge from the nest and begin learning how to fly. In fact, within an hour they were fluttering clumsily from branch to branch in the slash pines, squawking hungrily to tell their parents where to bring food.

Unfortunately, the racket also told a red-shouldered hawk where to find four tasty young fish crows to eat.

Red-shouldered Hawk

Buteo lineatus (BEW-tee-oh lin-ee-AY-tus)
Buteo = "falcon or hawk"   **lineatus** = "striped"

The red-shouldered hawk is also called a hen hawk, but it seldom eats chickens. It is the most common hawk in the swamps, and very important to the ecosystem, keeping mice, rats, insects, snakes and other reptiles from becoming too numerous. Fairly tame, it may let you get quite close before it flies. It's the only hawk in the area with reddish shoulders and a tail brightly barred with five to seven black stripes.

There are several races (a race is a group that is different in some way from others of the same species). The Southern Florida race is the palest, with grayish head and back. It may not have the breast streaks referred to in its scientific or *specific* name (see above, the *lineatus* part).

Red-shouldered hawks are noisy, especially during early spring breeding season. Listen for a **"kee-uckkk"** or **"kee-oooow,"** especially if you get too close to their nest.

Grasshopper Banquet

When grasshoppers are plentiful in the pinelands, flatwoods and scrub meadows surrounding the cypress swamps, red-shouldered hawk nestlings (and other species, too) are very well fed. Here are two grasshoppers that serve as food:

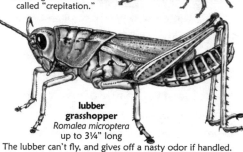

Carolina locust
Dissosteira carolina
actual size
The locust flies very fast, with a crackling sound called "crepitation."

lubber grasshopper
Romalea microptera
up to 3¼" long
The lubber can't fly, and gives off a nasty odor if handled.

Bird Fingers

Bones are heavy but birds must be light (see p. 16), so a bird wing has only a thumb and two fingers, each made of only one or two bones.

Feel your hand near where it joins your wrist. The lumps are your eight wrist bones, or *carpals* (KAR-pulz). A bird's carpals are fused into just a few light-weight bones.

Now, imagine having 20" feathers attached to your arms and fingers!

human arm

thumb

thumb
alula attaches here (see p. 66)

bird wing

human and bird **carpals** are shown in black here

Every one of **your** fingers has three bones. Bird "fingers" have only one or two bones.

Liveoak *Quercus virginiana*

notice the person

Huge, spreading evergreen oaks, often draped with Spanish moss, are called liveoaks because they look "alive" all year.

The Snatchers Toolbox

Hawks are *raptors*, an old word meaning "plunderer," or "snatcher." Raptors are also called *birds of prey*, which actually means "birds who eat other animals" Cypress swamps are full of good raptor food – mammals, birds, lizards, snakes, crawfish, fish and insects. Some major swamp raptors are: red-shouldered hawks, barred owls, ospreys, black and turkey vultures, bald eagles, kestrels and kites. To catch and devour prey, all raptors (except vultures) have hooked beaks, and their *talons* (TAL-unz = claws) are sharp and curved.

a red-shouldered hawk's hooked beak

osprey talons

huge rear talon hooks fish→

Population Explosion?

Do you hate the thought of raptors and other predators killing helpless victims? Try thinking of it this way: If a pair of warblers hatched two broods of four chicks each year and all of them survived to hatch two broods of four chicks for ten years, 19 MILLION warblers would result from just that original pair. Other animals are controlled by predators, too. If there were no predators, there wouldn't be enough food for them all, and they'd die slowly of starvation. That's no fun, either.

prothonot. warbler
Protonotar citrea

18. The Red-shouldered Hawk

The red-shouldered hawks had finished their rowdy courtship. In midwinter they had circled in the air over the massive liveoak tree, screaming and diving in noisy displays. For weeks they had guarded the empty nest they would use – a bulky, flat-topped mass of broken sticks about two feet wide, decorated with swags of Spanish moss. Occasionally one of them brought a sprig of wax myrtle to lay in the nest, perhaps to show that it had been claimed.

Now they were incubating three eggs. This morning the male had already delivered one mouse, two big lubber grasshoppers, and half a water snake (he was very good at catching water snakes) to his mate, who was keeping the eggs warm.

About mid-morning, he flew to the nest empty-beaked and lit on the edge of the nest. The female rose, fluffed her feathers and stepped aside while the male took over the incubating. She flew briskly off to catch a meal. Her mate had eaten most of the last snake before delivering it to the nest.

She heard the squawking fish crow fledglings from quite a distance, and lit in the top of a slash pine to look the situation over. Red-shouldered hawks are only a little bigger than a fish crow, so one of these big babies would be a handful. She watched the female crow arrive with a grasshopper for a fledgling, then fly away. As soon as the adult crow had flown out of sight, the hawk dived.

"CRAWWWWWWK!!!" screamed the young crow, as the hawk struck. The hawk strained upward, with her struggling lunch. The male crow was just returning with a crawfish when he saw his fledgling being carried away. He dropped the food and flapped furiously after the hawk. Without any cargo, he was faster than the hawk, and he swooped from above, striking fiercely at her head.

She folded her wings and dived, but the crow stayed with her, croaking, pecking, and snatching angrily at her back and head. Within moments, the noise had brought his mate and nine other fish crows from the nearby colony to join in the attack.

The hawk was outnumbered, outflown, out of luck. With a scream, she dropped the crow fledgling, which fluttered to the ground scratched and bruised, but very much alive. The frustrated hawk streaked into the trees, dodging pecks and wing whacks from the angry mob of crows.

Eastern Gray Squirrel

Sciurus carolinensis (sie-YUR-us cair-oh-lin-EN-sis)
Sciurus = "squirrel" ***carolinensis*** = "of Carolina"

The gray squirrel is a very important character in the hardwood forests. It buries acorns and nuts carefully, digging down one or two inches, placing the food in the hole, and ramming it in with its front teeth. Then it carefully replaces the dirt and leaves until the burial spot is hidden. A squirrel may forget where it stored the food, but it can smell an acorn under two feet of snow, so it finds *most* of them later.

The vast eastern oak, hickory and beech forests may have re-sprouted mostly from unclaimed squirrel dinners after Ice Age glaciers melted 10,000 years ago.

Squirrels also eat flowers, seeds, mushrooms, insects like beetles and moths, and believe it or not, nestling birds, baby rabbits, and lizards. Squirrels, in turn, are eaten by bobcats, hawks, minks, owls, and foxes, and by raccoons who snatch young squirrels from their nests.

Ox Beetle *Xyloryctes satyrus*

Ox beetles look vicious, but they're harmless. Males have longer "horns" than females. They are related to Egypt's sacred scarab beetles.

actual size

Safe Passage

Ever see a squirrel wearing a pink neck scarf? Look again – that's her *baby*. When danger threatens, she grabs it by the belly, then it wraps itself around her neck for a trip to another nest she has made ready.

She'll also move the babies if fleas get too thick at the old nest.

Leaf Ball

Look up into the trees for a leaf/twig ball. It may be a gray squirrel *drey* (nest). The inside, is insulated with moss and shredded bark, and so well-built it's rainproof.

hatching eggs

3" green caterpillar

a woven silk cocoon is glued to leaves and looks like a fat cigar

Polly Moth

Silk cloth is made from the cocoons of moths related to the tawny giant *polyphemus* (pahl-ih-FEE-mus) silkmoth. This caterpillar weaves its waterproof cocoon between leaves it has pulled together.

Antheraea polyphemus 6" wingspread

hawk nests are flat-topped

Who's Who?

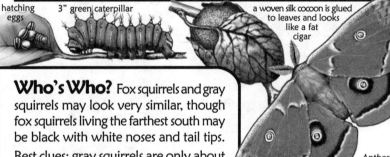

Fox squirrels and gray squirrels may look very similar, though fox squirrels living the farthest south may be black with white noses and tail tips.

Best clues: gray squirrels are only about 80% as big as fox squirrels, have longer ears, shorter tails, and silver-tipped fur.

Rodent Skulls

Squirrels are rodents. Rodent skulls are easy to identify because between the front and side teeth there is always the *diastema* (die-uh-STEE-muh), a **long** gap. Why rodents have this gap is unknown, but it does make a perfect space in which to carry nuts.

(So, is there a rodent skull on page 36?)

gray squirrel skull ¾ actual size

Resurrection Fern

This fern shrivels into a leathery, dead-looking curl when it dries out, but it "comes back to life" as a perky green fern at the next rain.

Green-fly orchids often grow on branches with resurrection ferns.

dried out

wet again

green-fly orchid
Epidendrum conopseum
This orchid has numerous ¾" yellow-green insect-like fragrant blooms clustered at the tips of 4 - 16" stems. These orchid epiphytes anchor to branches, but they don't hurt the tree.

resurrection fern
Polypodium polypodioides
½ actual size

gray squirrel track & scat

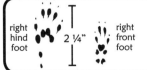

right hind foot

2 ¼"

right front foot

|·······24"- 36"·······|

gray squirrel scat actual size

48

19. The Eastern Gray Squirrel

Angry and smarting from the crow attack, the red-shouldered hawk dodged into the river bottomland trees where she finally escaped her pursuers. She perched on a sycamore branch, ruffled and hungry, trying to smooth her feathers back into place. Red-shouldered hawks don't like thick forest, and she was uneasy.

A rustling under the fan-shaped palmetto leaves below the tree caught her attention, and her sharp eyes quickly picked out a small brownish-gray shape crouched in the shadows. She squatted and dropped in a quick dive. Her target, a gray squirrel trying to pry open the tough wing covers of a very lively ox beetle, saw the movement and ducked out of sight beneath the spiky palmetto.

The red-shouldered hawk was half a second late, and her talons closed only on the papery fan of the palmetto leaf. With a frustrated scream, the hawk flapped back out to the scrub, with its sparse trees and open spaces where grasshoppers were easy to catch and where she felt more at home.

The gray squirrel, her heart beating wildly, huddled under the palmetto in a drift of dried leaves clutching her squirming beetle. When a cicada started up its shrill whine directly overhead, she knew it was safe to creep out cautiously. She quickly scrambled up into a nearby sweet-gum tree. Gray squirrels don't like to be surprised on the ground – trees give them a much better chance to escape.

She sprinted further up the trunk to where a side branch stretched out to meet the next tree, then she bounded over familiar moss-encrusted branches covered with resurrection ferns and green-fly orchids to the massive red oak tree and her leaf and twig nest. She stopped on a widened branch to pull apart and eat the beetle's soft parts, then popped into the nest to check on her babies.

The four squirrel kittens met her with enthusiastic squeaks, nuzzling her belly hungrily as she settled in beside them. It was cozy in the nest, with soft leaves, Spanish moss, and many of her long tail hairs creating both a soft mattress and a blanket. The squirrel nursed her babies until they fell asleep, then she crept quietly back out to forage for food. Nursing four pups requires a lot of energy.

Near the swamp, she ate fresh buds and trumpet vine flowers and a juicy polyphemus moth pupa she pulled from its cocoon. By this time of year she had already dug up and eaten most of the walnuts, beechnuts, pignuts and acorns she had hidden last autumn, so she was hungry again by the time she spotted a gray catbird trying to slip away from its nest without being noticed.

Gray Catbird

Dumetella carolinensis (dew-meh-TELL-uh cair-oh-lin-EN-sis)
Dumetella = " little thicket (dweller)" **carolinensis** = "of Carolina"

A catbird is a tidy bird, a little smaller than a robin. It is solid gray with a black cap and a reddish patch under its tail. You'll probably hear it before you see it – listen for a "lost kitten" in heavy shrubbery (see below), or a low **"kwirt."**

The catbird is found from Canada to Panama, often wintering in the Southeast. It definitely doesn't mind living in the suburbs.

In summer and fall, a catbird searches the shrubs, trees and vines for fruits and berries. Sometimes it pecks holes in the fruit in orchards and gardens, though it prefers wild groceries. In winter and spring, it eats ants, beetles, caterpillars and grasshoppers, silkmoths (see p. 48), other insects, and some spiders. These make good food for nestlings.

The catbird has strong parenting instincts and may feed other birds' nestlings if it sees them begging for food.

"Pucker Fruit" *Diospyros virginiana*

Wild persimmons were once a very important fruit to Native Americans in the Southeast. Persimmons are a favorite with catbirds, too, and they quickly learn to let the fruits ripen until late fall when the flesh is soft and orange. Your mouth will be puckered for a long time if you bite into an unripe one!

Tight Fit

The eggs of a catbird are shiny blue-green, usually laid in a nest two to ten feet above the ground in heavy shrubbery.

The nest is so deep that the mother catbird's tail and beak are pushed straight up by the sides of the nest when she is incubating the eggs.

A Family of Mimics

Catbirds, mockingbirds and thrashers all belong to the *Mimidae* family of birds. ALL of them are top-quality copycats, singing the songs of many other birds.

When staking out its territory and courting its mate, a catbird sings the songs of all of its musical neighbors – robins, warblers, thrushes – sprinkled with less lovely jay screeches, frog croaks, police sirens, dog yaps and cat meows. It may sing late into the night.

A disturbed catbird may fly off with a wren-like chatter. More likely, it will **"meow."** If you rush to rescue a kitten crying pitifully in a leafy shrub, you may find only a catbird meowing at you.

In the spring, catbirds sing loudly, with beaks wide open. But in fall, for some reason, a catbird may sing in a whisper, its beak barely open, its sweet secret song almost soundless from only a few feet away.

Best Friends?

While blue jays may join catbirds to mob a predator (see page 51), a jay will eat any unguarded catbird eggs or chicks it finds – so maybe it's not really what you'd call a first-choice friend.

Cyanocitta cristata

Cypress Knees

Poking up out of the swamp, cypress knees are a big mystery. Some scientists think these knobby enlargements on cypress tree roots help the submerged tree roots breathe, while others think they only help anchor the tree. Whatever they are, they make good "stepping stones" for wildlife moving through the swamp.

They also make safe nest sites for birds like prothonotary warblers (see page 46). Other plants and trees often take root on them.

Cat(bird) food

Carolina mantid
Stagmomantis carolina
This "praying mantis" hangs out on flower heads to grab visiting insects. Small mantids make excellent catbird food.

tiger beetle jaws close up

½ to ⅝"

tiger beetle
Cicindela species
Iridescent and colorful with light spots, tiger beetles are swift runners and flyers.

actual size

**subterranean
← termites**
Reticuitermes flavipes
After a rain, winged termite males emerge from their colonies. They pursue and mate with departing queens, who start new colonies.

20. The Gray Catbird

A squirrel will eat eggs, nestlings, and even an unwary adult bird if it gets the chance. The catbird's nest was built in a wax myrtle bush over the dark waters of the swamp, and the squirrel might not have noticed it if the bird had not moved.

The squirrel scrambled up into the fragrant bush with its reddish trim of young poison ivy leaves. The catbird chattered with rage from an overhead branch, but the squirrel ignored her as she crunched the catbird's four blue-green eggs. The male catbird arrived, hopping furiously from branch to branch above the squirrel with sharp cries of ***"TRAT! TAT-TAT-TAT! TRAT!"***

He dived at the squirrel's head, but she paid no attention. A cardinal and a jay joined the mob, but the squirrel scarcely noticed as she busily licked up the last dribbles of egg yolk. Finished, the squirrel scrambled up a tree, heading home to feed her babies as the mangled nest fell into the swamp with a splash.

The mob of birds drifted off, but the catbirds hopped mournfully about the shrub crying ***"miew, miew, miew,"*** and staring at the bits of nest floating below. Then, defeated, they left to search for a new nest site.

The squirrel attack may have changed her views about safe nest sites, for this time the female chose a much safer place. She found a cavity in a cypress knee, surrounded by water, and began to carry in nesting material – cattail leaves, frizzy strips of grapevine bark, coarse grasses and small rootlets for the lining. The male helped her build the nest, stopping to sing from nearby branches to declare ownership of the new territory. Nest-building took about a week, and the following week the female began to incubate new eggs.

As she sat, the male brought her food – beetles and caterpillars, wasps, walking sticks and spiders. He discovered a convenient snackbar – the dark water that formed a moat around the base of the hollow cypress knee that held the nest – where he could easily catch small swamp darter fish, diving beetles, and whatever else happened by.

One morning, the male catbird spotted a half-grown Carolina mantis struggling to free itself from a golden-silk spider web which stretched nearly five feet across a gap between two persimmon tree branches. Avoiding the sticky strands, the catbird hovered in midair to pluck it from the web. What a fine breakfast this would make for his hungry mate!

Golden-Silk Spider

Nephila clavipes (NEH-fill-uh KLAV-ih-peez)
Ne = "to spin" ***phila*** = "loving" ***clavi*** = "club" ***pes*** = "foot"

Hikers in swamps know the golden-silk spider well. Its golden webs may span more than three feet (often across a trail), causing unwary hikers to panic and "beat feet in retreat."

In the center of the wheel-spoked orb web perches the speckled orange-ish female spider with black-tufted legs, waiting for a victim to hit the web. Then she springs into action, wrapping her prey in tough silken threads whipped from her spinnerets by skillful hind feet. *Nephila's* web silk is the strongest known. *Nephila* and black widow spider web strands were once used for making the cross-hairs in gunsights.

Dazzled by her inch-long body (and her overall length of 3" from front toe to back toe), you might overlook the small, dark male golden-silk spider perched nearby on the web. It's only a fraction of the female's weight, and barely an eighth of an inch long. This species is found as far south as Central America.

Other Swamp Spiders

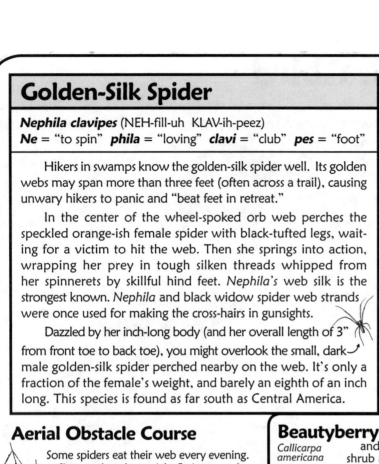

These spiders may be found in forests or in meadows near swamps in the Southeast. The black widow and brown *recluse* (REK-loos) spiders are most venomous. The brown recluse has a dark "violin" marking on its top. The black widow has a red "hourglass" beneath. All are shown actual size.

garden spider
Argiope aurantia

spiny-bodied orb spider
Gasteracantha cancriformis

flower crab spider
Misomena sp.

close-up of "violin" marking

☠ **brown recluse**
Loxosceles reclusus

male

☠ **black widow**
Latrodectus mactans
(underside of female)

female

Aerial Obstacle Course

Some spiders eat their web every evening. Since owls or bats might fly into a web overnight and rip it out, the spider eats the important nutrients it used to make the web so it can recycle them in making the next day's web.

Garden spiders weave messy white splotches (at left) into their patterns.

evening bat
Nycticeius humeralis
avoiding a garden spider web.

Beautyberry
Callicarpa americana

The leaves and twigs of this 6' shrub are munched by deer. Many birds and mammals eat its bright lavender berries.

Night birds and bats notice these splotches and avoid the webs. This saves the spiders a lot of time and energy. It must save small bats a lot of trouble, too.

Paper Makers
The mild-mannered, tiny-waisted paper wasp will let you come quite close without getting upset. Don't confuse it with the bad-tempered yellowjacket, which *usually* (but not *always*) builds its paper nest underground.

⊢ 1" ⊣

yellow jacket
Vespula sp.

paper wasp
Polistes sp.

paper wasp
actual size

To Build An Orb Web
Orb-weavers begin an orb by tossing a strand into the breeze or by dropping to the ground, walking to and climbing a distant upright, then pulling their web tight. After that, here's what happens:

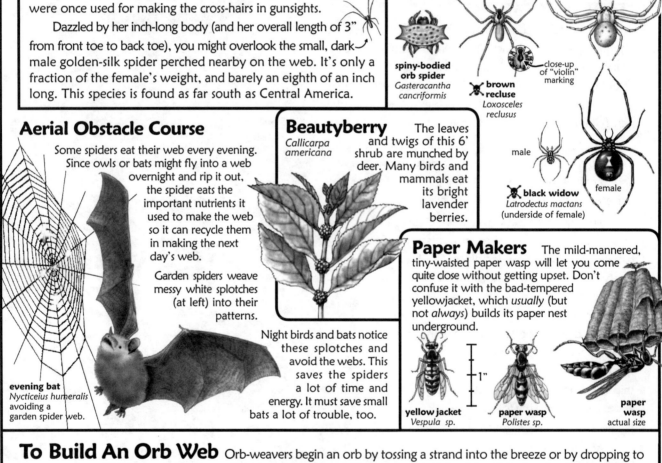

21. The Golden-Silk Spider

Within a few minutes she had mended the damage, eating loose and broken strands as she repaired the web. Then she settled down again in the center of her golden-stranded design to wait for prey.

She was rewarded an hour later when a paper wasp, carrying a mouthful of chewed-up bark fiber for its nest, blundered into the web a few inches away. She wrapped it, injected it with tenderizer, and sucked it dry to build her energy back up again.

Spider webs are fragile. They can get shredded by wind and weather, bats, birds, large insects and other catastrophes. The golden-silk spider had just snipped the drained body of the paper wasp out of the web when her entire web-world came crashing down about her. In fact, she was lucky to survive the event.

A whitetail deer had been browsing on a beautyberry shrub at the edge of a deep pool nearby, nibbling leaves and buds as she went. Reaching for tender leaves at the top of the shrub, she stepped up onto a mound of soil, leaves and twigs, not realizing it was the incubation nest of a large alligator. The mother alligator's sudden, hissing lunge from the depths of the pool in a sheet of foaming spray sent the deer leaping blindly in a mad scramble away from the water's edge – right through the web of the golden-silk spider.

The golden spiderweb clung and draped across the doe's face, ripping completely away from the persimmon tree. The spider was flung into the beautyberry shrub, stunned but not injured. She would rebuild her web from scratch, but since she couldn't eat the old one and recycle its protein into new webbing, the next web would be smaller. She climbed up into the persimmon tree to start all over again.

T he golden-silk spider was perched head-down in the center of her shining golden web when the half-grown young mantis on a twig overhead lost its grip while lunging at a hoverfly, and tumbled into the web near one edge.

The nearsighted spider tensed, pulling the signal threads of her web tight, feeling the size and strength of her prey through the vibrations.

Just as she decided the mantis was an easy meal, a ripping twang shot through the web, then a sudden sagging looseness. The spider knew nothing about catbirds – she only knew her prey was gone and she might be in danger herself. She raced up under a persimmon leaf and froze for a few minutes, waiting for more information. When the web remained silent and limp, she edged out onto it cautiously and inspected the gaping hole.

American Alligator

Alligator mississippiensis (AL-ih-gay-ter mississippee-EN-sis)
el lagarte (*Spanish*) = "the lizard" **mississippiensis** = "of Mississippi"

Alligators are important members of Southeastern swamps. Without the alligators, many birds, reptiles, fish, mammals, plants and others would not survive the frequent droughts. The alligator hollows out a pond, scooping it deeper during the dry season. This creates and maintains a pool where other animals can live and feed as well. The 'gator digs the pool for itself, of course, and may eat some of the other occupants that use it – fish, turtles, birds, snakes, mammals – but not enough to undo the good it does by providing the pool. A female may also may dig a long den.

Awesome bellows in the swamp are likely to be alligators, male *and* female (or bullfrogs – see page 14). But that's not all...

A courting male claps his jaws loudly, and his *subsonic* roars (*you* can't hear them) vibrate the water. Courting 'gators nuzzle, blow bubbles and wrestle. If the male proves too strong for the female to dunk, she may choose him for her mate.

'Gator Aid

Okay, you're canoeing through a swamp when suddenly the water ripples and you see two big 'gator eyes glowing at you. **Uh-oh!** How big is it? Here's a guessing aid: An alligator is about as many *feet* long as there are *inches* between its gleaming eyeballs and its nostrils: so...12 **inches** from eye to nose = a 12 **foot** 'gator. (And guess what else – its brain is only the size of a chicken egg yolk.)

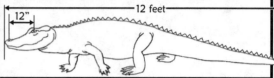

Alligator Freestyle

Since an alligator's feet aren't strongly webbed, it tucks them out of the way and wags its tail from side to side to swim. Its track through the water is a long, wavy line.

Raising Kids

A female alligator rips up plants and pond muck, piling up a mound two feet high and five feet wide at the edge of her pool. Then she hollows out the center and lays 20 to 70 tough white eggs, covering them with more plants and mud when she is finished. The muck heats up (composting) as it rots, keeping the eggs warm until they hatch two months later. Meanwhile, something amazing happens....

about ½ actual size

Giant Cane

Arundinaria gigantea

Two kinds of native bamboo, giant cane and switchcane, grow in the Southeast. **Giant cane** gets huge – up to 20' tall and 1" in diameter. **Switchcane** (a subspecies) reaches 8' with ½" stems. Both spread and multiply into huge thickets called *brakes*. Canebrakes were favorite hunting spots for ancient hunters.

If the nest's temperature averages below 86° during the first two weeks, the babies will be *females*. If it averages 93° and above, they'll be *males*. Temperatures between 86° and 93° produce *both sexes*.

The young hang out for years with mom, who protects them from many predators. But mother alligators don't usually argue with hungry black bears, who eat baby alligators and destroy many nests.

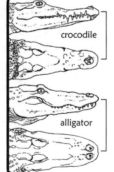

crocodile

alligator

Crocogator Rhyme

'Gators are not crocodiles,
although they do have similar styles.
A croc likes warm and salty water
in the tropics where it's hotter.
Florida's tip, U.S., Southeast,
is where you'll find **that** awesome beast.

A 'gator's nose is short and wide,
and hides the lower teeth inside.
The skinny nose of a crocodile
lets teeth poke **up** outside its smile.
But whether croc or alligator,
the best advice is: "see ya later!"

alligator track & scat

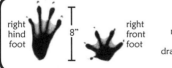

right hind foot

8"

right front foot

notice tail drag marks

toe webbing may not show

24" - 36"

alligator scat is usually a soupy glob in the water

22. The American Alligator

The deer had picked a bad time to step onto the alligator's nest mound – the babies were hatching. As late morning sunshine warmed the mound, the young alligators had begun to yip – faintly at first, but louder and more insistently every moment.

The mother alligator had been awaiting this moment for weeks. Just now she was basking near a towering patch of switchcane at the far edge of the pool, several yards away. She became uneasy as the deer got closer and closer to her nest. Sinking out of sight, she swam underwater toward the nest. As she rose silently to the surface near the mound she heard the muffled cries from her babies.

"Yurk!.................yurk!.................yurk!!" came yelps from inside the mound. The mother was electrified. Her young were hatching! They needed her help, and they were being invaded! She lunged from the water with a mighty swipe of her tail and tremendous shoves from all four feet.

A deep hiss, like the latte steamer in a coffee shop (but much louder), blasted from her throat. The deer stumbled backward in panic and scrambled away with a great crash of breaking twigs and branches.

The mother alligator followed for a few rushing steps, then swung back toward the mound. She scraped carefully at the muck with her long front claws and brushed it aside with her chin. Soon the nose of a tiny alligator poked into the air. One by one, the little hatchlings clawed their way out of their eggshells.

The mother carefully cracked open any unhatched eggs between her teeth and carried the still-moist hatchlings down the sloping mound to the tea-colored water in her huge but surprisingly gentle jaws. Some hatchlings crawled to the water by themselves.

Brightly striped with black and tan markings, the eight-inch-long alligators had charming "smiles" and tiny pinprick teeth that could cheerfully wrap around tadpoles, dragonfly larvae, and little fish. On land they would snap up dragonflies, grasshoppers and other insects. Soon they would eat larger fish, frogs, small turtles, mice and shrews.

Right now, as hatchlings, *they* were food for herons, snapping turtles, and even bullfrogs. In fact, they had barely gotten to the water when one little brand-new alligator came face to face with a hungry mink.

Mink

Mustela vison (mus-TEE-luh VEE-zon)
Mustela = "weasel" **vison** *(Swedish)* = "marten or weasel"

The mink is a beach bunny. It lives its entire life near the water – although it chooses ponds and streams rather than the ocean. It makes its home in hollow logs, muskrat dens or beaver lodges. Or it may dig its own den in a stream bank.

A mink comes out of its waterside den to hunt mainly at night. But when a mink is nursing young or is especially hungry, it may make daytime appearances to hunt rodents, rabbits, garter snakes, and a lot of other things.

Slightly webbed feet make the mink an excellent swimmer, and crawfish are a frequent dinner item. So are fish, frogs, small turtles, baby alligators and water birds. You might not expect a mink to eat plants, but sometimes it snacks on grass and leaves.

A mink, male or female, is very territorial. It marks the boundaries of its territory with scent from glands beneath its tail, and will fight any mink that doesn't respect its claim.

Plant Gourmet Food

Some bog plants eat meat – any insect that bumbles into them. But since they can't actually chew their buggy prey, they produce an *enzyme* (a chemical) to dissolve insects into liquid protein which the plant can absorb.

threadleaf sundew
Drosera filiformis
5" to 10"
A sundew has globs of goo at the ends of tentacles all along its leaves. Passing insects get stuck and the tentacles fold down to the leaf surface with them, where special glands dissolve and digest them.

← goo globs

pink sundew
Drosera capillaris
up to 3" across

pitcher plant
Sarracenia species.
12" to 30"

insects enter here

hollow tube

Pitcher plants attract insects down a tube into a pool of enzymes (see above). The tube is made from a single leaf fastened together down the front. Inside, stiff downward-pointing hairs keep any trapped insects from crawling back out.

Family Tree

Would you have guessed the mink is related to weasels and otters, skunks and badgers? They all use strong, musky scent glands to mark territory. Do you see other similarities? These are shown at comparative sizes below.

long-tailed weasel

striped skunk

mink

spotted skunk

river otter

(badgers are *Mustelids*, too, but they aren't shown here because they don't live in swamps)

Mink Skull
A mink has a long, narrow head, allowing it to enter tight tunnels in search of food.

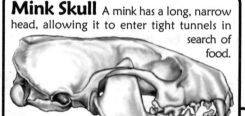

actual skull size

White-topped Sedge
Dichromena colorata

This sedge appears to have a white flower because the leaves at the top are white.

Marsh Rice Rat
Oryzomys palustris

nest

The 9"–12" (including tail) rice rat is a super swimmer, bringing water plants, snails, crawfish and fish up onto a grass platform to eat, as well as seeds, mushrooms, and fruits it carries in from drier areas.

A marsh rice rat may raise several litters of up to six pups in the volleyball-sized grass nest it hangs in the marsh reeds. Rice rats are a major part of mink diets.

mink track & scat

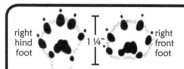

right hind foot

1 ¼"

right front foot

  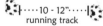 ···10 - 12"···
running track

mink scat
⅓ actual size

23. The Mink

The mink had heard the yips of the baby alligators even before their mother had. In fact, minks, raccoons, opossums and other predators are the very reason alligator mothers stick around to guard their eggs. By the time the hatchlings had all tumbled into the pool, the mink, who had been watching from a cavity beneath nearby willow tree roots, was famished. He slipped into the water under the cover of tall pickerel weeds, and swam cautiously toward a little alligator that had drifted away from the group.

SPLASH! A wave from the mother alligator's sweeping tail hit the mink broadside just as he grabbed the hatchling. The wave tumbled him over and over in a churning roll. Choking and spluttering, he dropped the little alligator and plunged for the shore with the mother alligator in hot pursuit.

Scrambling up the muddy bank, the mink bounded off across the bog, leaving a wet trail behind him. Well away from the alligator pond, he stopped to groom and recover from his close call. He was still very hungry, but wild animals must keep their coats clean and in order to stay healthy. So he shook briskly, licked the muddy water from his thick fur, and scratched vigorously until his coat was dry and fluffy again.

Then the mink resumed his hunt across the bog, twisting through clumps of white-topped sedge, sniffing where a mouse

had passed next to a pitcher plant, then stopping to lick off a paw that came up gooey from contact with a sticky sundew. He slipped quietly into a clump of cattails. A flicker of movement, a pounce, and the mink had a marsh rice rat by the tail. The rat thrashed back and forth in the dry cattails, nearly getting away, but the mink made a lightning-fast nip at the back of its neck and the rat was mink dinner.

The thumping and thrashing hadn't been very loud, but the noise had caught the attention of a pair of sandhill cranes feeding with their chick a few yards away. The cranes decided to check it out.

Sandhill Crane

Grus canadensis (GROOS can-uh-DEN-sis)
Grus = "crane" *canadensis* = "of Canada"

The sandhill crane is one of our biggest birds – about the size of a great blue heron, more than three feet tall. Its wings spread six and a half feet from tip to tip. Its close relative, the rare and endangered whooping crane, is much bigger, towering to four and a half feet with a wingspread nearly eight feet wide.

Once very numerous, sandhill cranes are now uncommon in most parts of the U.S. Great efforts are being made to preserve their marshes and wet prairies so they won't become endangered, too. Their numbers are beginning to increase.

Unlike herons and egrets which eat mainly fish and other water creatures, cranes forage for food in marshes and meadows, eating seeds, berries and roots, and catching grasshoppers, mice, snakes, lizards, crawfish and small birds.

Migrating cranes fly in a V-formation as high as two miles up, tiny specks in the sky but visible with binoculars.

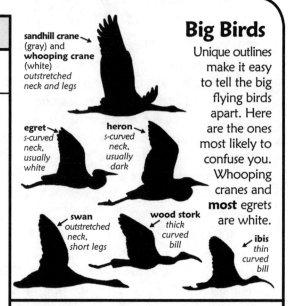

Big Birds

Unique outlines make it easy to tell the big flying birds apart. Here are the ones most likely to confuse you. Whooping cranes and **most** egrets are white.

sandhill crane (gray) and **whooping crane** (white) outstretched neck and legs

egret s-curved neck, usually white

heron s-curved neck, usually dark

swan outstretched neck, short legs

wood stork thick curved bill

ibis thin curved bill

Courtly Dances

Sandhill cranes leap and flap their wings in highly stylized dance routines to court their mates.

Bald Heads and Bustles

Adult sandhill cranes have bald red heads, long beaks, white chins, and greyish brown bodies. At a distance, you might think a crane is a great blue heron until you notice the "bustle," the puff of feather plumes that falls over its tail. Cranes walk a lot – their long dark legs may carry them several miles each day as they feed.

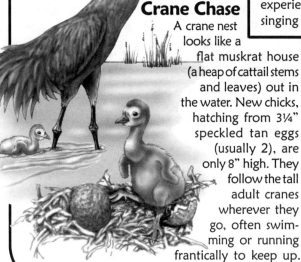

Crane Chase

A crane nest looks like a flat muskrat house (a heap of cattail stems and leaves) out in the water. New chicks, hatching from 3¼" speckled tan eggs (usually 2), are only 8" high. They follow the tall adult cranes wherever they go, often swimming or running frantically to keep up.

KAR-R-R-O-O-O-O.. KAR-R-R-O-O-O-O..

The rolling, rasping cry of a sandhill crane rings across the marsh like something from another world. You can try to imitate them by rattling your tongue as though you were trying to purr like a cat, while saying ***"karooo"*** (that will be pretty close, but not perfect). Listening to a flock of wild sandhill cranes is a fantastic experience. Imagine singing dinosaurs.

Sawgrass

Cladium jamaicense

leaf blade, actual size

Wet prairies may be covered with this jagged "lethal weapon."

It's a sedge, not a grass, and it grows ten feet tall in vast thickets.

If you try to walk through a clump, you'll end up bloody.

cross-section of leaf close-up

The Flyways

While most of the Southeast's sandhill cranes don't migrate, some cranes, as well as other kinds of birds, follow the seasons up and down the continent along the great flyways.

Central and Pacific Flyways are not shown here

Mississippi Flyway

Atlantic Flyway

Small populations of sandhill cranes live in Florida, on the Gulf Coast, and on the Atlantic Coast. Drained or polluted wetlands, rising seas from global warming, and hurricanes threaten their future.

24. The Sandhill Crane

The fuzzy, apricot-orange sandhill crane chick scrambled valiantly after the long-legged adults as they marched through the cattails toward the crackling sounds they had heard. The little one did its best to keep up. Where they waded through knee-deep pools, the chick paddled furiously through what seemed to be bottomless water. But that was easier than climbing through the tangles of dried cattails that covered the marsh between pools. The big cranes stepped easily over what must have seemed like big branches and logs to the small chick. He managed to catch up whenever they stopped.

Tall sandhill cranes have a big advantage over most of the marsh wildlife – they have an excellent view. The mink, concentrating on catching and eating the rice rat, didn't know they were coming until their red heads loomed above him, peering down.

For an instant, he froze. Then he whirled with the last bit of the rat clenched in his teeth, and slipped into the cattails leaving tufts of rat fur whirling up behind him like dried leaves. Two black bills stabbed into the mud where he had just been. But the mink was gone.

The crane chick finally arrived beneath his parents, gasping for breath. His mother caught and offered him a crushed grasshopper, which he devoured gratefully. Moving foward a few steps, she began digging up and eating small nutsedge tubers with her sturdy bill, while her chick watched and copied every move.

Investigating the mink had brought the cranes to the edge of the hardwood forest next to the marsh, and the male crane now noticed an oddly-moving leaf on a shrubby red maple a few yards away. The "leaf" bobbed again, and the crane approached the maple intently.

His target was a leaf-green anole lizard, and at a distance of several feet this was a problem. When the anole moved, the crane could see it. When it stopped, it blended so perfectly with the leaves that it seemed to disappear. When the crane approached within striking range, the anole leaped for another leaf, where it blended in again. This happened again and again. The frustrated, crane finally gave up and rejoined the hen and chick.

The anole settled down on some dark tree bark, its color slowly darkening from bright green to brown.

Green Anole Lizard

Anolis carolinensis (an-OL-iss cair-oh-lin-EN-sis)
Anoli (*West Indies word*) = "lizard" **carolinensis** = "of Carolina"

The green anole (uh-NO-lee) lizard (also called the Carolina anole) is native to the Southeast swamps and forests. Slender and six to seven inches long, an anole is about half tail. A bright pink throat-fan (dewlap) can be flipped forward below its chin when fighting or courting. Its head is a pointy, arrowhead-shaped wedge. Clingy pads on the anole's feet allow it to creep up on insects; it can even walk across slippery house windows.

The anole's color is sometimes brown, but it is usually lime green (sometimes with dark speckles), with white undersides, and often a row of light or dark "braided" markings down its back. When it's green, it has turquoise rings around its eyes.

You might mistake a green anole for a Cuban brown anole, which has invaded much of Florida in recent years. But the brown anole is *never* green, and its dewlap is yellow or orange, edged with white.

Reptile or Amphibian?

Here's how to quickly tell a reptile from an amphibian. These rules are **almost** always true.

REPTILES:

(lizards, snakes, turtles, alligators and crocs)
• have dry, scaly skin
• are born alive or hatch from eggs laid on land
• look like tiny adults at birth

AMPHIBIANS:

(frogs, salamanders, newts and toads)
• have moist, thin skin (it may be warty)
• hatch from eggs laid in water
• start out looking/acting a lot like fish

Herpetologists use the term **herptile** (HURP-tile), **herp** for short, to refer to reptiles AND amphibians.

most lizard tracks, including those of anoles, look similar to these

Chameleon or Not?

Pet shops may advertise anoles as *chameleons* (kuh-MEEL-yunz) because their skins can change color rapidly. But **real** chameleons live in Africa and Madagascar. Real chameleons change skin color instantly, while anoles take a while to switch.

The colors change with light, temperature, stress and other emotions. Chilly anoles are brown; upset anoles are brown, too. Warm anoles are green, and blend with bright leaves.

Parson's chameleon
Real chameleons have spiral tails, eyes that move like swivels, and very odd feet.

If two anoles fight, the winner turns bright green while the loser turns brown.

a patch of sunshine warmed up (and greened up) part of this chilly tan anole

anole actual size

How do they do it? *Pigment* (color) cells just below the skin surface are signaled by the lizard's *hormones* (body chemicals) to spread out and flood the skin with color, or to gather into tiny clumps to let the main body color underneath show through around them.

Dewlap Discussions

An anole "talks" to other anoles by flipping a flag of brightly colored skin back and forth under its chin. This dewlap is just stretchy skin that is stretched out when the lizard suddenly shoots its *hyoid* (HY-oyd) bone forward. Between encounters, the skin contracts and the splendid display disappears.

The anole's dewlap sign-language says things like "*Get outta here!*" or "***I'm** bigger than **you** are, NYAA-NYAA!*" or even "*I love you.*" Both sexes have dewlaps, but the female's dewlap is much smaller.

anole at rest

anole displaying

hyoid bone, flipped out

Red Maple *Acer rubrum* →

These small trees love swamps, and may even take root in cypress knees. Twigs, leaves, seeds, buds, flowers and bark are eaten by wildlife, although deer don't like them.

Red-blanket Lichen
Cryptothecia rubrocincta

White with crimson borders, this lichen → grows on the trunks of many swamp trees. A *lichen* (LY-ken) is the partnership of an *alga* (AL-guh = a simple green plant) and a *fungus* (FUN-gus = a simple non-green plant-like organism. Molds and mushrooms are fungi).*

Using *photosynthesis*, the alga creates food from sunshine to feed itself and the fungus, while the fungus provides the alga with water and minerals. Lichens attach tightly to trees, but don't harm them.

*Two or more alga are **algae** – AL-jee; two or more fungus are **fungi** – FUN-jie.

25. The Green Anole Lizard

The green anole had just caught and eaten a robber fly when the crane approached. Anoles are very alert, and they may leap quite a distance when alarmed. So by the time the crane finished chasing him, the lizard was outside his usual territory. He stopped short when a bright pink flag suddenly popped out from the trunk of a nearby red maple tree decorated with red-blanket lichens.

The flag was actually the dewlap (chin flap) on the male anole who claimed that particular patch of bottomland forest. The resident anole was brown because he had been resting in a shady spot when he spied the trespasser. In bright light, anoles usually become greener, but since he was annoyed, his skin remained brown even though he was standing in a spot of warm sunshine.

He tensed the muscles in his jaw so that his springy hyoid bone flipped forward, unfurling his pink dewlap like a flag. He stood tall on his stubby legs, lifted his tail into a curve and wagged it up and down.

"GO AWAY!" this display said, in anole body language which the trespassing green anole understood perfectly. He strutted forward and flipped out his own dewlap, jutting it back and forth a few times and wagging his tail. But he wasn't really interested in fighting, and after a few minutes of signalling, he headed back to his own territory at the edge of the forest.

When he reached his home in the corky sweetgum tree, he stopped short. Resting near his favorite basking spot was a small anole he had never seen before. He jutted out his dewlap vigorously – this was *his* tree and he *would* fight for his *own* property! The intruding lizard, though, didn't flip out a flag. She interpreted his display as courtship, so she turned her head to one side and peeked at him over her shoulder.

For a moment, the male anole paused in confusion. He had signalled to an "enemy" but she was reacting like a "mate." Then he understood. Moving closer, he flipped his dewlap in and out excitedly. When she didn't display her dewlap to warn him away, he grabbed the skin on her neck in his tiny teeth, lifted one leg across her back and tucked his tail beneath her body, choosing her for his mate.

61

White-tailed Deer

Odocoileus virginianus (oh-doh-KOY-lee-us ver-jin-ee-AY-nus)
Odous = "tooth" ***koilos*** = "hollow" ***virginianus*** = "of Virginia"

If you see a deer in the Southeastern swamps, you can know for sure that it is a white-tailed deer. The tiny endangered Key deer, found only in the Florida Keys, is just a small version of the white-tailed deer, weighing up to 60 lbs and about the size of a German shepherd. Some adults weigh only 35 lbs.

In the U.S., the other two deer species, the blacktail and mule deer, are never found anywhere near cypress swamps.

Deer are *browsers*, eating the leaves of shrubs, vines and trees instead of *grazing* on grass like cows. They wade out into the swamp waters to drink or browse (and swim sometimes, too) but they're mostly interested in swamp edges where there are many varieties of leaves within reach.

whitetail deer

Key deer

Deer Skulls

pedicel →

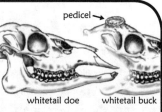
whitetail doe   whitetail buck

A deer skull without antlers is either a buck that has shed its antlers or a doe.

A buck skull has two flat *pedicels* (platforms) from which new antlers grow each year.

That Makes Scents...

Did you know a deer has ten scent glands on its body? Arrows point to them on the Key deer at left (they come in pairs).

Deer rub the glands against trees and rocks to mark their territory with their scent. And with every step they take, a gland behind each hoof leaves an odor. That's how they find each other in the forest. Pretty cool, huh?

What About Bambi?

It's a great tale, but the Bambi story leaves out lots of good stuff. *Before you read on, measure with your hands how tall you think a newborn fawn is.* Okay now, new fawns may be only twelve inches at the shoulder and weigh five to seven pounds. Were you close?

Newborn fawns have scent glands (see above), but they are scentless until fawns are old enough to follow mom. Predators would find and **eat** newborns if they had an odor. Later, mom can follow their trail if they wander off.

One final amazing thing: fawns have spots to *camouflage* (KAM-oh-flahzsh = conceal) them from predators like bobcats. Most predators can't see color, so the spots look just like leaf shadows and the fawn is nearly invisible.

Humming Along

The ruby-throated hummingbird is the only hummer in most eastern swamps, although other hummers may be spotted occasionally. Watch for the brilliant red throat and narrow black chin patch.

male ruby-throated hummingbird

Lyme Tyme?

Imagine this. You're sitting in a shrubby clearing and you notice a little critter hanging onto a leaf, waving its front legs. A closer look and – UH OH! It's a black-legged tick – waiting to catch a ride and suck some of your blood (see page 106).

↖ watch out for ticks between these sizes ↘

Ixodes scapularis close-up

Let's begin with a tick on a deer. A mature hungry tick, the size of a sesame seed on a hamburger bun, buries her snout into a deer and fills up with blood until she's about the size of your fingertip. A male finds her, they mate, then she drops to the ground, burrows under leaves, and later lays about 2000 eggs.

A hatching larval tick this size →· finds a host to suck. When it's full, it drops off and waits for another victim. Mice are major carriers of Lyme disease, so if it sucked on a mouse last time, look out – it could spread Lyme disease to its next host – you!

Carolina Ash
Fraxinus caroliniana

This ash is also called the water ash or pop ash. If growing in water, its base swells like a cypress trunk. Its winged seeds, called *keys*, are eaten by rodents, deer, bears, song birds and ducks.

whitetail deer track & scat

tracks may look like this

3"

or like this

when walking, rear hoof may step into front hoofprint

|······20"- 25"······|

deer scat actual size

26. The White-tailed Deer

If the anole lizards hadn't been interrupted, they would have mated and the small green female would have laid her eggs in a hole in the ground to hatch about two months later. But they didn't get the chance to finish their courting just then.

The white-tailed deer was approaching the sweetgum tree where the anoles were, followed by one of her twin fawns. It was nearly an hour since her alligator encounter and she browsed calmly on the leaves of a Carolina ash, nipping off a young leaf in one place and buds in another. The fawn followed her like a shadow. The anoles retreated higher up into the sweetgum for safety.

This was the fawn's first day of traveling with its mother. It was several weeks old, and until now she had left her fawns lying silent and still in two separate places while she went off to eat.

But shortly after her alligator encounter, when she returned to one of her fawns to nurse it, the fawn wouldn't lie back down when it had finished suckling. She butted it with her forehead and even pushed it back down with her forefoot, but it was ready to follow its mother and it wouldn't lie back down.

From now on it would remain by her side at all times (the other fawn would be ready to join them the next day) – until the next spring when she would chase both of them away just before the birth of new fawns.

Everything was a brand-new adventure to the little fawn. As it trotted along beside its mother, it carefully watched what she ate, copying her choices of leaves and buds. It sampled a red maple leaf, but immediately spit it out. Deer only eat red maple when there is nothing else to eat.

The fawn memorized the foods its mother chose, but it also explored and played in its new world, watching curiously as a ruby-throated hummingbird sipped nectar from the scarlet blossoms of a red buckeye.

At the edge of the boggy meadow, a patch of Queen Anne's lace, crawling with the striped caterpillars of black swallowtail butterflies, caught its attention.

The fawn lipped a caterpillar to see if it tasted good. But the caterpillar reared up its front end and inflated a pair of stinky scent horns just behind its head (see next page). The fawn snorted and backed away quickly. That smelly thing couldn't *possibly* be good to eat.

Black Swallowtail Butterfly

Papilio polyxenes (puh-PILL-ee-oh poh-LIX-en-eez)
papilio = "butterfly"   ***polyxenes*** = Achilles's girlfriend (myth.)

Swallowtails are found worldwide, but only a few live in the Southeast. Black swallowtail caterpillars feed only on plants of the carrot family. They're also called parsley caterpillars, for they eat parsley, anise and dill in peoples' gardens.

Swallowtail caterpillars have inflatable *osmeteria* (oz-muh-TEER-ee-uh). When the caterpillar is alarmed, these poke out and make a nasty stink.

The swallowtail butterfly is named for the long, trailing tags on its hindwings which look like the forked tail of a swallow (most, but not all, swallowtails have them). What are they for?

Have you ever seen swallowtail butterflies with raggedy rear wings, maybe even missing a "tail?" That's because birds grab the important-looking tail while the rest of the butterfly flies safely away. That's a sneaky trick to play on a hungry bird.

Butterfly Life Events

1st instar ¼"and up 2nd & 3rd instars ½"and up 4th instar ¾" and up 5th instar up to 2"

crysalis 1¼"

adult black swallowtail butterfly

Butterflies and moths go through three stages: egg, caterpillar or larva, and chrysalis before becoming butterflies. A black swallowtail egg is only this • big. Hatching into a small, fuzzy black larva (see above). Growing larger, it splits its skin and emerges (molts) as a black, tufted caterpillar with a white "saddle."

Several molts (instars) later, the much larger, smooth caterpillar binds itself to a twig with a silk thread and molts into a *pupa* (PEW-puh) or *chrysalis* (KRIS-uh-liss), inside which the butterfly develops. When the butterfly emerges, mates and lays eggs, the cycle repeats.

In the Southeast, this happens three times each summer. Eggs of the third generation (*caterpillar–chrysalis–butterfly*–**egg**; *caterpillar–chrysalis–butterfly*–**egg**; *caterpillar–chrysalis–butterfly*–**EGG**), hatch the next spring.

Here are some other common Southern swallowtail butterflies and their stages:

spicebush swallowtail
Papilio troilus
caterpillar: green and brown with golden eyespots
chrysalis: bright green
butterfly: black with white spots and bluish shading

zebra swallowtail
Eurytites marcellus
caterpillar: gray with black and yellow stripes.
chrysalis: looks like a folded green or brown leaf
butterfly: black and cream with long tails

pipevine swallowtail
Battus philenor
caterpillar: jet black, with long black "horns," and short bright orange bumps
chrysalis: tan, with humped back
butterfly: iridescent blue-black

Bitter Bites

Some butteflies (some swallowtails, for instance) taste bad because as caterpillars they feed on bitter, foul-tasting or even poisonous plants. If a bird eats just one pipevine swallowtail (adult or caterpillar), it will avoid other butterflies or caterpillars that look like that – even good-tasting ones – because they resemble the one that made it gag.

As a result, similar butterfly species live to produce more offspring that look just like themselves. These butterflies don't **plan** to copy bitter butterflies – it just happens. This is called *mimicry* (MIM-ih-kree = imitation).

The tasty **scarlet-bodied wasp moth** is safe because it has clear wings and poses to look like a dangerous wasp.→

Cosmosoma myrodora actual size

Most "bad guys" advertise their "badness" with bright colors or patterns. Predators learn these warning signs, and avoid similar brightly marked prey. Skunks, poison arrow frogs, and coral snakes are some non-insect examples.

Butterfly and Moth Equipment

Butterflies and moths have some interesting equipment. Here are some close-ups:

Scales:
Tiny, colorful scales cover the wings like overlapping shingles. ⟶

Antennae:
knob
Butterfly antennae have knobs. Moth antennae (see moth antennae above) don't.

Tongue: Moths and butterflies have coiled tube tongues for sucking up nectar or water. The tongue may be as long as its body.

coiled tongue
partly uncoiled

Transforming
Most caterpillar parts become similar butterfly parts, including the spiracles *(SPEER-uh-kulz = breathing holes).* Eyes, mouth parts and true legs *become more complex in butterflies. But* prolegs *are walking aids, and don't appear on butterflies.* Segments *on caterpillars may blend and be hard to count.*

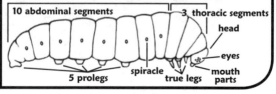

10 abdominal segments   3 thoracic segments
head
eyes
mouth parts
true legs
spiracle
5 prolegs

27. The Black Swallowtail Butterfly

By late afternoon, the steamy warm air above the Queen Anne's lace was alive with the flutter of swallowtails. The females were mostly black, but the males had rows of large yellow and orange spots on their wings. They flitted about the plants, courting and mating.

One female was laying round yellow eggs beneath the fern-like leaves.

Several males perched on the lower parts of the Queen Anne's lace, occasionally fluttering out to chase other males away from their chosen territories.

Pupae hung here and there along the stems, held in place with silken strings – more of them hung on twigs of the red maple and from palmetto blades nearby.

Caterpillars were all over the Queen Anne's lace, for it was both their home and food. They had hatched from eggs laid at different times by different black swallowtails, so there were many sizes, colors and ages of caterpillars on the plants.

The smallest caterpillars were fuzzy black with white saddles, but they grew and changed with every molt until, with the last molt, each caterpillar was jade-green and ringed with black stripes and bright yellow and black spots.

Each had two rubbery orange scent horns it could thrust from the skin just behind its head. The horns smelled terrible. If an attacker could be driven off by the nasty smell, the caterpillar might survive to become a butterfly. The caterpillars tasted fine, but they were protected by their bright colors.

A Carolina wren flying past in search of food noticed the big, fat caterpillars. Back at his nest were five hungry nestlings. The brightly striped caterpillars on the airy Queen Anne's lace would have been an easy meal.

But the little wren had recently tried to eat the striped caterpillar of a very similar butterfly, the pipevine swallowtail, and the taste had made him gag. He had drooled and wiped his bill on nearby twigs again and again, trying to get rid of the bitter flavor. Since then, the wren had avoided smooth, brightly-marked caterpillars.

He eyed the big clump of Queen Anne's lace nervously now, and flew widely around it and out into a forest opening. There he spotted a big leaf-footed bug (p. 72) sucking juice from a beautyberry bush stem. He snatched it without even landing on the bush, and headed for his nest of hungry chicks.

Carolina Wren

Thryothorus ludovicianus (thry-AH-thor-us lew-do-viss-ee-AY-nus)
Thryo = "reed" ***thouros*** = "leaping" ***ludovicianus*** = "of Louisiana"

For some reason, this large cinnamon-red wren first identified in Louisiana was officially named the *Carolina* wren. It's sometimes called the Louisiana or Florida wren, or the mocking wren – for its large collection of songs is similar to a mockingbird's. Some know it as "the jubilee bird," for one of its calls is ***"jubilee, jubilee, jubilee."*** It also sings ***"video, video, video."***

This is South Carolina's state bird. Common all over the Southeast, the Carolina wren is found year-round in dense, thickety places with lots of cover. You might call it hyper, since it is in constant motion, dodging into and under shrubs and brushpiles, flipping its tail and singing. Mated pairs may stay together all year, chattering and stopping to sing at any moment. They may even sing during snowstorms.

If you think you hear a cardinal or a titmouse singing ***under*** a bush, look for a Carolina wren instead.

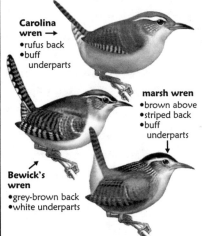

Carolina wren →
- rufus back
- buff underparts

marsh wren
- brown above
- striped back
- buff underparts

Bewick's wren
- grey-brown back
- white underparts

What Bird is That?

When identifying birds, it helps to notice **where** you see them. For instance, you won't see a marsh wren deep in a forest, and don't expect to see a Bewick's wren in a cattail marsh.

Three Southeastern wrens have *white eyestripes*, but only the Carolina wren also has a rufous (reddish) back **and** buff (tannish-pink) underparts. The marsh wren has a streaked back. Bewick's wren is white beneath.

Wren's Dinner

These are all wren food. Can you identify them? (Hint: many are in this book.) Wrens also eat stinkbugs, cockroaches, weevils, leafhoppers, scale insects, moths, leaf-footed bugs, flies, sowbugs, snails, millipedes, lizards, treefrogs, snakes, berries and seeds. Plus other stuff.

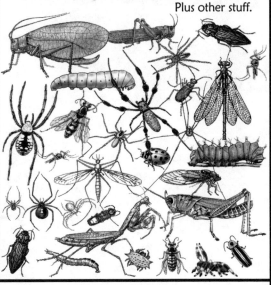

Brave or Foolish?

Pretend you are a Carolina wren and you live in the woods near a farm. Do you think you should build your nest:

a. in a quiet, safe, thorny shrub
b. in a cavity under an uprooted tree
c. in a tractor being used every day

Did you guess c.? Not only did one wren nest in a tractor, but she successfully raised her chicks in that nest. What a childhood *those* nestlings must have had. Wrens usually choose nesting sites more like a. or b.

Dinosaur Feathers

Scientists have found that if chick embryos (still inside the egg) don't get certain proteins, their leg scales (scutes) become feathers. Some scientists think *all* scaly dinosaurs had feathers (the first feathers may have looked more like chick fuzz) although BIG dinosaurs may have been nearly bare like elephants and rhinos. Modern birds probably developed from **small** *Velociraptor*-type dinosaurs, which ran swiftly on long hind legs.

Fossils of feathered wren-sized birds, *Iberomesornis*[1] (eye-BAIR-oh-mes-OR-niss) and *Eoalulavis*[2] (ee-oh-AL-yoo-lah-vis) have been discovered in Spain. *Eoalulavis* lived during the Cretaceous period more than a hundred million years ago and had tiny spiky teeth. Shrimp fossils were found in its fossil tummy. (Just for fun, pretend the next small bird you see is an *Eoalulavis...*)

Eoalulavis
Notice the claws on the wing.

Eoalulavis is the earliest bird fossil ever found with an *alula* (AL-yoo-luh) feather just like alulas on modern birds.
Like the flap on an airplane wing, an alula guides the flow of air over the wing to stabilize the bird during slow flight, take-off and landing (see p. 46).

alula on a wren wing

[1]*Ibero* = "Spain"   *mes* = "middle"   *ornis* = "bird"
[2]*Eo* = "early"   *alula* = "thumb feather"   *avis* = "bird"

28. The Carolina Wren

The male wren was very busy – he had to find food for the chicks in the first nest, for the female brooding the eggs in the second nest, and for himself.

Sometimes he stopped to sing his bright call of **"jubi-lee, jubilee, jubilee,"** but he always got right back to the business of food-gathering. There wasn't much time for anything else.

The male wren was not having a good morning. While nabbing a grasshopper he had been kicked in the eye, and the teary, bleary eye made searching for insects more difficult. He stopped repeatedly to blink and rub his beak and eye against twigs in an effort to clear it, and only now, af-ter nearly an hour, was his vision al-most back to normal. He crammed a small millipede into his beak along with the leaf-footed bug, but there was no way to add a delicious cranefly he saw fluttering in the dark hollow of a tree stump, so he memorized its position for the next trip.

He flew back toward his nest with a full beak, but a few yards away from it he braked to a halt in midair and dropped into a concealing holly shrub, staring around in dismay. His nest! What had happened to his nest? The entrance gaped blackly and the grasses, twigs, pieces of shed snakeskin, dead leaves and Spanish moss that had formed the cozy nest were scattered all over the forest floor.

Dropping his beakful of food, the little wren stut-tered out an alarm call. He flitted from bush to bush, moving closer to the wreckage with each short flight, peering at the mess in confusion. But nothing moved; no chicks chirped noisy demands for food. His fledg-lings were gone.

The male Carolina wren was taking care of a nest full of fledglings all by himself. The female had helped him feed the nestlings at first, but Carolina wrens often overlap their broods so that they can raise more chicks. The first nest was tucked snugly into the tangled roots of a tree blown down by a hurricane some years before.

The male had built a second nest in the base of a palmetto while the female was brooding the first chicks. A week ago she had left the first chicks, who were almost ready to fledge, to lay more eggs and start another family in the new nest in the palmetto.

Long-tailed Weasel

Mustela frenata (mus-TEE-luh freh-NAH-tuh)
Mustela = "weasel"   *fren* = "bridle"   *atus* = "provided with"

Mustela also means "one who carries off mice," which describes a weasel pretty well. Like the mink (see page 56), the long-tailed weasel is a member of the strong-scented *Mustela* family. The scent comes from two glands under the tail which activate at six weeks, just before the young leave the nest.

In areas with cold winters, weasels' brown summer fur is replaced with white winter fur. White fur makes them hard to see on snow, which helps them sneak up on prey. It also makes it difficult for other predators, like hungry owls, to spot them.

White weasels are called ermines (UR-minz). Their furry pelts have been used to decorate royal garments for centuries.

In the Southeast, weasels remain brown year-round, and their underparts range from white or cream to deep yellow. The "bridle" in their scientific name (see above) refers to the white bridle-like face markings found on weasels in the Southwest.

Milkweed *Asclepias sp.*

Look at milkweed flowers close up – they're lovely. Parachute-like seeds burst from big, warty pods.

Bringing Home the Bacon

Carrying food home could be a big problem if the weasel's neck were any shorter.

Low-Life

A weasel lives close to the earth. Like a furry, four-legged sausage, it follows its keen nose down rodent tunnels in search of mice and rats, but it also climbs trees, where it feeds on nestlings and squirrels. Rabbits, too, become dinner sometimes. A long-tailed weasel may attack something even larger in self-defense, or when angry or protecting its young, but since it is only ten inches long (plus a five-inch tail) it usually hunts smaller prey.

A weasel needs a lot of fuel and has to eat about forty percent of its own weight every day. That means a nine-ounce male (females are only half that size) must gobble about 3½ ounces of meat daily to survive – that would be four or five cotton mice at almost an ounce apiece or one cotton rat weighing three to four ounces.

A weasel may travel more than **three miles** every twenty-four hours searching for food. That's the same as if an eighty pound person ran fifty miles cross-country daily while finding, catching **and eating** about ten wild bunnies (that's about forty-five cheeseburgers). GULP...

A Weasel's "Cotton Candy"

cotton mouse
Peromyscus gossypinus
body 4,"
tail 3½"

Two main weasel snacks are the cotton mouse and the *hispid* (coarse-haired) cotton rat. The cotton **mouse** is the southern version of a deer mouse. The cotton **rat** is grizzled black and gray, and lives in grassy areas. The "cotton" refers to cotton plantations where both were first recorded.

hispid cotton rat
Sigmodon hispidus
body 7"
tail 5"

Skinny Skull

Weasel skulls are tough and flat, perfect for forcing passage through narrow mouse tunnels.

actual size

1 ½" - 2"

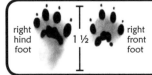

right hind foot

1 ½

right front foot

weasel track & scat

12"

weasel scat actual size

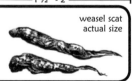

29. The Long-tailed Weasel

The long, yellow-bellied weasel sniffed for prey in the broken roots of the big sycamore oak tree. He didn't know a nest full of wren chicks was tucked into a cavity in its tangled roots just above him.

Bird nestlings are usually silent when their parents are away. They sleep, preen their pinfeathers and quietly stretch and flap their wings.

But the wren chicks were hungry. Food had been coming less often now that only one adult was feeding them.

Away through the forest, several minutes passed as the father wren detoured around the Queen Anne's lace then found and snatched the leaf-footed bug. The hungry little wrens were wide awake and impatient for their food. Even so, they remained quiet.

But when the weasel leaped up onto the rootball, the nest vibrated slightly. The chicks snapped to attention – that felt like father arriving! The weasel brushed against a wiry root which twanged back into place. That was the sound their father would make brushing past the rootlets to bring food. Five yellow beaks opened wide as the nestlings began to chant their **"FEED ME"** call.

They made a good breakfast for the weasel.

To make sure he had missed nothing, the weasel ripped the nest apart. Then, satisfied that he had eaten every bite, he bounced away with looping zigzag leaps, poking into every nook and cranny in his path. Coming out into the meadow, the weasel ducked behind a patch of blooming milkweed. He had seen something move in the nearby marsh.

A moorhen was scrunching down nervously in her dried-cattail nest. Spotting movement in the meadow, she had instantly squatted low and spread her wings out protectively over her just-now-hatching chicks. But it wasn't enough.

Originally the nest had been surrounded by water. But hot weather had dried the marsh until now the nest was exposed on the cracked mud like a footstool, framed by tall, green cattails. The weasel dashed toward the nest, sending the moorhen, followed by six tiny newly-hatched black chicks, squawking and flapping into the surrounding cattails. In the nest was a single unhatched egg. The weasel crunched it open and gulped the gooey contents. Then, full-bellied and drowsy from his morning's hunt, he curled up amid the empty cinnamon-spotted eggshells and slept.

Common Moorhen

Gallinula chloropus (gal-IN-yew-luh   KLOR-oh-pus)
Gallinula = "little chicken"   **chloros** = "green"   **pous** = "foot"

The common moorhen is named for the moors (marshes) where it lives. You'll notice the bright-red, yellow-tipped beak right away. The red forehead shield is part of its beak, and male moorhens (males are called moor**hens**, too) display it to their ladies when courting, even though females also have one.

Common moorhens are brown with black heads, bluish chests, white on their sides and undertail, and yellow legs. Coots and purple gallinules (GAL-in-yools) look similar, but coots have white beaks, while purple gallinules are bright purple and green.

The common moorhen is also called a common gallinule, blue rail, chicken-foot coot, red-billed mud hen, water chicken, and other names. One name, Blue Peter, came from the fact that its long toes spread its weight so that it can walk around on floating lilypads and other water plants and debris – it appears to walk on water like Saint Peter in the Bible.

Cattail Deli
Typha latifolia

Many kinds of freshwater insects and small animals shelter in the water at the bases of cattails. Cattail roots anchor the shoreline, and the leaves and stems (up to eight feet tall) cut the wind and calm the water. They multiply quickly, and can fill up a pond or marsh.

Both Native Americans and white settlers ate cattail parts, grinding the starchy roots into flour, eating young shoots like asparagus, and nibbling the young boiled flower spikes like corn-on-the-cob.

Goofy Chick

A newly-hatched common moorhen chick is almost the size of a farmyard chick. It is sooty black and fuzzy, with dark legs and feet and long, black skinny toes. Its bald head looks pretty funny – you can see candy-pink skin through the short fuzz on top, and blue skin on the forehead and around the eyes. The bill is lipstick red, but after a few weeks it fades to greenish yellow. The bright red color will return when it gets older.

Common moorhen chicks are *precocial* (pree-KO-shul = downy and fully active when hatched) unlike *altricial* (al-TRISH-ul) chicks, such as robins, which are nearly naked and helpless when they break out of the egg.

On Shaky Ground
Some marshes have islands that **look** solid, with trees, shrubs, grasses and small plants growing on them. But if you step on them they jiggle like jelly and you may plunge right through. These floating islands are made of peat moss and tangled root masses. If the plant roots reach the bottom, it may become a permanent island. If not, it drifts around, changing the scenery.

One swamp is named for an Indian word meaning "land that trembles." Since 1780 the name has changed from Enkanfinaka to Eckenfinooka to today's Okefenokee (OH-kee-fen-OH-kee) Swamp.

This snail is **spiraled.**

operculum (lid)

This snail is **coiled.**

Snips & Snails & Gooey Slime Trails
Swamps, calm and muddy bottomed, make good habitat for snails (moorhen food). These important members of the clean-up crew have big, fleshy "foot-tongues." A snail scrapes off decaying underwater objects and algae with its *radula* (RAD-yoo-luh = a small raspy ribbon lined with teeth).

A snail views the world with eyes and antennae on long stalks. Scare a snail and it sucks its soft parts in and slams shut its *operculum* (oh-PUR-kew-lum) or lid.

A snail slides along on a slime trail produced by its muscular foot. Amazingly, a snail can actually slide along the *underside* of the water surface, upside down.

Mnemonic (nih-MAH-nik) Devices
How do YOU remember important stuff? You could use a *mnemonic device* – a memory helper. For example, if a plant looks like this → you probably call it "grass." But it could also be a *sedge* or a *rush*. How can you tell? Memorize this mnemonic device: ***Grass leaves are flat, rushes are round and sedges have edges.*** Roll a piece of "grass" between your fingers and look at it carefully. Which is it? Another clue: true grasses have *jointed stems* (a reed is a grass). By the way, cattails stand alone – they're not grass, rush, or sedge.

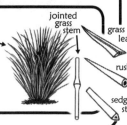

jointed grass stem

grass leaf

rush leaf

sedge stem

30. The Common Moorhen

The tiny moorhen chicks scattered to hide under mats of dried cattails as their mother splashed noisily across the open marsh water to a small vegetation island, hoping to distract the weasel. The weasel ignored them all, busy eating the egg, then it curled up out of sight in the nest. After several minutes, the mother moorhen quietly called her chicks. Soon, six muddy, long-toed chicks crept silently to the water's edge and paddled hastily to their mother across ten feet of water. This was their first swim, for they had hatched from their eggs only that morning, but they didn't hesitate.

"*queep? queep?*" They clustered about her legs, frightened and confused by their rough welcome to swamp life. She clucked soothingly, and finally, under her protective breast, they calmed down and began to groom their downy black fuzz until they were clean and dry and fluffy. They were ready to get on with life.

The youngsters grew fast in the sunny shallow waters of the swamp. Late spring turned to summer, dry and hot. Cicadas buzzed high in the trees during the muggy days, and frogs chirped, croaked, twanged and clicked all through the nights. Owl calls echoed through the swamp at all hours.

With their long toes splayed out, the moorhen chicks could trot over the tops of the waterlilies, eating water insects, tiny fish trapped in the shrinking pools, worms and snails, and seeds and grasses that grew in and near the water. Their mother abandoned them when they were about a month old and started another brood, but they scarcely noticed.

The young birds chased each other like giddy ducklings, beating the water with their pinfeathered wings. They dived for seeds, bits of water plants, and rootlets on the muddy bottom. Sometimes their racket attracted a gar or an alligator, and they raced for shore to hide in the cattails, their feet clutching the roots and their heads barely above water. Sometimes one of them didn't reach shelter in time, but these grim episodes faded quickly from the minds of the remaining chicks. Within minutes they would be back in action as though nothing had happened.

The chicks often chased water striders, paddling so fast that they rose out of the water and seemed to run on the surface.

Water Strider

Gerris remigis (JAIR-iss   REM-ih-jiss)
Ger = "to carry"   **remigium** = "to row"

What's that four-legged bug skating over the surface of the water? Call it a skipper, a pond skater, or a Jesus bug (for walking on water) – a lot of people call it a water strider. It may look only four-legged, because it often folds its front legs under its chin, ready to reach out to grab and carry food. The middle pair flicks back and forth to move the strider across the water. The hind legs guide its movement like rudders. Some striders are wingless. Others can fly off to a new pond if their birth pond dries up.

Male striders tap out vibrating ripples to attract females. After mating, the female glues about a hundred eggs to plant stems at the water's edge. The eggs hatch two weeks later.

Water striders are attracted to bright lights, and oddly, this helps them find their food. They automatically race toward the sparkles of sun reflecting off ripples caused by injured insects struggling on the water's surface.

Water World

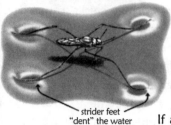

strider feet "dent" the water

To us, water is thin and splashy. To a small insect, the water's surface (*meniscus*) is a rubbery sheet. If an insect breaks through the surface, it will get stuck in it like fruit bits in warm jello. It's really a different world.

The undersides of a water strider's lower legs are thickly covered with tiny hairs that act like snowshoes, keeping the strider's sharp feet from piercing the water's surface. Look at the dents made by the feet of the strider above – you can actually see how the meniscus bends under the weight of the waterstrider.

Leaf-footed Bug

Leptoglossus phyllopus

This bug gets its name from big, colorful leaf-like blades on its hind legs. It's very common in the Southeast, living on shrubs where it sucks juices from plant stems and leaves.

actual size

Wearing Armor

Water striders, spiders, crawfish and lots of other critters are *invertebrates* (in-VER-tuh-bruts = without backbones). They wear their skeletons on the *outside* and store their squishy body parts safely *inside*.
Imagine if YOU were made like that!

Invertebrate kid pats invertebrate cat

King of the Air

The eastern kingbird is the terror of all the swamp insects. Perching on a twig over water, the black and white kingbird drops and swoops, plucking its prey out of midair.

It also eats wild fruit and berries. Listen for its **"kit-kit-kittery"** cry.

Eastern kingbird
Tyrannus tyrannus
6¾" to 8½" long

It's a Wing Thing

Beetles are *Coleopterans* (ko-lee-OPP-tur-uns) *koleos* = "cover," *ptera* = "wing"

A beetle's hard top wings lift out of the way so the underwings can fly (see p. 18). Beetles mostly bite and chew.

stinkbug actual size

Bugs are *Hemipterans* (heh-MIP-tur-uns) *hemi* = "half."

Bugs may have bright red or orange markings. A bug's top wings are leathery at the front and see-through at the rear. Where they meet, the edges make an X or Y marking on its back.

Bugs have mouthparts that pierce and suck, much like a mosquito's. Some bugs drink plant juices, others drink blood.

But some insects that **aren't** really bugs are **called** bugs.

Below: is a **ladybug*** a bug? What about **lovebugs***?
If you aren't sure, check the wings.

mouth parts

lady bug and mating lovebugs actual size

Water Dragons

Water striders share the water with some ferocious swimming companions. The insects below are carnivorous. Don't "bug" them – two of them may bite.

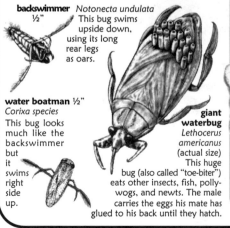

backswimmer *Notonecta undulata* ½"
This bug swims upside down, using its long rear legs as oars.

water boatman ½"
Corixa species
This bug looks much like the backswimmer but it swims right side up.

giant waterbug
Lethocerus americanus
(actual size)
This huge bug (also called "toe-biter") eats other insects, fish, polly-wogs, and newts. The male carries the eggs his mate has glued to his back until they hatch.

Lizard's-tail

Saururus cernuus

Since it doesn't mind "getting its feet wet," the lizard's-tail plant often grows at the edge of water. Do you see the "lizard's tail?"

***Ladybugs** (*Coccinellidae* species) are beetles, not bugs.
***Lovebugs** (*Plecia nearctica*) are flies, not bugs.

31. The Water Strider

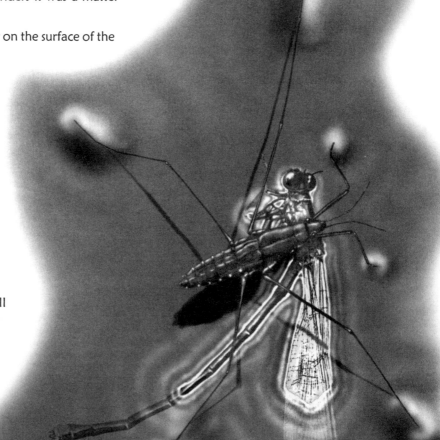

Although the common moorhen chicks seemed to think it was terrific fun to chase the water striders, to the water striders it was a matter of life or death.

The striders could travel swiftly on the surface of the water, either by sculling (rowing) with their center pair of legs or by hopping. When sculling, the two hind feet were braced against the water. The bugs skittered across the surface like skaters on an icy skating rink.

But the pursuing moorhen chicks were speedy, too. It was a lucky water strider that reached the safety of the cattails, rushes, cane, or some other shelter before a racing chick could snap it up.

There were water striders all over the water, out in the sunny marsh and in the swamp where trees made dappled shadows on the dark water. Wherever there was food for the striders – dead, dying or unlucky insects struggling in the film of the water's surface – the striders cruised for their dinner.

Near a lizard's-tail plant at the water's edge, a turquoise and black Rambur's forktail damselfly, knocked into the water by a young Eastern kingbird, struggled weakly.

The sensitive hairs on the legs of a nearby female water strider picked up the vibrations. With a swift kick, she skated forward. Her front legs unfolded swiftly to reach out and pull the damselfly beneath her.

She poked her sharp mouthpiece into the damselfly, injecting a fluid to dissolve its insides. Within moments, its organs turned to liquid, and the strider sucked until the body was an empty husk. She released it, her hunger satisfied, and drifted away on the slow swamp current.

Earlier that spring, the strider had mated, then glued her eggs – nearly a hundred of them – to lizard's-tail stems at the edge of the warm, shallow water. Now they were hatching into tiny, half-inch copies of the adult strider.

They hunted mayflies, mosquitoes and other tiny prey. Then, in turn, they became food for other hungry creatures such as catfish, frogs, and birds, including hungry wood ducks.

Wood Duck

Aix sponsa (AIKS SPON-suh)
Aix = "water bird" **sponsa** = "bride" (dressed beautifully)

The wood duck almost became extinct. In the 1800s it was slaughtered in huge numbers for the Eastern meat markets. Even worse, the hardwood forests with the old hollow trees it needs for nesting were heavily logged and nearly wiped out. By the time market harvesting of wild birds was outlawed in 1918, there were few left. Something had to be done quickly.

People incubated eggs, raised and released wood ducks, and provided nesting boxes to replace their missing hollow nest trees. Now the wood duck is one of the most plentiful ducks in the eastern half of the U.S. But it was a close call.

The wood duck's other common names are woody, swamp duck, whistler and squealer (from its **"ooo-ee-e-e-e-k"** call), acorn duck (it *gobbles* acorns), bridal duck (from its *specific* name, see above), tree duck (it roosts and nests in trees) and summer duck (it's one of the few ducks to nest in the southern U.S).

Dump Nesting

A wood duck's **ideal** nest is hidden thirty feet up, in a hollow tree at least 100' from water. If a nest is easy to see, other wood ducks looking for a nesting cavity will pop in and "dump" an egg in the nest. In time, there may be as many as fifty eggs in this "dump nest." The nesting duck can't keep all the eggs warm, so many of the dumped eggs will never hatch. Some people still hang nest boxes at the edges of ponds, but the news is getting around that nests must be hidden so they won't be used as dump nests.

Dude!

The female wood duck is a Plain Jane. Only a white eye ring and speckles dress up her soft grey-brown feathers. But the male – what an incredible rainbow!

This guy really overdoes it. His head and long crest are iridescent green with white markings. His eyes are scarlet, and his beak is red, gold, white and black. Next, a speckled brick-red breast, stripey tan sides, white and brick undersides, and an iridescent blue-and-black back with white accents...
Wow!

Life is Short

That fuzzy cloud swirling over the water may be mayflies that have molted from their underwater nymph skins and are mating in swarms. They can't eat – they have no mouths – so they only live a few days (they only eat during their nymph stage).

adult mayfly actual size

Mommy?

Lost woody ducklings may be adopted by mallard duck hens. Until it is three weeks old, a lost woody might *imprint on* (attach to) a mallard hen, thinking she is "mom." Imprinted *male* woodies may later mate with mallard hens, producing infertile hybrids. Imprinted *female* woodies don't get confused – when they mature. they mate with wood ducks as they should.

They lay eggs in the water for the next year's mayfly swarms. Then they all die and are gobbled up by ducklings, fish, and other hungry critters.

mayfly nymph, actual size

Fuzzy Down

Except for their long, sharp toenails (useful for climbing up out of hollow tree nests) wood ducklings look like most other wild ducklings with lots of fuzzy *down* (fluffy pre-feathers). The soft down keeps them warm, and it also cushions the ducklings' landing when they leap from the nest.

Surprisingly, down isn't a special kind of baby feather – it's just the fluffy tip of an ordinary feather, the first part to sprout out. Six weeks later, the downy tips will be worn away and the ducklings will be feathered like adult hens.

Males will sprout their bright feathers after the first molt.

Wanted/Country Homes

Rural, hidn. in forest nr. wtr. in gd. nbrhood – no snks., flckrs., sqrls, mnk., hwks., rcoons., crws., fxs., big fsh., snpping. trtls., allgtrs., cats or dgs., nearby. Prefr. wdpckr. style bdrm., Mnufctured. home w/3½" door ok. Non-smoker w/kids.   #56

Modrn. new nest in rd. mpl. tree, big den mdrn ktchn. remodld

32. The Wood Duck

Fourteen wood ducklings hatched one morning inside a down-lined, hollow, red oak branch twenty feet up in a tree that grew in the forest about a hundred yards from the edge of the swamp.

The following morning the mother wood duck perched in the long horizontal opening of the cavity and cooed softly until the ducklings clawed their way up to the opening using their long, sharp toenails.

Without warning, the mother wood duck spread her wings and jumped. She landed beneath the tree and looked up at her ducklings calling **_"Kuk-kuk-kuk!"_**

In the warm, early-morning mist, the forest floor and the ducklings' mother seemed very far away. The ducklings fidgeted uneasily, staring down at her. Suddenly one brave duckling launched herself into the air, her stubby wings flipping violently, her legs spread and webbed toes outstretched to make tiny sails. She landed with a soft thump on dry leaves, moss, and the cushion of her own downy feathers. She was followed by first one, then the rest of the ducklings, until they were all clustered excitedly around their mother.

"Pee–ee.....peee–eee.......pee–eee," the mother wood duck walked away, calling softly, and the ducklings toddled along behind her to the swamp. It was a long trek through the woods, over dead branches, under cinnamon ferns, through southern blue flags, and around trees and other obstacles. They finally arrived at the water's edge, peeping anxiously.

Barely pausing, the mother wood duck launched into the water, and the tiny ducklings followed. The moment they hit the water, it seemed as though they'd been swimming a thousand times before. They bobbed and paddled, swimming expertly, ducking under to snap up insect larvae and snails. They pecked mayflies, beetles and other insects from the stems of the waterlilies and other water plants above and below the water surface. Soon they would be chasing and catching water striders whenever they could, just like the moorhen chicks.

But in the very beginning, the small group of fuzzy ducklings would stick close to their mother. She could protect them if they stayed together, warning them of approaching alligators, gars or other dangers. She could lead them to safety on shore or onto a log, or later, when they got their feathers, to take flight.

Sometimes the male wood duck shared in the care of the little flock. But even the adults' sharp eyes couldn't always spot the perils lurking below the surface of the dark swamp water.

Snapping Turtle

Chelydra serpentina (KELL-ih-druh sur-pen-TIE-nuh)
Chelydr = "water serpent" *serpentina* = "snake"

The snapping turtle's scientific name (see above) probably has more to do with its looks than its bad attitude. In the water, snappers are cautious and rather timid. Out of the water, though, watch out! Hungry snapping turtles aren't very picky about their food. Looking more like mossy rocks than hungry predators, they eat fish, ducklings, fishing spiders, insects, smaller snapping turtles, vegetation and carrion (KAIR-ee-un = dead meat). Snappers probably find decaying food in murky water by tasting it, and they eat some really disgusting (to us) stuff. These scavengers play a major part in keeping swamp and pond water clean and pure.

But can't snappers "bite through broomsticks?" Well, snappers do have a tough, bony mouth with cutting edges. Even with no teeth, tearing apart meat is doable (by using their sharp claws), but chopping wood? Sorrrrry. It's just a myth.

Mobile Home

A turtle's ribs flatten and widen, growing together into a solid sheet to support the outer shell.

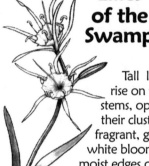

ribs

neck

Most turtle necks curve into an "S" inside the shell when the turtle pulls in its head. Most shells also provide room to tuck in legs.

Lilies of the Swamp

Tall lilies rise on thin stems, opening their clusters of fragrant, glowing white blooms at the moist edges of southern swamps, ponds and creeks.

spider lily
Hymenocallis species

swamp lily
Crinum americanum

Snapper Duo

Snappers aren't very, well, **sociable**, except when mating or when large numbers gather together in winter to hibernate.

When the weather warms, they get snappish and vicious, and wander far and wide overland, looking for a pond with fewer ferocious fiends in it.

Book Him!

Here's what you get when you fingerprint a snapping turtle.

An *alligator snapper* invites lunch (like this **swamp darter**) into its mouth by wiggling a wormlike lure attached to the tip of its tongue.
Then...... **SNAP!!**

alligator snapping turtle
Macroclemys temmincki

common snapping turtle
Chelydra serpentina

Snappers (there are two kinds) can become gigantic whoppers. In about fifty years, a well-fed **alligator snapping turtle** could reach 300 lbs. and be 30" long. A **common snapping turtle** may have an 18" shell and weigh 60 lbs. Do you see other differences, too?

Whirligig Beetles

air bubble

Watch for clusters of these shiny black beetles twirling about on top of calm water.

They have two sets of eyes – for looking above and below the water surface at the same time.

When diving, they carry along a bubble of air to breathe.

Snapperettes

actual hatchling size

plastron

baby snapping turtles

Unlike other turtles, snappers have such big heads they can't pull them inside their shells. They rely on their swift bite for protection. Even newly hatched snappers, fresh from round, creamy 1" eggs, can nip hard. A snapping turtle has a very small *plastron* (PLASS- trun = the bony shield covering its belly). This allows the snapper to move its legs easily. If a turtle looks several sizes too large for its *carapace* (KAIR-uh-puss = shell), it's *probably* a snapping turtle.

33. The Snapping Turtle

Down on the soft muddy floor of the swamp, a snapping turtle lay very still, waiting. He was a smallish snapper – his shell was only about nine inches long – and he was nearly fifteen years old. His mouth was open, his eyes were beady bright.

He had awakened early that morning as the sunshine turned the dark water to amber tea. Spidery white swamp lilies growing at the water's edge were reflected like stars in the dark water.

Dragging slowly through the swamp, raking past the stems of arrow arum with the long, sharp nails on his webbed front feet, he had pulled himself into a shallow spot where the sun-warmed water would heat his muscles enough to activate them.

He snaked his head up for a breath of air, then settled back down, mouth open, to wait for something to come close enough to snatch. He could dart his long, warty neck and head out nearly two-thirds the length of his body. This allowed him to catch something far above or in front of

him without even moving his shell. Overhead, he saw only shiny black whirligig beetles twirling on the water's surface, and the gently moving shadows of the arrow arum leaves. Then he sensed something else.

A fluttery vibration of splashing, paddling sounds came from near the muddy bank of the swamp. One large oval shape and fourteen small balls floated together on the water. It was the family of newly hatched wood ducks, but what the snapping turtle saw was the compact cluster of dents their bodies made in the water, and thirty churning feet.

The group of ducklings looked like one large creature, much too big and dangerous for the snapping turtle to eat.

He pulled his head back as far as possible into his shell, compressing his neck into a tight S-curve. The raft of ducklings drew closer, unaware of the hazard in the dark water just inches below. The mother passed overhead safely. So did thirteen of the chicks. The fourteenth chick lagged behind, exploring a floating leaf here, a waterlily there, every new thing in sight. The dent it made in the water didn't look large and dangerous at all. When you go swimming, it's wise to stay with the crowd. This duckling was about to learn the hard way.

River Otter

Lutra canadensis (LOO-truh can-uh-DEN-sis)
Lutra = "otter"   ***canadensis*** = "of Canada"

The otter spends some time on dry land, but it's more at home in water where it finds its food, socializes and plays. It can hold its breath for up to four minutes when swimming.

The river otter has ear and nose flaps that close underwater. A *nictitating* (NIK-tih-tayt-ing) membrane (a transparent eyelid) pulls across each eye to protect it. Its tail steers like a rudder as the otter tucks in its front paws and kicks with webbed hind feet to chase, catch and eat fish, crawfish, frogs, snakes, salamanders, turtles, birds, muskrats and aquatic insects in the swamp.

You'd think a swimming otter would get wet to the skin, but its fur is so thick the water can't get in (hey, that rhymes). An otter has more hairs growing on one square inch on its body than you have on your *whole head*. Warm air, trapped in the thick fur by water pressure, keeps the otter toasty and dry even when the water is chilly.

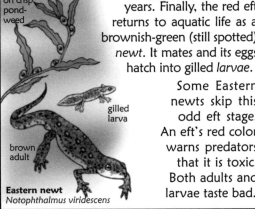

red eft

eggs on crisp pond-weed

gilled larva

brown adult

Eastern newt
Notophthalmus viridescens

An Odd Lifestyle

The Eastern newt's lifestyle is strange, even for a newt. The newt starts out as a gilled *larva* in a pond, then it absorbs its gills and lives on land as an *eft*, crimson with black-ringed red spots, for up to seven years. Finally, the red eft returns to aquatic life as a brownish-green (still spotted) *newt*. It mates and its eggs hatch into gilled *larvae*.

Some Eastern newts skip this odd eft stage. An eft's red color warns predators that it is toxic. Both adults and larvae taste bad.

Slip-slidin' Away!

Otters play a **lot** – it seems as though they try to make everything **FUN**. They play with their food, dropping and catching it, tossing it into the air, and, if it's alive, toying with it like a cat with a mouse.

They play games underwater with other family members, and sometimes use unwilling neighbors such as turtles, fish and crawfish as toys.

Since they are skillful hunters and food is pretty easy to find, life is just one big party. Otters like to climb up a muddy bank at the water's edge, getting it slick and wet, then swoosh down their home-made slide again and again on their bellies.

Southern Blue Flag

Iris virginica

Watch for these lavender or blue irises near shallow water. Their leaves may rise 24."

Otter Utterings

To sound like an otter: With your lips shut, say **"hm"** 6–8 times (very quickly) in your deepest voice. Make it sound buzzy.

You otter try it. (Sorrrrrry)

45-Cent Cutie

Otter kits are born toothless, blind and furry. They are about 5 inches long and weigh 4½ ounces, about as much as 45 pennies. Their eyes open at one month, and they leave the den at about three months. Very young otter kits are afraid of the water, and must be taught to swim.

A seven-week-old otter kit stretches and yawns.

Streamlined Skull
An otter's skull is wide and flat. Only an otter's lower front teeth are arranged this particular way.

actual size is about 4"

Giant 2nd incisors grow in **behind** the other front teeth.

river otter track & scat

right hind foot

3 ½"

right front foot

tail track

bounding, 16"- 30"

otter scat about 4" long, full of bones and crawfish pieces

Watch for this: a trail of bubbles on the water's surface may mean an otter is swimming along below.

34. The River Otter

Releasing the coiled S-curve of his neck and head, the snapping turtle struck at the last duckling, catching it by a toe and dragging it under the water. The mother wood duck, turning in the water, saw only a bubbling mound of water and a scatter of frightened ducklings. With a sharp cry and flapping wings, she herded her flock to the safety of the shore.

The snapping turtle sank back to the bottom with the struggling chick flopping in his beaky jaws. But just as he started to gulp down the fuzzy duckling, something grabbed his long warty tail and gave it a sharp tug. His mouth flew open in surprise and the duckling popped back up to the surface with only a snipped toe to show for its close escape.

"Weeek! weeek! weeek! weeek!" the lucky duckling shrieked, paddling hastily after its family.

Meanwhile, the turtle-tail-puller, a river otter just looking for fun, dodged the angry turtle's snapping jaws. She yanked the snapper through a billowy cloud of muddy water. A frightened Eastern newt and several startled water insects scattered off in all directions.

The turtle hooked a claw on a submerged log and swung around to strike at his tormenter. Dodging skillfully, the frisky otter teased the snapping turtle awhile longer, then she shot away to torpedo out of the water on a slimy mud chute used by turtles, alligators and minks to enter and leave the swamp.

The watery explosion of her exit rocked the pool, spreading arcs of waves across the surface. The surge sent a yellow-bellied slider turtle and a chicken turtle plopping in a panic off their floating basking log into the water.

The otter rose on her hind legs to check out the sudden movement of a cautious stinkpot turtle dropping from a tree limb into the swamp. Dropping back to all fours, she spent a few minutes rolling in a patch of sun-dappled grass to dry her shining dark-brown coat. Then she prowled along the bank sniffing her territory markers – a tuft of white-topped sedge, a half-buried broken branch, and a pile of her own droppings made highly visible by the pink and white bits of crawfish shell they contained.

But no one else had visited recently. She freshened the musk scent on the markers with squirts from the gland under her tail, then she nosed sleepily into a jungle of ferns and mint.

Playtime was over. The otter was ready for her afternoon nap.

Chicken Turtle

Dierochelys reticularia (die-air-AH-kel-iss reh-tik-yew-LAIR-ee-uh)
Diero = "nimble" ***chely*** = "tortoise" ***reticularius*** = "netted"

Chicken turtles are common in the still waters of southern swamps and ponds. *Reticularia* refers to the yellow net-like markings on the dark shell. A favorite food of many swamp dwellers, few chicken turtles reach their maximum possible size of ten inches.

Here's the best way to identify a chicken turtle: A chicken turtle's neck is very long – three-fourths the length of its shell – and striped yellow and black. Its plastron is yellow-orange. But unless the turtle "sticks its neck out," you'll have to look instead for narrow yellow stripes running from upper to lower shell between the hind legs.

The shell of the similar **yellow-bellied slider** (see below) is rounder than the chicken turtle's (which is much longer than it is wide, and widens out over the hips – see above).

Life.In.The.Slow.Lane.

Because turtles are reptiles, they're "cold-blooded" or ectothermic (*ecto* = outside, *thermic* = temperature) and can't regulate their own body temperatures.

They need sunshine to warm them up enough to keep moving. When the sun heats them up, they plop into the water to cool off or forage for food. A diving turtle can hold its breath for a lo-o-o-o-ng time because its slow metabolism (meh-TAB-oh-lizm = life process) doesn't use much oxygen.

Living slowly means turtles may live a very long time, too. In fact, turtles have been known to live for more than a hundred years.

This Old House
(a poem)

A turtle lives
inside its shell
Like a lizard
under a cup.
If it "turns turtle"
(upside down),
It's hard to turn
right-side-up.

Double-hinged **box turtles** can close up completely

A **chicken turtle** struggles to upright itself

Yolk Tales

Chicken turtles carrying ready-to-lay eggs can wait up to six months until the weather is right for laying them. A baby turtle may hatch with its yolk sac attached, but it will soon be absorbed.

newly hatched, actual size

yolk sac

Help Me!
Many turtles are killed by cars while crossing roads. If you stop to help, carry the turtle to the side of the road it is trying to reach. Otherwise it will just try again – and next time it may get mooshed.

Tortoise or Turtle?

•**Eastern box turtle**, which lives <u>mostly</u> on land, is a turtle, not a tortoise.

•**Chicken turtle**, <u>often</u> seen on dry land, is a turtle.

•**Gopher tortoise** (TOR-tuss) the Southeast's only tortoise species, avoids water entirely. Its deep burrows provide valuable habitat for many other animals as well.

Eastern box turtle
Terrapene carolina – 8"

<u>**Remember this:**</u>

~**Turtles** live in the *water* at least part of the time

~**Tortoises** live only on *land*.

gopher tortoise
Gopherus polyphemus – 14½"

Eternal Cypress

Cypress wood is very slow to rot, especially when it is under the water. Since the 1800s, loggers have "mined" swamps for cypress trees that may have died hundreds of years before.

Some hollow cypress logs used as water pipes in New Orleans in 1798 were still usable when they were dug up in 1914. Cypress shingles have been known to last as long as 250 years.

Other Turtles Found in Swamps

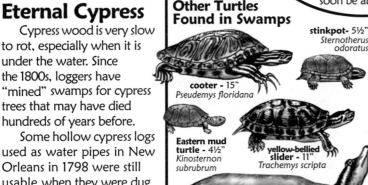

cooter - 15"
Pseudemys floridana

stinkpot- 5½"
Sternotherus odoratus

Eastern mud turtle - 4½"
Kinosternon subrubrum

yellow-bellied slider - 11"
Trachemys scripta

softshell turtle
20" *Apalone spinifera*

turtle track & scat

right hind foot

1 ¾"

right front foot

5"

tail track

toenails may scrape long grooves as the turtle moves forward

turtle scat about 1½" long. It may have a white blob at one end like a bird or lizard dropping.

35. The Chicken Turtle

The shell of a turtle protects it against most predators. The large chicken turtle that dived off the log had once been chewed on by a small alligator. The 'gator's sharp teeth had punched several holes in his shell and cracked some of his upper plates before it finally gave up. The holes and cracks had healed over, leaving only scars, but now any suspicious movement in the water or on shore caused the cracked turtle to plop off his basking perch and disappear into the depths.

Chicken turtles spend more time on land than most turtles. They hibernate and lay their eggs as far as a thousand feet from water, so their habitat must have large swamp margins undisturbed and untrampled by people or other animals. This chicken turtle had been ducking danger on land and in the water for more than twenty years, and his extreme caution was one of the reasons he had lived so long and gotten so big – nearly ten inches.

Some kinds of turtles like to bask together. This is a good plan since at least one turtle is usually watching for trouble while the others nap. Although the otter wasn't any real danger to the slider and the chicken turtle, they slid off the half-sunken cypress log and sank down to the muddy swamp bottom, waiting for it to leave.

Startled by the otter's splashy exit from the pool, a small stinkpot turtle, basking on a nearby tree branch hanging over the water, also dived for the swamp. It hit the water with a solid smack and sank like a rock, leaving a stinky trail in the water from the musk glands beneath the rim of its shell – the stinkpot turtle's usual response to danger.

When nothing had moved for a long time, the turtles rose from the mud and paddled to the surface. Their eyes and nostrils barely broke the surface of the water as they searched the scene for danger. Finally, seeing no threats to their safety, they swam back toward their basking log.

The cracked turtle stopped on the way to eat, munching down a tadpole then chomping his way up a white waterlily stem. A curled-over edge of the water lily leaf was being used as a hiding place by a fishing spider. As the leaf slithered into the turtle's mouth, the spider leaped out onto the surface of the water and raced away.

Six-spotted Fishing Spider

Dolomedes triton (doll-uh-MEE-deez TRY-tun)
Dolomedes = "wily" **triton** = (myth.) "demigod of the sea"

For the six-spotted fishing spider, which walks on water like a water strider (pp. 72, 73), "skin-diving" is a way of life. This spider hunts with its toes – feeling the water for ripples created by prey that falls onto the water or is swimming below. Then it races or dives to catch it. Able to stay underwater for up to an hour, it clings to plants and breathes air trapped among its body hairs. The fishing spider is sometimes preyed upon by a hunting wasp, *Anoplius depressipes* (uh-NOP-lee-us dih-PRESS-ih-peez) which follows it into the water, stings and captures it, then carries it up and away to its burrow to feed to its young.

Openings on the spider's legs "smell" pheromones (p. 18) drifting past in the water, letting a male know if a possible female partner is nearby. He beats a special rhythm with his body on the water to get her attention, then follows the dragline web she has laid across plants and water until he finds her.

Spin Offs

spider spinnerets

A spider's web comes from *spinnerets*, a group of nozzles on its abdomen. Some nozzles produce sheet-web, others make sticky web, dragline (p. 20) or other kinds of web (pp.52, 53). Although there are seven known types of web, most spiders make only a few kinds, pulling web from the nozzles with their hind feet.

Fishing spiders spin mostly dragline silk. But the female builds a pouch for her eggs with sheet-web, binding the eggs into a waterproof ball which she carries from her fangs until they begin to hatch. Then she weaves a "nurseryweb," releases the babies into it, and leaves them to their fate.

fishing spider
carrying egg sac

Mythical Fire Fetcher

Cherokee Indians honor the water spider because in their legends a brave water spider raced across a lake to fetch the first fire to their ancestors. It carried the coal of fire in a bowl it wove from its web and carried on its back.

water spider
on a
shell pendant

Fragrant Floaters

white waterlily
Nymphaea odorata

floating hearts
Nymphoides aquatica

Pond plants make a roof on the quiet waters of swamps. They offer shade from the sun, hunting blinds for predators, and hidey-holes for their prey. They are ladders up to the airy world for morphing insects. Their flowers, stems and roots are food for many. The flat, shiny green leaves of **white waterlilies** (also called fragrant waterlilies) are round, six to twelve inches across, and purple beneath. The spiky flowers are white.

Floating hearts is a pond plant with heart-shaped, six-inch leaves. It has clusters of crinkly white, five-petaled flowers which are less than an inch wide.

The Hunters

Fishing spiders, wolf spiders and lynx spiders all chase their food instead of snaring it in webs. They aren't dangerous to humans, but because they are so big and swift (and hairy) they look a bit scary. These are shown actual size.

Spooky Hairdo?

It's too bad most people think hairy spiders are _so spooky_. Hairs are the spider's "survival kit."

The fishing spider breathes air trapped among its body hairs. This allows it to stay underwater a long time. So that's cool – nothing spooky there.

A tarantula vibrates its feet against its abdomen to flick out a cloud of stinging hairs onto an attacker. But that's just self-defense – not really spooky, right?

And *all* spiders have special hairs on their bodies to detect vibrations. One type, stiff, springy leg hairs in sockets like car gearshift levers, detects movement and the location of nearby insect prey. Is *that* spooky?

Decide for yourself.

a close-up look

green lynx
Peucetia viridans
(bright green)

Carolina wolf spider
Lycosa carolinensis
(brown)

six-spotted fishing spider
Dolomedes triton
(brown and white)

36. The Six-spotted Fishing Spider

The fishing spider moved easily on the surface of the swamp, much like a water strider. Sometimes she caught food on top of the water – striders or emerging dragonfly nymphs. But other times, she would crouch on a leaf with two or more legs dangling in the water like probes. When she felt vibrations made by prey, she would feel around underwater to snag a pond plant with the sharp hooks on her feet, then she'd pull herself down underwater to seek her prey.

If she didn't see her prey immediately, she would tuck herself out of sight in some leaves or stems and watch.

If nothing came along, she might hide in a different place, staying underwater for several minutes. In an emergency – if, for instance, she herself were being hunted by a fish, wasp or giant diving beetle – she could stay under water much longer by breathing the air trapped among her body hairs, drawing it in through the lung slits on her abdomen.

Now, to flee from the turtle, she hauled herself down the stems of a clump of floating hearts until she was safely out of sight under the water. And while she was there, she began to watch for prey.

*THRUMMMMmmm...*her leg bristles vibrated violently so she knew something fairly large was passing nearby.

At first she saw only a purplish-gray blur in the dim underwater light. Then there was a flash of silvery belly, and the spider tensed herself for action as a tubby tadpole wallowed into range.

Hanging tight to the plant stem with her rear feet, the fishing spider pounced and grabbed the plump tadpole.

She jerked it close to her body and thrust her fangs into it, injecting enough venom to kill it. Then she released her hold on the plant, and the air trapped among her body hairs brought both tadpole and spider bobbing to the surface of the swamp.

Hauling the tadpole alongside a lilypad, the fishing spider injected an enzyme into her prey. She paused, motionless,

waiting a few moments for the insides to become liquid, then she began to suck up the body juices.

Focused on her food, the fishing spider didn't see the dark shape looming up out of the swamp below. The mouth of the bluegill fish opened, his flashy turquoise gills flared wide, and the fishing spider and tadpole were instantly sucked inside.

Bluegill

Lepomis macrochirus (leh-PO-miss muh-KRAW-ker-us)
Lepomis = "scaly cover" ***macro*** = "large" ***chirus*** = "like a hand"

The bluegill is a sunfish, related to bass. It has stiff spines on its fins, and a black "ear-flap" that juts off the rear edge of each gill cover. With a black spot at the base of its pectoral fin (see **Bluegill ID** below) and black stripes on its sides, a bluegill is easy to identify. Breeding males have gleaming coppery chests, and blue gills and chins. Females are paler.

Bluegills are called bream, brim, gill, redbreasted sunfish, baldface, sunny, yellowbelly, plum granny, copperhead, blue-mouth sunfish, kivver, sun perch, roach and other names. They are native only to the East and South, but have been released by sportsmen into swamps, ponds and lakes all over the U.S.

Shaped like a big, flat egg, a six-inch-long bluegill may weigh two pounds. That makes it a favorite "panfish."

Bluegills prefer still or slow-moving water where vegetation above and below the water offers feeding and hiding places.

Fishy Groupies

Bluegills feed, court, nest and spawn in groups. In spring, when morning water temperatures in the shallows reach 70°, the males whisk aside the silt on the swamp floor with their tails to create saucer-shaped nests about a foot wide. Nests are packed so closely together they may even touch each other.

Big "bull" (male) bluegills compete with each other for the safest nest spots at the center of the bed. Hungry wading birds, bass, gar and snapping turtles eat their fill on the smaller bluegills around the edges of a colony.

Aerial Attack

Bluegills are great bird-food. They may be eaten by cormorants, anhingas, herons and egrets. Osprey and bald eagles dive and snag them up out of the water.

osprey
Pandion haliaetus

Blue Sneakers
When bluegills are spawning, a small "sneaker" bluegill sometimes slips in to add his sperm to fertilize the female's eggs (she lays up to 60,000 eggs, mostly during the full moon). When the eggs hatch, some will have been fathered by the sneaker bluegill. This trick gives the *larvae* (LAR-vee = newborn fish) a wide mix of genes, but at the same time makes sure the strongest dad guards the nest.

actual size

bluegill eggs and recently-hatched larva ↗ (close-up)

Doin' the t w i s t . . .

a fish swims by flexing its body from side to side

Swim Fins

Fins have many tasks. A bluegill's **tail** fin swishes sideways to move the fish forward.

Dorsal fins and **anal** fins work like rudders to keep the fish from tilting to the side.

Pectoral and **pelvic** fins brake, turn, reverse, and help the fish balance.

Fossils show that the fins of some ancient fish (called **lobe-fins***) worked as limbs to let them walk on land.

dorsal fin
tail fin
pectoral fin
anal fin
pelvic fins

ancient lobe-fin fin bones
upper leg
lower leg
ankle bones
foot and toe bones
land animal limb bones now

*Lobe-fins had **bones** in their fins instead of **cartilage rays** like most fish. All lobe-fin fish except the *coelacanth* (SEE-la-kanth) and the lungfish have become extinct.

Fish Food
(not shown actual size)

Bluegills have small mouths, so they eat small food such as:

worms, zooplankton, small crayfish, small tadpoles, minnows and fry, snails and clams, fish eggs (even their own), aquatic insects and larvae, plus algae and vegetation when protein is scarce.

Arrow Arum
Peltandra virginica

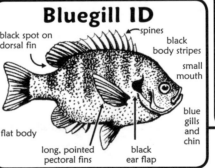

The Algonquin name for arrow arum (AIR-um) is "tuckahoe," and the roots are edible by humans. The 12" leaves shade the water, make good insect, spider and frog perches, and supply cover for swamp dwellers.

Bluegill ID

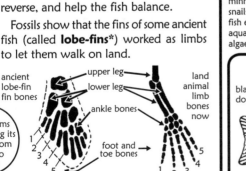

black spot on dorsal fin
spines
black body stripes
small mouth
blue gills and chin
flat body
long, pointed pectoral fins
black ear flap

37. The Bluegill

The fishing spider and its tadpole prey were a big meal for the little bluegill. As usual, he was patrolling the edges of the bluegill spawning grounds where about forty bluegill bulls were tidying their nests, fanning fresh water over their eggs, or courting female bluegills for a chance to spawn.

Too small to defend a territory against bigger bluegill males, the little bluegill (known as a "sneaker") had to dodge danger and find food wherever he could, while still staying close to the safety of the crowd.

The small bluegill was eager to mate, but the females ignored him. They wanted BIG bluegills to mate with – males with good nests near the center of the colony. These strong males would court them and fertilize the eggs. And when the eggs hatched they would be good fathers to their young fry, chasing away predators fiercely.

But sometimes something different happens. This lovesick little sneaker was about to make a very daring move.

In the tawny water, sunlight sparkled off two spawning bluegills near a patch of glossy, big-leafed arrow arum rooted in the silt-covered sand. The swaggering male flashed his coppery chest and displayed his large, sturdy body while grunting tenderly. The female was impressed. She tilted her body to one side and released her eggs into his nest.

The big male was so busy courting that he didn't notice two things. He didn't notice the small sneaker that slipped in on the opposite side of the female and squirted his milt (sperm) over the eggs to fertilize them before dashing to safety in the thicket of arrow arum stalks.

And he didn't notice the other intruder which had stealthily approached the colony from behind the patch of arrow arum. He didn't see the tall black legs rising out of the water or the long, sharp bill that was poised to strike. He didn't understand why his new mate and all the nearby bluegills suddenly streaked away.

But it was a false alarm. Great egrets don't eat big fish. The egret's yellow bill slashed down only to pluck a small frog from an arrow arum stem.

Great Egret

Casmerodius albus (kaz-mer-OH-dee-us AL-buss)
kosmetos = "decorated" **herodius** = "heron" **albus** = "white"

The beautiful feathers of the great egrets (EE-grets) almost caused their extinction. Why? Some of their other names – plume birds, big plume birds, and long whites – give us a clue. In the 1840's it became fashionable to decorate ladies' hats with feathers, and by 1903 the lovely, flowing plumes of the great egret and snowy egret were worth $32 per ounce, twice the value of gold. But by then the egrets were almost wiped out. When the Audubon Society publicized their pitiful plight, laws were passed and the sixty-year slaughter stopped.

Although pesticides poison their food, and the draining of wetlands reduces feeding and nesting sites, they have made an amazing recovery. Watch for them in swamps and marshes.

A great blue heron's white phase, in south Florida, may be mistaken for a great egret. But the great egret's legs are black, while the "white" great blue heron's legs are yellow.

Aigrette Plumes

The egret is named for the white feathers, *aigrettes* (ay-GRETS = a French word for "a spray of feathers"), which grow from its back. As many as fifty delicate plumes flow down behind like a fringed cape. When courting or excited, the egret fans them upward in an airy rosette over its body.

Take-Out Bag

Many birds carry along a kind of "doggy bag" (called a **crop**) to tote home extra groceries. Where is it? It's at the base of the throat. → Food is stored in the flexible crop to digest. If they have chicks at the nest, they take it home to urp up for the kiddies' snack-time. YUM!

to the mouth

to the stomach

Hurricane!

A hurricane is the most dreaded event of a Southeast summer – according to humans. Animals just hunker down until it passes. If they survive, they get on with living.

A hurricane changes the swamp's scenery. As in a theatrical drama, the characters' lives may change for better or worse; some even die. But ultimately, the swamp is refreshed with new growth, and the curtain goes up on the next act.

Mint, Rosemary & Thyme

Were you ever taking a walk when you suddenly smelled "*peppermint tea!*"? Is it possible you just stepped on a mint plant? Mints are closely related to thyme, rosemary and lavender, and all give off a strong scent (especially when they're mashed).

If it has a square stem, it's a mint.

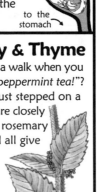

Family Feud

Great egret chicks often commit *siblicide* (SIB-lih-side). That is, stronger nestmates often murder smaller nestmates

They peck with their saber-sharp bills, beat with their wings, and shove the smaller nestlings out of the nest. Weaker chicks may trip and fall from the nest.

These chicks are very hot-tempered. It's not just simple hunger. Even fat chicks have three or four knock-down fights every **day**.

Half of the chicks in a nest may die during their first month. This ensures that the strongest chicks will be well fed and strong, and more likely to survive.

Two to four eggs hatch in the order they're laid, so the oldest chick may be much larger than the youngest. If there's extra food, the last-hatched chick **may** get some. Otherwise...

Grooming Guide

Because it catches and eats slimy, gooey things (fish, snails, etc.), an egret must have some way to get its feathers clean again.

It combs its neck, face and chin with a special toothed edge on the outer rim of each middle claw. That helps, but the comb can't get off all the goo, slime, and fish grease. A shampoo would be perfect.

But Big Bird can't trot off to the beauty salon, so these dirty birds have evolved another way to clean their grubby plumage.

Patches of "powder feathers" on breast and back erode into a film of waxy powder as they emerge.

With its bill, the egret spreads the waxy powder around to blot up dirt and to waterproof its feathers.

Do you think it would work to powder **your** hair when it needs a shampoo?

38. The Great Egret

The great egret had tensed, body stretched, neck coiled in an S-curve, inching closer and closer to the frog. At exactly the right instant, her neck uncoiled like a spring, shooting her bill forward like open scissors. As bluegills flashed away in panic, the yellow bill snapped shut on the frog, jerking it out from under the protective leaves.

The egret flipped the frog into the air, then caught it just as its head pointed toward her body. She snapped, gulped and the frog rippled visibly all the way down to her crop at the base of her throat. For a moment she stood, opening and closing her bill and swallowing, then she sprang upward, flapping her wings heavily in the steamy air.

Her crop was full. In addition to the frog, she had swallowed three dragonflies, a cranefly, a cotton mouse, and several mosquitofish. Returning to her treetop nest in the island rookery, she flew tilted slightly forward from the weight in her crop, her splendid plumes flowing behind like a silvery scarf.

Hurricane season had arrived, and all afternoon the sky had been filling with dark menacing clouds. The air felt hot and full, and the swamp water, flat and oily-looking, reflected the gloomy overcast sky.

As she arrived at the rookery, the egret was slammed by a gust of hot wind. All around her, egrets, white ibises and herons hunched down in their nests, facing into the rising wind. She landed awkwardly on the tangle of nest sticks that held her three chicks as it swayed springily from side to side with each new gust.

"KUK.....KUK.....KUK!" she yelped, struggling to keep her balance. Her three pushy chicks swarmed around her, poking at her bill, squawking and pecking fiercely at each other – each was determined to get *all* the food.

She arched her neck and regurgitated a glob of partly-digested dinner into the bill of the most persistent chick. The two smaller chicks buffeted their mother and the lucky chick with their wings and bills, but in the blasting wind the smallest chick lost its balance and tumbled over the edge of the nest. Not yet able to fly, it landed in a crumpled heap in the peppermint plants at the base of the tree and did not move again.

The chick's family barely noticed. But its unfortunate plunge was observed with great interest by a bobcat, patrolling her territory with her two young kittens.

Bobcat

Lynx rufus (LINKS ROO-fuss)
Lynx = "the wildcat" *rufus* = "reddish"

Bobcats RULE in many places where humans don't even suspect they exist. They weigh from 15 to 30 lbs, measure about 2' long with 5" tails, and are tan, camouflaged with dark spots. When they hold still, they're nearly invisible. Around humans, they sleep during the day and come out mostly at night to hunt, so no one realizes they're around. They will eat almost anything small that moves, so they can nearly always find food.

In remote swamps and other places where they don't feel threatened, bobcats may go hunting during the day. Seeing movement and depending on its "camo-spots" to hide it, a bobcat creeps up on its prey and pounces without warning – unless its twitching, white-tipped tail gives it away.

Bobcats are found from Canada to Mexico. Southeastern bobcats living in dim, warm swamps are darker and not as thickly furred as bobcats living in other areas.

The Hunting Game
Like all kittens, young bobcats are natural hunters. But they have a lot to learn. As soon as their eyes open, the mother bobcat releases live insects and small animals in the den so the kittens can practice stalking and pouncing.

At about two months, they join her as she hunts, learning how and where to find and catch live prey.

White fur on her tail and on the backs of her ears makes her easier to follow in the dark.

Safe House
An island rookery (bird nesting place) is useless if predators like bobcats can reach the nests. If the water dries up or a bridge forms, the birds may leave to find a safer nursery.

Skullduggery
A skull's shape, teeth, and other bony parts tell a lot about the animal that "wears" them – how it hunts or forages, what it eats, its courting habits (head-banging bighorn sheep have thick skulls), etc. A skull also gives clues about what the living animal looks like.

bobcat – 6½"

Shape is your first clue. For instance, a short-faced bobcat has a short-faced skull, while a fox has a long, skinny skull.

domestic cat – 3" (see ruler below)

Meat-eaters have sharp canine teeth (front fangs) and pointy molars (for cutting and chewing) (compare on pp. 36 and 92).

red fox – 5½"

Size is also important. A skull is a little smaller than the live animal's head. A puma's skull is 7 – 10" long. It's living head could be as long as this book is tall!

molars
canine teeth

ruler, actual size 1" 2" 3"

Chuttering?
If you ever saw a cat stare at something just out of reach, chatter its teeth, and make a weird smacking sound, it almost certainly cracked you up. It's nutty.

Oddly, there is no word for this unique activity. If you think the word *"chutter"* sounds about right, use it and pass it on.

Cat Antennae
A bobcat wouldn't be able to hear quite as well without the tuft of long black hairs that projects from each eartip.

The bobcat can detect sound vibrations with them.

Winged Sumac
Rhus copallina

Growing in shrubby thickets, winged sumac (also called dwarf or shining sumac), has velvety stems with winglike flanges, and clumps of fuzzy red fruits in autumn. In winter, rabbits, deer and songbirds eat the berries and twigs, which are rich in Vitamin A.

bobcat track & scat

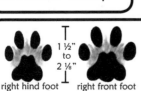

1 ½" to 2 ⅛"

right hind foot   right front foot

no claw marks

8"–16" walking

hair marks may show between toes and pad

rear pawprint may cover front pawprint

bobcat scat ¼ actual size probably contains feathers or fur.

39. The Bobcat

From the edge of the meadow, the mother bobcat watched the egret chick fall. There was a narrow strip of water between her and the island, but predators normally wouldn't cross over into the rookery because of the alligators. She studied the duckweed-coated water and chuttered wistfully at the dead egret chick just twenty feet away. She paced back and forth in frustration. Her two kittens watched curiously.

The wind rose to a howl, flattening the bobcats' spotted fur. The rookery trees swayed and creaked.

KRAAAAAAAKKKK! A large branch split and snapped off the trunk of one of the guano-killed trees (see p. 30). It caught the wind and flew a dozen yards, landing with one end on the island and the other in the water so close it splashed the bobcat family. They streaked for the shelter of a fetterbush a few yards away.

After a bit, the mother bobcat crept cautiously back to the water's edge. The egret chick was still there, and she noticed that the end of the branch, just a few feet away, gave her a bridge to the island.

She stared across at the chick, kneading the soft ground with first one front paw then the other. The end of the branch was not very far away. She could leap to it. Yes.... yes, she could. She did.

The bird cries in the nest trees overhead rose above the howl of the storm – INVADER BELOW! – but the birds didn't dare fly from their nests in the high wind.

Pulling the dead chick from the fragrant, guano-spattered peppermint, the mother bobcat bounded back across the tree-bridge and leaped to land right next to her kittens. They examined the nestling eagerly, nipping at the dangling legs, plastering their tongues with downy feathers. The wind was now tossing big splats of rain, so the bobcat mother clamped her teeth firmly on her prize, ducked into a thicket of winged sumac veiled with a net of morning glory vines, and dropped it onto the ground.

The hungry kittens pounced on the egret chick, growling fiercely as they tugged and ripped at their meal. The mother bobcat watched them, not joining in the feast. A few minutes later, only a few soggy feathers showed where they had eaten.

It was then that the kittens noticed the other storm victims in the thicket.

Cardinal

Cardinalis cardinalis (kar-dih-NAY-lis kar-dih-NAY-lis)
Cardinal = named after red-robed Roman Catholic cardinals

The male cardinal is a gorgeous bird, a bright splash of black-masked red against the green of forest or yard, a loud joyful singer – and although a little skittish, it's likely to hang around where you can see it. Most schoolkids can identify a cardinal, even if they've never seen one before, and seven states in the U.S. have made it their state bird (that's a record).

The female cardinal isn't red, but she's beautiful. Mostly golden tan, she has a bright coral bill, reddish feathers on her crest, wings and tail, and wears charcoal eyeshadow.

Cardinals were once found only in the Southeast. In 1886 they were seldom seen north of Kentucky. But they're now found in Canada and even in the Southwest – partly because people keep bird feeders filled all winter. Cardinals eat seeds and fruits (about 70%) and insects (about 30%) including everything from dragonflies to beetles.

The What-cheer Wheetio Birdee

Cardinals gather in flocks in the winter, and males are not especially friendly to females that come close. But in spring, the male begins to court the female, even putting seeds into her mouth and singing love songs, low and soft. If the female likes this, she replies with the same songs, and they sing back-and-forth duets until nesting time.

Then it's time to defend a nesting territory.

"what-cheer! what-cheer! what-cheer!" they both sing. Some other favorite calls are *"bir*dee*, bir*dee*, bir*dee*, bir*dee*"* *"whit–whit–whit–whit–whit,"* and *"wheet*io*, wheet*io*, wheet*io*."* They sing more than twenty different songs, and some of them may be whispered or sung at night.

Seeing Red

Cardinals hide their nests full of brown-speckled eggs deep inside shrubs.

But even though the nest and eggs are hidden, you can spot a cardinal easily against green leaves. A bright red bird at the nest should be easy for predators to see, right? *Wrong.* **Only insects, birds, reptiles, monkeys, apes and humans can see color.** And in a black & white world, *red and green appear the same shade of gray.*

Hey, Baby!

It isn't really unusual for an animal to nurse a baby of a different species. If a needy tot shows up when an adult animal is feeling "parental" (like a parent) it may get adopted.

At times, really strange adoptions occur. Chickens might adopt ducklings or kittens. Cardinals have even been seen feeding goldfish!

But imagine the hen's puzzlement when her ducklings go swimming or her kittens catch a mouse. Do you suppose the cardinal wonders why its little fish won't fly?

Bills 'n' Beaks

Raptors (birds of prey) have "beaks." All other birds have "bills." The shape and size of a bird's beak or bill always matches its lifestyle.

- a hooked raptor beak rips and tears
- a cardinal's sturdy bill mostly cracks seeds
- a bluejay's bill has no special shape. It's a multipurpose bill
- a long, thin hummingbird bill sips nectar
- a strong, blunt woodpecker bill hacks holes
- a long, sharp anhinga bill stabs fish

Spittlebug

Philenus spumarius

nymph begins foam home

15 minutes later

in about half an hour the nymph has created a fizzy new domain

Adult → froghopper leaves home (actual size) .

Imagine living in a house you built yourself out of gooey, bubbly, sticky spit. Imagine.....no, that is just <u>too</u> yucky! But spittlebugs do it.

A spittlebug is a froghopper nymph. It sucks up plant juices and pumps out a froth of bubbles inside which it then lives safely while it matures. Even hungry cardinals don't think this looks good to eat, so the spittlebug is safe in plain sight.

Ivy-Leafed Morning Glory

Ipomoea hederacea

This hairy twining vine has sky-blue morning-blooming flowers that soon fade to lavender purple.

40. The Cardinal

The cardinal nest had been poorly made. It was the female's first nest and the result was a see-through saucer. It lasted through the brooding and three days of squirming chicks. But as the sumac branches whipped and thrashed in the wind, the nest came apart and the chicks tumbled to the ground.

As the bobcat kittens sat washing their faces after eating the egret chick, they heard the cardinal nestlings chirping from the remains of their fallen nest on the far side of the sumac thicket. With great excitement, they crept through the thicket of sumac stems to make their first stalk-and-pounce.

The cardinals were hopping anxiously around on the ground beside their dumped nestlings as the kittens crept closer. At the last moment, to save their own lives, they fled to the shelter of the bottomland forest nearby, their distress cries blowing away in the wind.

The kittens ate the small nestlings. Then, purring softly, they cuddled against their mother as she crouched motionless, keeping a wary lookout from the safety of the sumac bush as the wind shrieked overhead.

After the hurricane, the adult cardinals began a new family in a nest in a Carolina allspice shrub. The new nest was much more skillfully built.

The male cardinal fed his mate faithfully as she sat on the new eggs, but the loss of their first nest had one strange result. Because the male was still programmed to feed a BIG family, he was catching far more insects than he and his mate could eat.

One morning while passing a nest full of hungry mockingbird nestlings, the confused cardinal stopped and thrust his bundle of unwanted insects into an open mockingbird chick's mouth. He immediately felt better. He brought a load of insects to his mate, ate some, then delivered another load to the mockingbird nestlings. He fed the mockingbirds regularly until the peeping of his own newly hatched chicks turned his efforts back to his own nest.

Sometimes life is very strange indeed.

Marsh Rabbit

Sylvilagus palustris (sill-vih-LAY-guss puh-LUS-tris)
Sylvi = "woods" **lagos** = "hare" **palustr** = "marsh"

Marsh and swamp rabbits have similar habits. They're related to cottontails but they don't act or look like any cottontail you ever saw. For instance, they live in wet places and swim readily. The marsh rabbit lives in the Atlantic coastal lowlands from Virginia and around Florida to Alabama, while the swamp rabbit (*Sylvilagus aquaticus*) is found more westerly, from South Carolina to Texas. In places where their ranges overlap, the marsh rabbit's smaller size, shorter ears and all-brown tail can help you tell them apart.

In contrast, the eastern cottontail never gets wet willingly. If you see a rabbit swimming or diving (the swamp rabbit frequently dives, coming up under dark overhangs to keep out of sight – the marsh rabbit dives in emergencies), it's probably a marsh rabbit going about its regular aquatic routine. Marsh rabbits may be eaten by owls, alligators, hawks, gray foxes and snakes.

Is It A Rabbit Skull?

Lagomorphs (LAG-o-morfs = hare-shaped) – a group that includes the rabbits, hares and *pikas – have double upper front teeth. The small pair behind the big pair probably braces and strengthens them for tough gnawing. *Lagomorph* teeth, like rodent teeth, don't stop growing. If the front teeth don't meet, or if the animal doesn't chew a lot of tough stuff to grind the edges off, its teeth will keep on growing – out of its mouth in a big curl. *Then* what do you suppose happens?

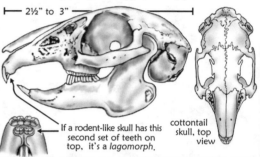

├── 2½" to 3"

If a rodent-like skull has this second set of teeth on top, it's a *lagomorph*.

cottontail skull, top view

Bunny Bones

A rabbit is born to bounce. Its curved back is like a coiled spring and its heavy-duty oversize hind legs supply power and traction. A five foot standing broad-jump is *kid stuff* for a four-pound bunny. Can YOU do that?

NOT Your Average Rabbit

Even when it's not soaking wet, a marsh rabbit does not look like a cottontail or swamp rabbit. Its bristly fur and tiny tail are dark reddish brown. Its head is boxy, it's rear toenails are very long, and its ears look *way* too short.

Cottontails usually look, well, you could say "cute." Marsh rabbits are NOT cute.

Southern Flying Squirrel
Glaucomys volans

These nocturnal dark-eyed beauties are so shy that you could spend years out in the swamp and never see one.

Ghostly Islands

Dead plants form mats on the swamp bottom. In warm water, decay creates gasses which float the mats. When it cools, they often sink again. Plants like sweetspire and swamp redbay take root on vegetation islands, which *may* later become solid land (see p. 70).

swamp red-bay
Persea palustris
This tree's leathery evergreen leaves have a spicy scent. Wildlife eat the blue-black fruits.

sweetspire or Virginia-willow
Itea virginica

Plumes of star-shaped flowers on this 6' shrub make lovely white arches.

The marsh rabbit sometimes walks upright on its hind feet. If you see a walking rabbit, it's probably a marsh rabbit.

rabbit track & scat

right fore and hind foot

3½"

here is how a rabbit's hind tracks get in front of its front tracks

├── up to 5" ──┤

marsh rabbit tracks, walking upright

rabbit scat
⅓ actual size

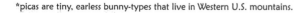

*picas are tiny, earless bunny-types that live in Western U.S. mountains.

41. The Marsh Rabbit

When the end of the falling branch hit the ground on the rookery island, it flushed a small rabbit from his snug retreat in a clump of shrubbery. The rabbit dived without hesitation into the water to escape, but hastily changed direction as he spotted the bobcat. He paddled quickly around the end of the island to keep out of sight.

The rabbit wasn't fluffy with a poofy white tail as you might expect a rabbit to be. Instead, he was brown all over, including his tail, with very short ears and a coarse, spiky coat. He was a marsh rabbit.

Marsh rabbits are good swimmers. They often avoid danger by taking to the water, swimming confidently with only their eyes and nose above the surface. But in this wind-whipped swamp, *nowhere* seemed very safe to the little rabbit. For awhile the rabbit floated in the water beneath a fringe of willows, watching fearfully for the bobcat, but after awhile his dense fur soaked through and he began to shiver. He crept up onto a tiny floating vegetation island (see p. 70), warily eyed a cottonmouth snake at the base of a sweetspire shrub, then settled down right next to it.

The cottonmouth snake also swims regularly. It even hunts in the water, catching frogs, fish, other snakes, and small mammals like cotton mice, cotton rats and baby rabbits. But the marsh rabbit knew he was much too large for the snake to eat. They ignored each other.

A blast of high wind split apart a hollow tree above them, and a flying squirrel, blown from its nest, landed almost on top of them. After a few moments of shivering, the squirrel and rabbit edged closer and huddled together for warmth.

The summer rainstorms were late this year and the hot sunshine had evaporated much of the swamp water, drying it up in many areas. But with this wet, blasting hurricane, the drought was over. The water in the nearby riverbottom had risen fifteen feet and the flood was pouring into the swamp. Now it ripped up the roots of the little vegetation island, and set it adrift with its three refugees.

A hailstone the size of an acorn struck the swamp, splashing up a fountain of tea-colored water. Another splatted down a few feet away. Suddenly the whole swamp surface was bouncing with icy balls and spouts of water. As the gale caught the floating island's shrubs and whirled it around, it rocked, dipped and partly sank for a moment, then drifted closer to the muddy bank. With a grunt, the drenched marsh rabbit flattened his short ears against his neck and leaped for solid earth.

Cottonmouth Snake

Agkistrodon piscivorus (ag-KISS-tro-dahn pie-sih-VOR-us)
Agkistr = "fish hook" ***od*** = "form" ***pisci*** = "fish" ***vorus*** = "eater"

Perhaps the most feared snake in the swamp, the cottonmouth, also called the water moccasin, is often mistaken for a copperhead (which may be in the same area). When young, cottonmouths and copperheads look similar, with bright brown and tan markings. The copperhead keeps its bright color as it matures and has two small black dots on its head. The cottonmouth darkens with age – sometimes to nearly black – although it usually shows the cream-bordered black stripe behind its eye.

If it opens its mouth, the white interior is a good identifier. But you don't want to be hanging around when it opens its mouth, so don't depend on this sign. Both snakes are venomous, the cottonmouth even more than the copperhead.

Give them both a lot of space, but don't kill either one. Both have important roles in the swamp – they're needed there, and if they're missing, the swamp gets out of balance.

Swimming Serpents (a helpful poem)
To watch for a cottonmouth, you should know
That most snakes swim with their heads down low.
But a cottonmouth swims with its head up high.
(Is it trying to keep its "cotton" dry?)

Skin & Bones
A snake's skeleton isn't joined together like other animal skeletons. For instance, the lower jaw bones are held together in front with just an elastic band. And only skin and muscles hold a snake's guts in. So a snake can easily gulp gigantic food into the stretchy tube of its body. Its fangs fold up against the roof of its mouth when not in use.

Some pit vipers have spare fangs that drop down to replace fangs that break off.

spare drop-down fangs

Cottonmouth snakes eat small turtles and alligators, fish, lizards, birds, snakes, frogs and small mammals.

elastic band

Which is the Coral Snake?
(the *other* snake is a scarlet kingsnake)

red
yellow

red
black

Snake Eggs
Baby pit vipers are "live-born" instead of hatching from eggs. The black, red and yellow coral snake is the <u>only</u> **venomous** (VEN-uh-muss) snake found anywhere near swamps which hatches from eggs, although **non-venomous** snakes may hatch from eggs, too. Memorize this jingle about snakes:

Red by yellow, kills a fellow.
Red by black, venom lack.

Ain't That the Pits?

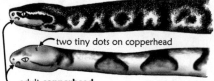
adult **cottonmouth**

two tiny dots on copperhead

adult **copperhead**

The only other pit vipers in the U.S. are the rattlesnakes.

Pit vipers get their name from the deep "pit" found between the eye and the nostril. This facial pit is a heat sensor and helps the snake "home in" on its warm prey. The pit may not be obvious, so memorize the other signs so you can avoid **all** pit vipers.

triangular head

thin neck

thick body

pit between nostril and eye

vertical slit pupils ("cat-eyes")

Beware U.S. snakes with cat-eyed pupils! The coral snake is the only venomous round-pupilled snake in the U.S. By the way, snakes are *venomous*, not *poisonous*. **Venom** is a toxic bite or sting – **poison** must be swallowed.

Gone Huntin'
The cottonmouth may curl up on stumps or cypress knees surrounded by water for days or weeks without eating, but when it gets hungry it waits beside an animal trail where it smells animal odors. Its infra-red-sensing facial pits can sense the heat of something warm that passed by within the previous half an hour or so.

A cottonmouth strikes and injects venom into small prey, then hangs on. But if the prey is big enough to cause injury, the snake bites quickly, injects venom, then lets it escape.

Then, following the heat-and-scent trail, it soon tracks down its doomed dinner. Snakes bite humans in self-defense, not for food. See p. 107 for advice on dealing with snakes.

Virginia Creeper
Parthenocissus quinquefolia
This woody vine "snakes" up trees and shrubs, clinging with adhesive discs at the ends of tendrils. The leaves turn brilliant red in the autumn. Birds love its berries.

42. The Cottonmouth Snake

The cottonmouth needed shelter too. Since a reptile can't control its own temperature, staying too long in cold water can chill its body until it may have trouble reaching dry ground.

The swamp had chilled considerably from all the hailstones. But more than that, the cottonmouth had snake eggs inside her body that were almost ready to hatch.

The cottonmouth slowly unwound from her heat-conserving coil and slipped into the water. Head held high, she wove through the water between the floating island and the bank, sliding up onto the sand and continuing on toward the vegetation where the slash pine/palmetto flatwoods began.

The afternoon light had darkened into a dirty dusk of howling wind filled with small branches, twigs, leaves, and banners of Spanish moss. The hail was quickly melting, but the dark sky was threatening heavy rain.

Slithering up the bank through leaves and over pine needles, the cottonmouth came face to face with a small opossum baby, lost by his mother hours before.

Before the hurricane struck, the cottonmouth had been hungry – and the baby opossum was the perfect prey size. But the hurtling branches and twigs made finding cover much more important now.

Alarmed, the snake drew back into a coil, hissed and vibrated her tail. The small opossum arched his back and hissed too, but with fright. Then he suddenly slumped to the ground.

Sluggishly uncoiling, the snake watched the still form warily. But the small opossum didn't move again. After watching for several minutes in the pelting rain, the snake glided off through the palmettos. She was looking for sanctuary. A cavity in a stump, a crevice covered with Virginia creeper vines, a hole in the ground, a thick pile of palmetto leaves she could slide under – any of those would do.

There, in the midst of the hurricane, her tiny pencil-thin babies would be born into the protective coil of her thick, brown-patterned body.

Virginia Opossum

Didelphis marsupialis (dih-DEL-fis mar-soo-pee-AY-lis)
Di = "two" ***delph*** = "womb" ***marsip*** = "pouch" ***alis*** "relating to"

Once known as *Didelphis virginianus*, the opossum is the only *marsupial* (mar-SOO-pee-ul = pouched, like a kangaroo) in the U.S., and has been renamed to mention its pouch. It eats insects, eggs, birds, crayfish, mammals as big as chipmunks, earthworms, snakes and toads. Berries, fruits, nuts and greens are also eaten. Maybe you've seen one at night (perhaps mashed) on highways, where it was patroling for road-kills. Its coarse silvery fur gives it a ghostly look.

A male opossum can weigh fifteen pounds, twice as much as a female the same age. When frightened it may growl, hiss, gape widely to show all its teeth, and drool massively. If the danger remains, the opossum collapses unconscious, its heartbeat slows, and its tongue hangs out as it "dies." Many predators won't eat an animal they didn't kill themselves, so they leave. After awhile, the opossum wakes up and trots off as though nothing happened. Opossums die of old age when only two years old (*really*).

A Possum of Little Brain

An opossum's brain is about the size of a large peanut or an acorn. If you find a skull with fifty pointy teeth, little pockets for lower incisors to fit into and a high crest along the top to which big jaw muscles can attach, it's an opossum's skull.

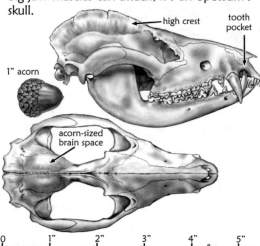

high crest — tooth pocket — 1" acorn — acorn-sized brain space

0   1"   2"   3"   4"   5"

Possum Paws

right hind paw — thumb — thumb close-up. See the "fingerprint" on the tip? — right front paw

An opossum ("possum" for short) has a thumb on each hind foot that helps it hold on when climbing trees for fruit. It also has a wiry tail which grabs branches and can support the opossum's full weight (but it **doesn't** sleep hanging from a branch as shown in cartoons).

Pignut Hickory
Carya glabra

Slow-growing hickories may live 250 years. The pignut hickory nut looks delightfully like a tiny pig's head, with ears and snout. Related to pecans, the smooth, dark, snouted nuts are good wildlife food.

pignut — pig

"....& a taile like a Rat"

Captain John Smith (Pocahontas's friend) wrote, in 1612, "An Opossum hath a head like a Swine & a taile like a Rat."

Its tail truly IS ratlike, but by using its hairless, scaly "taile" like a *hand*, an opossum can hang onto branches with it like a monkey would, and may coil its tail around packets of leaves to carry them to a new nest site.

Pouch Pups

Barely as big as raisins at birth, newborn opossums have only tiny bumps for eyes and ears. But their front claws are fully formed, because the pups need them for crawling into mom's pouch where they can connect to her nipples to drink and grow.

newborn, actual size

At ten weeks, as many as thirteen mouse-sized babies creep out of the pouch to ride on her back, clutching her fur as she travels. The old story that they dangle in a row from her tail is not true, but they do grab it with hands or tails to hang on.

a 3-week-old opossum baby is much cuter than a newborn!

opossum track & scat

right hind foot — 2¾" — right front foot

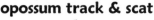 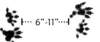

┈ 6"-11" ┈

opossum scat about ½ actual size. Appearance depends on what the opossum last ate.

43. The Virginia Opossum

By now, the mother opossum was far away, fighting her way through the wild wind and rain as she searched for a safe place for herself and the mob of babies that clung to her fur.

In the gusting wind, she hadn't noticed when one little opossum had lost his grip and trotted along behind, gasping in alarm, trying to grab her tail. When she climbed over a series of broken branches, he fell behind and finally stopped in confusion. The mother opossum waddled out of sight, leaving the baby far behind. Then the snake came.

At the cottonmouth snake's hiss, the small opossum jerked back, petrified with fear. Then, without any warning, he fell unconscious as opossums may do when they become very frightened or threatened. But this time, because of the drenching rain and the nervous shock of losing his mother, his system would close down completely. He would never awaken.

As the wind rose to a howl, the mother spotted

a tangle of roots from a blown-down pignut hickory tree, and she crept into a small cavity beneath it, dragging her remaining babies along with her. She curled protectively around them and soon the small cavity grew warm and snug. After a while, the opossums unwound from their tight clump and began to groom themselves dry.

Outside in the high wind, trees were crashing down on all sides. The mother opossum ventured a few feet from the cavity, her youngsters clinging on tightly, but a palmetto fan rattled past, slapping them wetly. She retreated to the safety of the tree roots.

For a time, she stood looking out through the overhanging roots, sniffing anxiously, her nose dripping a long silver dribble. Then she lay down to wait out the hurricane. The babies snuggled tightly against her. Their warmth seeped into a southern toad, half-buried in the soil at the rear of the cavity, and it awoke for a moment, then slept again.

Black Vulture

Coragyps atratus (KOR-uh-jips uh-TRAY-tus)
Korax = "raven" *gyps* = "vulture" *atratus* = "black"

Black and turkey vultures both live in the Southeast and often soar and feed together. Both have excellent eyesight and can spot a carcass from a great distance. The turkey vulture can also locate hidden meat by smell once it begins to stink. Black vultures are aggressive, chasing the more timid turkey vultures away from a carcass if food is scarce.

Together they fill an important role in the ecosystem, keeping things cleaned up and preventing the spread of diseases. Even cholera, anthrax, *E. coli* and other nasty microbes are killed by the vulture's super-strong digestive juices.

Black vultures, also called "black buzzards" and "carrion crows," are fairly tame, but turkey vultures usually fly off if people approach. To take off in still air, vultures may have to run twenty or thirty feet, flapping heavily the whole time, to leave the ground. But once aloft, they can float for hours.

Big Bald Birds

Why do you think vultures are bald-headed? What would happen if they had **feathery** faces? They'd NEVER get cleaned up, that's what.

see-through nasal opening

A **turkey vulture** has bright red wrinkles and a few scattered hairs.

A **black vulture** has black, raisin-like bumps and scattered hairs.

A turkey vulture's larg[e] nasal (NAY-zull = nose) opening helps it sme[ll] food, while black vulture[s] hunt only by sig[ht]

Vulture legs look white because vultures cool off and kill germs on their feet by pooping down their legs.

You DID want to know that, didn't you?

All vultures are raptor[s,] but their beaks an[d] feet are not shar[p] and hooke[d] like a hawk'[s]

They must wait for toug[h] meat to rot and softe[n] before they can dig i[n]

Nest Quest
Eggs hidden in holes don't need protective coloring, so as a rule, birds that **always** nest in cavities lay white eggs. Black vultures may lay their eggs in hollow trees, but sometimes nest under leaning trees or palmettos, or even on bare ground in cane thickets or caves. Eggs are camouflaged with blotches. Chicks are buffy-pink with bald black heads.

black vulture egg and chick actual size.

Chick Check
Never get close enough to a rookery (or ANY bird nest) to make the adults fly away – if they rush off in alarm, eggs and chicks can be injured or knocked from nests. Those chicks may die of exposure or be eaten by vultures, raccoons, crows or snakes. Just to make sure you won't cause problems, **keep your distance and use binoculars to watch chicks in a nest.**

Soar Point
How can birds stay up in the air for hours at a time just by holding their wings out? With five- to six-foot-long wingspreads, and weighing only four to six pounds, vultures are easily lifted up by thermals (THUR-mulz), rising warm air heated by the sun. To help them steer, wingtip feathers spread out like fingers to guide the airflow (swifts and swallows tilt their entire bodies).

Black vultures are heavier, with shorter wings and tails than turkey vultures, so they must flap their wings more often to stay up.

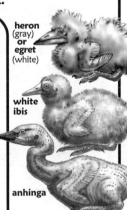

heron (gray) **or** egret (white)

white ibis

anhinga

Which Vulture Is It?

In flight, the heavier **black vulture** flaps and soars, **flaps and soars.**

Flying profile is almost flat.

The light-weight **turkey vulture** soars for long periods **with only occasional wingflaps.**

Flying profile is a shallow, tippy V.

• **BLACK VULTURE** has a **short tail, gray or black head,** and **white patches in its wings.** Its feet may stick out past its **short tail.**

• **TURKEY VULTURE** has a **long tail** and a **small, red head** Young turkey vultures have gray heads like black vultures, so check the **long tail.**

Tulip Tree
Also called "yellow poplar," this tree's big orange-and-green tulip-like flowers show its relationship to magnolias. Native Americans once used the trunks for canoes. Squirrels and birds eat the seeds.

Liriodendron tulipifera

44. The Black Vulture

By morning, the hurricane was history, but nothing looked the same in the rookery. Just the day before, it had been a thriving bird nursery with nests in nearly every tree. Now the trees lay splintered, broken, and uprooted all around. Black and turkey vultures perched near the nests of herons, ibises, anhingas and egrets in trees that had survived the storm. Parent birds hovered protectively over the few hungry nestlings that hadn't fallen to their deaths.

The bobcat's bridge still stretched between the rookery and the pine flatland, and more nestlings in the following days would be eaten by predators who found the bridge. Next year the rookery would be abandoned because of this. But for now, a foggy mist rose from the wet earth as the air warmed.

WHUP WHUP WHUP WHUP. Heavy wings beat as vultures dropped from the trees and gulped down the smaller dead chicks. Other vultures, with hisses and sharp barks of ***"Wahh! Wahh! Wahh!"*** tugged and jerked at chicks too large to swallow in one piece.

Gorged vultures flapped heavily upward and sat in the trees with bulging crops, digesting their brunch. Others flew off with full crops, carrying the feast back to their nestlings. By noon, the vultures nearly had the rookery tidied up.

All day long the big black hunters flew lazy circles in the clean blue sky over the shattered swamp, pine flatwood and hardwood forest. Turkey vultures, whose excellent sense of smell allows them to find hidden rotten meat, had no advantage over the black vultures today. Many animals had been crushed or injured by falling trees and branches, so there were gory picnics spread out in plain sight for miles around.

Swallows and swifts, darted through the air snapping up disoriented insects. Other insects hovered in bewilderment where sheltering trees or shrubs, now broken and flattened, had once stood. Near dusk, the vultures headed for their big tulip tree roost which still survived upright in the hardwood forest. Swifts and tree swallows swooped into their nestholes and roosts in old snags – if they were still standing. Others searched for temporary nooks and crannies in which to pass the night.

Much habitat had been lost. Only a few refugees would find new homes, for most other habitats already had residents who would not welcome newcomers.

Against the sunset, the silhouettes of bats began to flutter through the sky.

Seminole Bat

Lasiuris seminolus (laz-ee-YUR-iss seh-mih-NO-luss)
Lasios = "shaggy" **oura** = "tail" **seminolus** = for Seminole Indians

The Seminole bat belongs to a group called "hairy-tailed bats" – the top of the tail and the entire membrane stretching between tail and legs is covered with a shaggy fuzz (most bats have no hair on their tail membranes).

This solitary bat may be the most abundant bat species in the Southeast. It prefers to roost alone in Spanish moss within twenty feet of the ground. In May or June, up to four young are born and cling to their mom, even while she hunts, until they weigh more than she does. They are able to fly barely a month after birth.

The mouse-sized Seminole bat is a lovely silver-frosted mahogany-red. It has rounded, reddish ears and its nose is velvety black. The black wings stretch about twelve inches from tip to tip. Females are usually a little paler than males.

Beware of any bat lying on the ground – it could be sick (p. 106). It may bite you if it is frightened, so **don't handle it.**

Dusky Flyers

Bats share the twilight sky with swifts and swallows, all searching for food on the wing.

You won't see bats fly in the daytime, but at dusk, a flying figure that zigzags and flutters is probably a bat. Each zigzag means another insect is caught and eaten.

Birds fly more evenly than bats. Watch for these swallows and swifts around swamps and marshes:

chimney swift
Chaetura pelagica

tree swallow
Tachycineta bicolor

rough-winged swallow
Stelgidopteryx serripennis

barn swallow
Hirundo rustica

purple martin
Progne subis
(martins are swallows)

Seminole bat fast food →
Swift-moving bats are usually only flickering silhouettes in the dim evening light.

Gotcha!

catching a cranefly

Seminole bats eat dragonflies, beetles, bugs, flies, bees, wasps and crickets. They will land on leaves to snatch some, but most prey is caught in midair, scooped up by a wing or in a basket formed by the hind legs and tails. The bat pinpoints an insect's position by *echolocation (EK-ko-lo-KAY-shun)*, making incredibly loud squeaks, and flying to where the echo bounces off an insect (see p. 101). Then it sweeps dinner into its mouth.

The squeak is as loud as a jet plane engine, but it's too high for human ears to hear.

To a bat or insect, "a quiet evening in the swamp" must sound more like the Miami International Airport. Can you even imagine it?

During echolocation, a bat squeaks,...
Then it listens for an echo.

Bat Food

Ichneumon (ick-NOO-mun= "tracker") wasps are sometimes bat food, for they may be out after dark. Some fly to lighted windows at night. The ichneumon wasp shown below is parasitic (pair-uh-SIT-ick) – its larva attaches to a "host" and eats it alive.

The female "listens" with her antennae for a horntail wasp larva tunneling in a log or branch.

She plunges her *ovipositer* (OH-vih-pah-zit-ur = eggplacer) *through the wood* into the larva (see at right), lays an egg on it, then flies away. When the ichneumon larva hatches, it eats the horntail larva, matures into a wasp and digs its way out.

ichneumon wasp
Megarhyssa
laying egg

in flight long, ovipo may s 3" behi

Hats Off To Bats (a poem)

BIG teeth help bats crunch tough insects

People fear bats; they think bats will attack
or get caught in their hair. That's not true.

Bats eat winged insects and gobble mosquitos –
twelve hundred per hour! That's a FEW!

Half of our bats are endangered or missing.
For people use strong pesticides

Which ruin the delicate balance of nature –
and wreck ecosystems, besides.

So throw out the bug spray to help our
night flyers. Protect them from predators (cats).

You'll give them a boost if you hang up a roost*
for those great insect hunters, the bats.

Slurpeeeeee

It takes great skill to fly over water, open your mouth, and scoop up a drink without taking a sudden bath.

But a bat, clumsy on land, has to do this whenever it gets thirsty, for if it lands to drink, a predator may grab it.

"Hand Wing"

A bat wing is really just a hand with webbed fingers.

To work like a bat wing, **your** fingers would have to be about twenty inches long with really stretchy skin between them. For you to be light enough to fly, your legs would have to shrink to about twelve inches long and be *very skinny.*

* find information about bat houses on page 109

45. The Seminole Bat

As the sun sank behind the trees, a Seminole bat dropped from her roost in a tattered swag of Spanish moss hanging from a liveoak tree at the edge of the swamp.

Beating strongly with her wings, she fluttered up into the night sky. Her usual route along the edge of the forest was impossible tonight, and she dodged broken branches blocking her path. She flew cautiously through and around the tangled landscape, noting fresh landmarks and checking out new open areas in which to hunt.

And the hunting was good. Unlike the vultures, she wasn't seeking carcasses – her prey must be alive. But some insects seemed to have been disoriented or injured by the hurricane, making them easy to catch. She filled the evening air with bursts of sound which bounced off the flying insects, then she followed the returning echoes to her prey. It was done swiftly, each insect detected and eaten in seconds. She chased a big night-flying ichneumon wasp, but it dodged and escaped. Spotting a katydid, she lit on a leaf and chomped it down, then she swooped from the tree and headed out over the swamp on a mosquito run.

The Seminole bat dipped and fluttered as she chased insects through the warm dusk. Around her, red bats and evening bats darted and swooped as they too caught their dinners. She scooped up a drink of warm swamp water tea to wash down her food.

The bat's usual Spanish moss night roost (Spanish moss is a favorite roost choice for Seminole bats) had been damaged in the hurricane. The wind had flapped and buffeted it about, sometimes even whipping it out horizontally. The bat had clung tightly to the strands inside and had safely weathered the storm, but a large section of the big clump had torn away and now lay in a soggy heap far downwind.

When the bat's belly was full of insects, she flew back to what was left of her roost. But as she was climbing up inside, her eye caught the bright flicker of a firefly passing the roost – so much moss had blown away that she could see right through the side. She paused nervously, looking around. The rising moon made lacy patterns where she usually hung in total darkness. This was not good

Dropping back out, she fluttered along the oaks at the edge of the swamp, searching for another large, dense clump of Spanish moss. Soon she would bear young, and she needed a snug home. As she searched, the twangy **"wenk.......wenk.......wenk"** of green treefrog calls filled the steamy swamp with sound.

Green Treefrog

Hyla cinerea (HIE-luh sie-NEER-ee-uh)
Hyla = "of the forest" *cinereus* = "ash-colored"

The green treefrog is one of the noisier members of the swamp. It belongs to a group of frogs known as "rain frogs," because it sings mostly during wet weather (but other times, too). Because of its nasal **"wenk, wenk, wenk"** call, it is also known as the "bell frog" and the "cowbell frog."

The green treefrog may reach a bit more than two inches in length. Like other treefrogs, its color can change from bright yellow-green (when singing) to dull gray (when hiding). There is usually a creamy, black-outlined stripe down its side, and gold spots may dot its back. The similar squirrel treefrog is smaller.

The light-weight green treefrog's blobby, sticky toes help it navigate and cling to the undersides of slick leaves without falling off. It blends so well with the water plants and lily pads of its watery habitat that it is seldom seen there. So watch for it to come catch insects on glass windows at night.

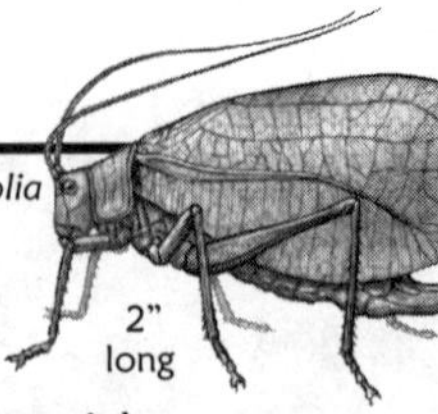

Night Noises

Frogs aren't the only noisemakers in the Southern night. Alligators bellow. Owls whistle, hoot and gabble. Whip-poor-wills and chuck-will's-widows call their own names endlessly. Herons and other waterbirds squawk, cluck, gurgle and yelp. Mockingbirds, thrushes and catbirds may sing at night, but they tend to have more mellow songs.

You can't always guess what's making the calls, though. Some toads sound like crickets. Some crickets sound like katydids. Some katydids sound like frogs (or clackety hedge trimmers). Saw-whet owls also sound like frogs, while some frogs sound like crickets, squirrels or pigs. Is this **totally** confusing, or what?

Try creeping up on these little music-makers with a flashlight to discover who's who. If the music stops, hold still and they'll probably call again. For more frog info, read page 14.

Small Frogs

chorus frog
Pseudacris species, ¾" to 1⅜"
"**tk-tk-tk-tk-tk**"

cricket frog
Acris species, ⅝" to 1⅜"
"**click–click-clickclikliklik**"

green treefrog
Hyla cinerea, 1¼" to 2½"
"**wenk, wenk, wenk**"

spring peeper treefrog
Pseudacris crucifer, ¾" to 1⅜"
"**queep, queep, queep**"

Tree Toes

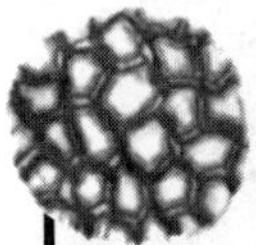

close-up of green treefrog toe pad

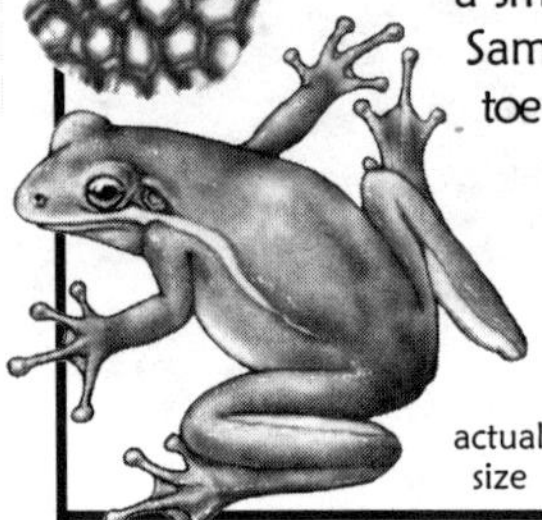

Hanging onto the underside of a leaf is easy if you only weigh about as much as a quarter. But how does it work? Have you ever noticed how a wet glass sticks to a smooth surface? Same thing. Each toe has lots of smooth pads with spaces between, like tire treads.

To disconnect, the treefrog tilts its foot until the tiny pads peel off, one by one, to release the connection.

actual size

Boom Box

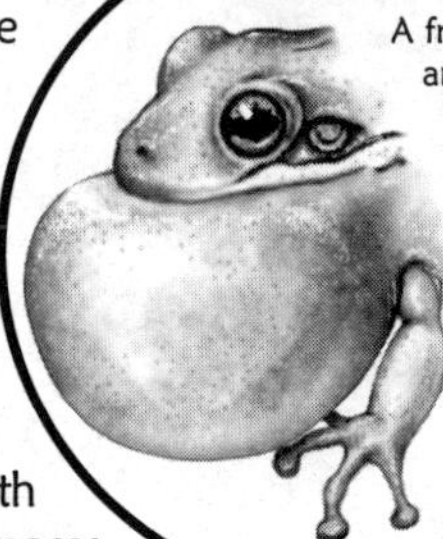

A frog's song is amplified by the bubble-like pouch under its chin. Some frogs have double bubbles, one below each eardrum or *tympanum* (TIM-puh-num), the flat circle behind each eye.

Frogs in Danger

Miners used to carry a canary underground with them. If the delicate bird fainted, they knew the mine was dangerous and they got out fast. Frogs may be our Earth's "canaries." They are disappearing everywhere and there are many reasons:

1. Frogs are **losing habitat** as humans drain their wetlands. **2.** People release into their habitats **alien species** which may compete with them (see pages 104–105). **3.** A frog's super-absorbent skin soaks up poisons from **polluted water**. **4.** Poisons from **polluted air** enter a frog's skin while on land. **5.** Pollywogs are herbivores, and adult frogs are carnivores. So a frog eats **contaminated food** of *both kinds* during its life. **6.** The ozone hole causes a frog's delicate skin to get *way* too much **ultraviolet** (a frog can't wear sunscreen), so its immune system has trouble resisting fatal infections. **7. Acid rain** kills frog eggs. **8.** Stress may make frogs susceptible to a **chytrid fungus** which appears to keep their skins from absorbing oxygen. **9. Global warming** is drying up swamps, while rising sea water may completely cover low-lying wetlands.

If frogs **are** Earth's canaries, we'd better pay attention – we may be next!

Pickerelweed

Pontederia cordata

Hummingbirds and butterflies visit the plumes of purple flowers on this big-leafed three-foot-tall plant. Frogs, fish and insects hide under the leaves.

Compare with **duck potato** on p. 26 and **arrow arum** on p. 84.

Oak "Apples"

Sometimes an oak tree looks as though it has sprouted apples. But don't eat one – you'll get a mouthful of worm and dry foam! The "apple" is a *gall* – a puffy growth formed by the plant to wall off an intruder. Triggered when a parasite injects the plant with chemicals, the gall grows around the larva or egg, making a cozy "house" in which the larva feeds and matures. Spiders, mites, fungi, nematodes and bacteria also cause galls, each choosing a particular plant and triggering a unique gall shape.

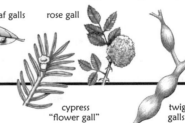

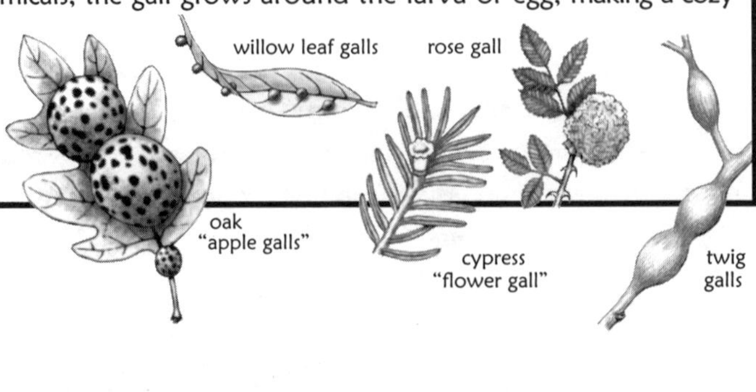

willow leaf galls

rose gall

oak "apple galls"

cypress "flower gall"

twig galls

46. The Green Treefrog

The hurricane had broken the drought, and now the summer rains would begin in the swamps. In the silvery moonlight, clinging to twigs, branches and leaves above the water, the slim green treefrogs' wonky calls rose in a clanging chorus as they called for mates.

The symphony had begun with a single call, then the song had been taken up by several more frogs until perhaps a hundred green treefrogs were calling every second. Unlike most other frogs, they didn't call in unison, so the air was filled with a hundred nasal clanks and clunks, all at different times and on slightly different notes in marvelous concert.

"wahnk .. wahnk wahnk wahnk wahnk"
"wonk wonk wonk wonk wonk wonk wonk"
"wenk.. wenk.. wenk"
"Wonk:.... wonk:......wonk :.....wonk:......wonk"
"wahnk...wahnk...wahnk...wahnk...wahnk...wank..."
"wenk..wenk..wenk..wenk..wenk..wenk"
"wenk....wenk....wenk....wenk....wenk....wenk"
"wonk......wonk......wonk......wonk......wonk"

Each frog had spent the day silently hidden near the water's edge under shrub leaves or beneath the petals or leaves of spatterdock, pickerel weed, cattails or water-lilies. Now the little frogs' bubble-like throat pouches pulsed with sound and gleamed like pearls in the light of the full moon as they edged into sight.

The chorus stopped suddenly for reasons known only to the frogs, and the air was heavy with silence. Then a single frog called, and the music began again. This pattern would continue far into the night.

The warm, steamy marsh and swamp vibrated with sound. Chorus frogs rasped out a tinkly *"tk-tk-tk-tk-tk-tk-tk" "tk-tk-tk-tk-tk-tk-tk."* like a thumb run across comb teeth.

"Click–click–click–click-click-click-click-clickliklikk" went the cricket frogs, making a sound like small stones or marbles clicking together at the water's edge, starting slowly and increasing to a clickety trill. The shrill chorus was interrupted every few minutes by the loud **"OINK!   OINK!   OINK!"** of a pig frog in deeper water.

A plucked banjo sound, **"glunk, glunk, glunk,"** twanged from a large green frog.

Now and again a bullfrog would tune its bass fiddle with a loud, stuttering **"UH-UH-UH-RUHHNN!"** while a pale green tree cricket shrilled *"chrrrrrrrrrrrrrrrrrrrrrr"* from cattails at the edge of the marsh.

Deep in the swamp an alligator rumbled like the roar of a faraway lion.

The hurricane had passed. The swamp, marsh, scrub and bottomlands had all survived. Summer in the cypress swamp was in full swing, and life, as always, continued on.

Aliens – Non-native Plants and Animals

Humans have a habit of taking plants and animals which they find beautiful, interesting or useful along with them when they move to a new place. In this way, many natural habitats have been invaded by species that take over and push out native species.

Many alien species have been purposely introduced by good-hearted people who thought the new species would be a big benefit to the neighborhood. Occasionally, they were right. But when they were wrong, great troubles followed.

Now it is illegal to release many species of plants or animals into new habitats. But lots of them still get there accidentally as stowaways when people move or ship items, or when people release or plant them where they shouldn't be, or when they escape from captivity.

The starling is a good example of an animal invader – people thought these beautiful birds from England would look good in America, so they imported and released them into their neighborhoods. Now starlings live everywhere from coast to coast. They chase native birds from their territories, take over their nest holes, kill their nestlings and eat their food.

A clear example of a plant invader is kudzu, which covers entire forests in the south like a huge, smothering green blanket. Kudzu vines were quite welcome in the South at first, since they made quick shade for porches and hay for cattle. And they were beautiful and smelled good.

However, when the vines buried peoples' houses, crowded out crops, and crawled over railroad tracks, causing trains to jump the tracks, it became clear to some people that they were more trouble than they were worth.

Still, kudzu was promoted by the government in the 1930s to control erosion along southern roads – and now it covers trees like a huge green blanket along many southern highways, killing everything beneath. Unfortunately, kudzu is almost impossible to get rid of since the roots must be totally removed, and some of them go down as deep as twenty feet and weight 200 pounds. The soil conditions, insects, and diseases that keep kudzu in check in its native Japan don't exist in the Southeastern U.S.

The Southeastern U.S. has a warm, welcoming climate. Many aliens have nearly taken over some habitats. In their native habitats, other species would have evolved along with them to eat them, slow their growth, or otherwise hold their numbers or growth down. In a new habitat, with nothing to stop them, their numbers explode and they overwhelm everything else.

Whole books have been written about them, and some people have spent their lives trying to poison, capture, burn out, chop or uproot them – doing whatever it takes to stop these plant and animal invaders.

You can find out more about these aliens in the library or online. With an online search, you'll get better results if you use the specific name (for instance, look for "*Solenopsis invicta*," rather than "fire ant").

Here's a partial list of some of the nastiest invaders in the Southeast. There are many more.

melaleuca - *Melaleuca quinquenervia*
casuarina - *Casuarina equisetifolia*
kudzu - *Pueraria montana*
water hyacinth - *Eichhornia crassipes*
Chinese privet - *Ligustrum sinense*
Japanese honeysuckle - *Lonicera japonica*
Japanese climbing fern - *Lygodium japonicum*
Chinese tallow - *Triadica sebifera*
Florida elodea, hydrilla - *Hydrilla verticillata*
bamboo - *most species*

Asian tiger mosquito - *Aedes albopictus*
red imported fire ant - *Solenopsis invicta*
Asian long-horned beetle - *Anoplophora glabripennis*
Formosan subterranean termite - *Coptotermes formosanus*

rusty crawfish - *Orconectes rusticus*
walking catfish - *Clarias batrachus*
cane toad - *Bufo marinus*
greenhouse frog - *Eleutherodactylus planirostris*
Cuban treefrog - *Osteopilus septentrionalis*
brown anole - *Norops sagrei*

European starling - *Sturnus vulgaris*
wild boar - *Sus scrofa*
nutria - *Myocastor coypus*

Good sources for finding information and pictures of invasive plants and animals are *www.nps.gov/plants/alien* and *www.invasivespeciesinfo.gov*. There you'll find information about how to identify them and what to do about them.

You might wonder what the big deal is if you don't know the details. It has taken biologists a long time to sort through the information and figure out where things went wrong. But they've gotten a pretty good list of problems now, and you can see some of the details on the next page.

In a natural situation, without alien invaders, the plants and animals in an ecosystem grow up together, learn to get along, and adjust to each other's habits and tricks. They learn what they need to live, and they find ways to get what they need. If they are in a safe spot, they get rid of defenses they don't need in order to save energy. They adapt perfectly to fit in their world, even if sometimes there is drought or flood. They're ready for anything. Except alien invaders.

Here are some things that get changed when aliens invade:

~fires become hotter and more frequent when highly flammable invaders take over
~entire ecosystems get replaced by a single aggressive invader
~invaders hybridize with natives, changing their genetics
~wildlife starves or does poorly because unsuitable non-native foods replace their usual foods
~natives starve or die out when invaders take over water and food resources
~invading trees and shrubs shade or crowd out native species

Here are some things that get interrupted when aliens invade:

~natural plant growth and replacement are interrupted
~plant-animal pollination and seed dispersal are interrupted
~invaders prevent seedlings from rooting and growing

Here are some things that get lost when aliens invade:

~native plants, insects, birds, mammals, reptiles and amphibians lose habitat.
~natural parasite hosts and life processes don't happen
~plant/pollinator relationships of insects and mammals are lost or can't function
~entire species disappear, eaten or crowded out by invaders
~important functions once done for the ecosystem by specialized native plant and animal communities don't get done
~streambanks and beaches erode away when native plants that stabilized them disappear

Here are some things that get added when aliens invade:

~new diseases cause natives to sicken or die
~invaders serve as new hosts for diseases which previously didn't bother native species
~invaders stress out natives, which weakens them

When alien invaders appear alone, without the usual things that keep them from multiplying, they can take over a natural habitat. By eating the natives' food, sucking up their water, creating shade where none was before, bringing along diseases, and by many other means, animal invaders shove out other animals, and plant invaders shove out other plants, reducing the kinds and numbers of native plants and animals in a habitat.

As you can see, alien invaders are a huge problem. Although people try to root them out, some of them are here to stay.

One of the simplest things you can do to help with the problem is to not release animals, plants, or seeds into places where they don't normally live.

Even if they are available in a plant nursery, not all plants you can buy there should be planted in your area. For instance, bamboo is a popular ornamental plant sold by nurseries, but it doesn't always stay where it is planted. Its roots travel underground and new bamboo plants pop up yards away. Bamboos grow in dense clumps that crowd out other plants, and they're not good food for most native wildlife. Other plants, such as pampas grass, become problems when their seeds are spread by wind or water. Water hyacinth, which escaped from backyard ponds, now chokes southeastern ponds and lakes, multiplying so quickly it can't be controlled.

People planting their yards should first check to see whether the plants they are interested in have invasive habits. If they do, they should not use them (or should contain them carefully). A good way to find out is to go online and do a search for, for example, "invasive plants Alabama" (but using your own state's name).

You can have an effect on animal invaders, too. For instance, if you go fishing, make sure you don't dump live bait (crawfish, fish, etc.) into the water – they might become invaders and take over the habitat of the fish or other creatures who live in that water system.

Don't pull sticky seeds off your clothes and drop them where they didn't grow before. That's one sneaky way plants manage to spread, so don't help them out. Instead, drop the seeds into your pocket to put in your campfire if you're camping, or take them home to put into the garbage can. What other ways do seeds get around?

If you like to raise caterpillars, don't release non-native butterflies or moths outside. They could crowd out, eat, pass on diseases, or otherwise damage native insects and plants.

You can probably think of some other ways to prevent alien invaders from entering a new habitat, and you can also probably think of some ways to combat them if you find them trying to take over.

If you discover an invader in a new place, tell authorities (such as County Agents) so that they can find ways to keep it from getting a firm hold on the environment. Remove invaders yourself when you find them.

Who knows? You might save the environment!

Swamp Safety

Swamps are cool places to explore, and people have lived in and around swamps for hundreds of years. But you do need to be alert, keep your eyes open, and be smart.

WALKABOUT: put the following things in your kit, or wear them when you go out hiking.

~full water bottle – there are too many people and animals around swamps for the water to be safe, so don't drink it.
~long-sleeved shirt to keep off sun and bugs
~sunscreen – be sure to put some on before you go
~insect repellent – enough for several applications
~lunch and energy bar – just in case you get lost
~whistle – to call for help if you get lost or break a leg
~poncho – in case it rains and to keep you warm if needed
~a hat with a brim to see better into dark places
~a headband or bandana to keep sweat out of your eyes
~map and compass – it helps if you know how to use them
~potty kit (see next page)
~binoculars, camera, notebook or journal to keep notes
~a flashlight to see into dark places, or in case you don't get back before dark

MOSQUITOES: Before you even go out, smear on mos-

quito repellent. Even if mosquito bites don't bother you a lot, or don't often bite you, some mosquitoes carry diseases, such as malaria and West Nile virus, that can make you quite sick. Mosquito repellent will keep them away, although you'll need to smear on some more if you sweat a lot, or get wet and it gets diluted or wiped away. Don't forget to carry repellent with you. (Mosquitoes are most active at dawn and dusk, so you will get fewer bites if you stay inside then.)

SUNSCREEN: While you're putting on the repellent, also apply some sunscreen to protect your skin if you'll be out in the sun without protection for awhile. Sunshine is good for you, and builds up the Vitamin D in your body, but it can also burn you, so be smart. It is definitely not smart to get sunburned.

a chigger

TICKS & CHIGGERS: Ticks and chiggers are common

a tick

around swamps, too. Chiggers are only about this · big, and ambush you from the grass. They burrow under your skin and itch like crazy, but probably won't give you a disease.

Ticks hang around on tall grass and shrubs, waiting for you to come along so they can hitch a ride. Then they'll look for a nice tight, warm spot, like under your belt or in your armpit, to suck some blood. While they're doing that, they're injecting tick juice which may carry disease (see page 62.

WHAT TO WEAR: Even if it is hot outside, dress so that the little guys won't bite or attach to you. Wear long-sleeved, long-legged light-colored clothing and tuck your pants legs into your socks.

INSECT REPELLENT: Spray your clothes with insect repellent to guard against ticks, chiggers and mosquitoes. When you get back home, check your whole body, including your scalp, for ticks, and remove them as soon as possible.

REMOVING A TICK: To remove a tick, grasp its body with tweezers *as close as possible to its head*, and pull gently until it lets go. If the head breaks off under your skin, dab it with antiseptic but don't worry about it – it won't poison you. Wash your hands and the bite site with soapy water to clean away any infected juices, particularly if you squash the tick with the tweezers.

BUG ZAPPERS: Zappers, the kind that electrocute insects with a snap and flash of blue light – are **bad news**. Research done on six zappers placed within two miles of streams and marshes showed that of 13,789 insects they zapped, only 31 were mosquitoes or biting flies. The rest were important insect food for other species. Zappers don't kill many mosquitoes, but they do kill insects that normally eat mosquitoes, plus other insects that are important native wildlife food. Leave the "zapping" to the birds, bats, fish, and insects who eat those flying insects for survival.

WHAT ABOUT RABIES?: Rabies is transmitted by such mammals as opossums, raccoons, foxes and bats (not usually squirrels, rats, or mice). Rabies infections happen only rarely.

You can get infected if saliva from a rabid mammal (wild or a pet) gets into a sore, scratch or wound. Avoid any animal that acts odd, seems to be choking, or drools, all signs of rabies (although opossums normally drool when they snarl).

If you get bitten by any mammal, don't wait for symptoms to occur – get advice from your doctor.

ALLIGATORS: One of the cool things about swamps is that there are REAL monsters out there. It makes for good goosebumps when you want to scare yourself, but if you pay attention you will stay safe. Remember these things:

~A mother alligator will charge at you to protect her babies (read page 55) so keep away from alligator pools with nests in them.

~Avoid cute little baby alligators because mom could be out of sight but ready to come save them.

~Alligators can run really, REALLY fast for a short distance, and they love dogmeat. So leave your dog at home or keep it on a leash when you're around swamps.

~Don't swim or wade in alligator pools.

SNAKES: You are very likely to see snakes in a swamp, and they could be venomous. Read page 94 for information on the most common venomous snakes you might encounter in swamps.

There's a lot to see in a swamp, so keep your eyes open, and while you're doing that, you'll probably spot any snakes hanging around. They would rather avoid you, and they're generally not looking for trouble, so leave them alone. This is important, because the snakes play an important role in the swamp and the other animals need them to keep things in balance. So please respect them.

SNAKE RULES: (memorize these)
~Watch where you step, especially when crossing over logs.
~Never poke fingers into dark places without checking first.
~Wear shoes or boots. Most snake bites occur below the knee.
~After dark use a flashlight. Try to finish hikes before dark.
~If you meet a snake, hold perfectly still until it moves off or, if you are 3' – 4' away, back up slowly.
~If a snake bites you, tie your bandana or headband around your body between the bite and the heart – but not tight enough to cut off the blood supply. Don't run. That pumps the venom through your body faster.
~Walk slowly toward help and blow your whistle to get someone's attention. If possible, apply ice to the bite until you arrive at the hospital.

While most swimming snakes are non-venomous watersnakes, cottonmouth and copperhead snakes also swim, so avoid swimming snakes just to be safe. A snake swimming with it's head held high out of the water will be a cottonmouth (see page 94).

FROGS: You may need to wash your hands after handling frogs. Some people get a nasty rash from frog slime. Frogs are fragile, so you really shouldn't handle them, anyway.

COLLECTING: it's okay to pick up some things to take home (leaves, acorns, etc.), but most things you should leave in the swamp where you find them.

Many animals and plants are protected by law, and it is illegal to collect them or remove them from their habitat. However, if you take a camera with you when you go swamping, you can make an awesome photo collection instead. This is even better in lots of ways – you can take the photos to school to share with friends and you never have to feed them or clean their cages. A photo of a snake will never bite you. And photos won't take up much space in your room, either.

Take a sketchbook or journal with you when you go to the swamp. Making drawings instead of a collection will leave you with great memories of the occasion, especially if you write about it in your journal (see page. 109 for some ideas).

Did you know it's against the law to collect most kinds of bird feathers? That's because some people kill birds to get their feathers. If you have a feather it might mean you killed the bird – so it's against the law to have feathers of most kinds. Game bird feathers (duck, quail, etc.) and chicken feathers are okay to have, though.

It's also against the law to pick many kinds of flowers. Some plants are protected because there are very few of them left in the wild. Go ahead and sniff them and enjoy them, and take a photo (great idea!), but don't trample them or pick a bouquet or you might accidentally wipe out an entire species.

WHEN YOU GOTTA GO: When hiking, _always_ carry a "potty kit" in your pocket. In a sealable plastic bag, put about six feet of toilet tissue folded up small. Also add a second small plastic bag into which you can tuck _used_ tissues.

Gotta go? Try to find a high spot at least 200' (about half a city block) from any water, where no one is likely to walk and where the next heavy rain or flood won't wash it out. If you can't get that far away from water, either wait until later or just do the best you can (if you can't put it off.)

With a stick, dig a "cathole" about six inches deep and six inches wide. Use it. When finished, push the dirt back into the hole and hide the spot with leaves or natural debris.

Tuck used tissues into the second plastic bag and put it back into your potty kit, then into your pocket If you leave the tissue in the hole it will be dug up by animals – ICK!

If you only need to pee, don't dig a hole. Dispose of your used tissues back at camp, at the car or at home.

Things to Do

After many projects you'll see page numbers in parentheses. Look on those pages in this book for more information. Some projects in this section will refer you to websites for more information. If these don't work, do a search for other sites for additional help.

Swamp and Wetlands Activities

• <u>Bird Pellets</u> Collect owl or other bird pellets. Soak pellet in warm water, then see what kinds of bones, insect legs, etc., are inside. The pellet is sanitary, cleaned by strong stomach acids, so you don't need to worry about diseases, but wash your hands when you are finished. (pp. 16, 44)

• <u>Wet It & Watch</u> Dribble water on resurrection ferns, Spanish moss, lichens, and mosses, then watch to see what happens. Careful, Spanish moss may harbor "biters." (p. 48)

• <u>Rushes are Round,</u> sedges have edges and grasses are flat. See if you can find one of each. (p. 70)

• <u>Look for Crawfish Chimneys</u> Drop in tiny twigs. (p. 38)

• <u>Color a Chameleon</u> Find an anole lizard basking in the sun. Arrange a leaf so that it casts a sharp shadow across part of its body. Watch that part get darker. (p. 60)

• <u>Nature Rubbings</u> Find a leaf, or a bark or log with beetle tunnel patterns on it. Press a sheet of paper onto your subject and rub across the pattern with a crayon or pencil – the pattern will appear on the paper. (p. 30)

• <u>Making Tracks</u> Find animal tracks in mud. Mix plaster of Paris and pour it into a track. Wait until cool, lift the plaster, wash off, and the track is done. *More information is at www.bear-tracker.com/plastertracks.html*

• <u>Spit Home</u> Look on grass or plants for a glob of spit. Inside is a spittlebug larva. If you remove the spit and if you wait patiently you can watch it build a new spitty house. (p. 90)

• <u>Natural Flashlight</u> After dark, catch fireflies in a jar and use it as a flashlight. Release them before bedtime in the same area you caught them so they can go on with their lives. (p. 32)

• <u>Nest ID</u> Look for bird and squirrel nests. How many kinds can you find? A squirrel nest is spherical – most bird nests are flat on top. (p. 48)

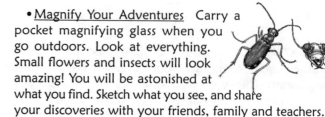

• <u>Magnify Your Adventures</u> Carry a pocket magnifying glass when you go outdoors. Look at everything. Small flowers and insects will look amazing! You will be astonished at what you find. Sketch what you see, and share your discoveries with your friends, family and teachers.

Swampy Projects

• <u>Sun Tea</u> Wet leaves make swamp water tea-dark. Make some *drinkable* "swamp water" (sun tea) with 2 qts. of water, 3-4 black tea bags and mint sprigs if you have some. Let it sit in the hot sun for 3-4 hours, cool, sweeten it if you want, and drink. Only make as much as you can drink in one day. Caffeine (but not herbal) teabags prevent bacterial growth for a few hours. (p. 24)

• <u>Do-it-yourself Swamp</u> Take a big plastic jar with a lid to the edge of a nearby swamp or pond. Fill it half full of water, add pondweeds and some mud from the shallow water. Screw the lid on tightly. At home, empty the container into a bigger jar or aquarium and add water. As it clears over the next week, strange and mysterious things will appear like magic. Record them, and sketch what you discover. Make sure hatching things can escape to freedom. (pp. 12, 14, 34, 42, 44, 72, 109 etc.)

• <u>Mosquito Patrol</u> Search your yard for buckets or cans holding rainwater, then empty them so mosquitos won't breed there. Some states provide free mosquito fish to put in ponds or water gardens to eat the mosquitoes. The mosquito fish (gambusia) is native to southeastern states but would be an alien invader in other states, so make sure it can't escape. (p. 34)

• <u>Create a Wildlife Habitat</u> Start your own backyard swamp (or nature refuge). By 2008, the National Wildlife Foundation had certified more than 100,000 backyard wildlife habitats. *See www.nwf.org for more information.*

Craft Projects

• <u>Make an Atlatl</u> (say *at-LAT-tul*) Early hunter-gatherers made these tools to give their throwing darts more power. Caution: use it responsibly! (p. 28) *More directions here: www.primitiveways.com/atlatl_branch.html*

• <u>Make a Unique Walking Stick</u> Find a branch about six feet long which has been decorated by beetle-chewed tunnels. Cut off side branches, saw it to the correct length for you, then smooth it with sandpaper and oil it. (p. 30)

• <u>Make a Cattail Duck</u> Native Americans used cattails to make decoys to attract waterfowl when they hunted. These are beautiful and fun to make. *See directions here: www.nativetech.org/decoy/DUCKDECOYS.htm*

• Make a Bone Model Next time you nibble a chicken wing, nibble carefully and save all the bones. Clean off all the meat, dry the bones, and glue them to a piece of cardboard. Label carefully. (p. 46)

• Frog Banjo Create a frog banjo with a cardboard box and rubberbands. Just stretch several different-sized rubberbands tightly around the box, then pluck – each will twang like a different size of frog. A different box size will produce different twang tones. Experiment.

• Frog Comb Band To sound like a chorus frog, pull your thumb across the teeth of a comb, going from the large teeth to the small. *To hear this frog call, go to www.uga.edu/srelherp and click on "Amphibians," then "Frogs & Toads," then "Southern Chorus Frog.* (pp. 14, 15, 102, 103)

Other Interesting Things To Do

• Raising Caterpillars If you find a caterpillar, you can watch it turn into a butterfly or moth, then release it where you found the caterpillar. *See www.butterflyschool.org/teacher/raising.html* (p. 64)

• Make a Bat House Bats need homes, and you can help by making a bat house. Get an adult to help you. *Plans are here: www.batcon.org or www. batconservation.org (p. 100)*

• Make a Bird House Birds need homes, too, and you can make a bird house with help from an adult. *Plans are here www.50birds. com/D50BH.htm (p. 74)*

• Grow Gourds Growing gourds is like growing pumpkins, except that you let them get hard and dry on the vine. Then you can make them into bird houses, bowls and water jars like early Native Americans did. *www.americangourdsociety.org/FAQ/ birdhouse.html* (pp. 40, 41)

• Make a Collection How many kinds of pinecones or acorns can you find? (p. 8) There are many kinds of galls – make a collection and identify them when they hatch out. (p. 102) Collect bark beetle etchings – learn which beetle makes each design. (p. 30) Make a seed collection – seeds come in some really strange shapes and sizes. (p. 22, 62, 96). Make sure it's okay to collect that item, though. Be sure to NOT collect feathers. It's against the law to keep most kinds of wild bird feathers, especially songbirds and raptors! (see page 107)

• Record Your Adventures Describe what you see and do in a notebook or journal (unlined is best if you'll be sketching in it). Draw pictures and write about things that interest you.

If you have a camera, photograph interesting things and add the photos to your journal.

Pressed leaves and lichens also make cool additions.

Write poems about what you see or how you feel about it. Your poem can be beautiful, or spooky, or funny, or sad – do whatever you want.

Sketch things you see, even if you don't think you're a very good artist. You'll get LOTS better with practice.

Below is a page out of Irene Brady's sketchbook. She sketches all the time, so she gets lots of practice, but it's okay if a picture isn't finished or doesn't turn out very well – the important thing is to just draw and write about the things you discover. You might enjoy learning to sketch from her book, **Illustrating Nature** ~ you can find it at *www.natureworkspress.com.*

Swamp Highlights ~ Where Are the Swamps?

You can find thousands of swamps, marshes, bogs, and wetlands of all kinds throughout the south. Some are easy to visit and popular, others are hidden and almost unknown. Some are huge, others are tiny remnants of what they were in the past.

On the following pages, a few of these wetlands have been described to give you an idea of what you might find if you are looking for a swamp to visit.*

You'll find a description of the swamp and the typical animals and plants you'd find there today. You'll learn a bit about its ancient human inhabitants and how they lived in the swamp long ago, then what happened when early European settlers moved into the area.

You'll also find information about how each wetland formed ages ago, and how it is doing today. Most of these swamps have visitor centers or stores where you can buy maps, guides, books, and sometimes even food if you are camping. Some of them have campgrounds, others are near campgrounds where you can stay if you want to spend more than one day exploring.

Each one is different, with its own particular geology, history, wildlife and plants, but all of them are well worth a visit.

There may be other swamps and wetlands even closer to where you live. On the map below, the gray area shows areas of the southeastern United States that are are low enough to have swamps and other wetlands.

These areas extend well away from the coast into parts of the country most people wouldn't think of as "swampy." For instance, did you know there are cypress swamps in Illinois, Tennessee, Maryland, Missouri, New Jersey, Virginia, Kentucky, Oklahoma and Delaware? And swamps can show up in other unexpected places, too – within the Baton Rouge city limits in Louisiana, for example.

There are alligators in many of the southern swamps, although they are rare or missing in more northerly swamps. But with or without alligators, swamps are wild, wonderful, mysterious places. Go and see for yourself!

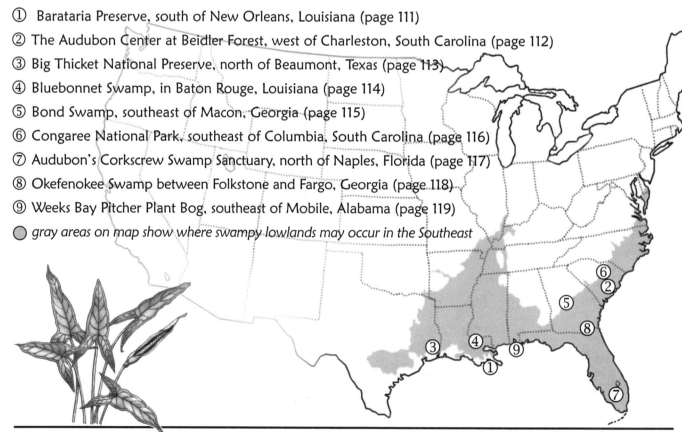

① Barataria Preserve, south of New Orleans, Louisiana (page 111)

② The Audubon Center at Beidler Forest, west of Charleston, South Carolina (page 112)

③ Big Thicket National Preserve, north of Beaumont, Texas (page 113)

④ Bluebonnet Swamp, in Baton Rouge, Louisiana (page 114)

⑤ Bond Swamp, southeast of Macon, Georgia (page 115)

⑥ Congaree National Park, southeast of Columbia, South Carolina (page 116)

⑦ Audubon's Corkscrew Swamp Sanctuary, north of Naples, Florida (page 117)

⑧ Okefenokee Swamp between Folkstone and Fargo, Georgia (page 118)

⑨ Weeks Bay Pitcher Plant Bog, southeast of Mobile, Alabama (page 119)

⦿ *gray areas on map show where swampy lowlands may occur in the Southeast*

---

*Information on the following pages was provided by the organizations represented.

Barataria Preserve is part of Jean Lafitte National Historical Park and Preserve, located about sixteen miles from New Orleans. The preserve contains about 20,000 acres of bottomland hardwoods, tupelo-cypress swamp, and marsh. There is a Visitor Center, an Environmental Educational Center for special programs, two canoe launches, and dirt and boardwalk trails. One of these trails enables visitors to experience all three ecosystems within a one-mile walk.

Barataria Preserve is a microcosmic example of a flood plain delta, created thousands of years ago as the Mississippi River flooded and deposited silt from upriver. Bayou Des Familles, once a segment of the Mississippi River, cuts sluggishly through the preserve. Early Native Americans lived on the high ridge embankment created by this bayou more than 2000 years ago. Their shell middens, as well as archaeological sites containing European artifacts, have been found throughout the preserve. Early French and Spanish farmers tried to farm this forest only to be periodically flooded out. Jean Lafitte and his pirate crew hid in and smuggled goods through the swamps. Their spirits still haunt the preserve in stories and folklore.

By the 1900s, Barataria's large cypress trees had been felled and canals had been dug to carry out the logs. Oil was discovered, and pipelines, more canals, and drill sites disrupted the environment. People who depended on the bounty of the swamp for their livelihood began to see changes and losses. Concerned citizens petitioned Congress, and a National Park was created in 1978.

Today, the canals in Barataria Preserve are now canoe paths where alligators dwell and wading birds dance. Trails and boardwalks follow old roadbeds, and delight visitors with an array of plants and animals.

In August of 2005, Hurricane Katrina knocked down 60% of the trees, mostly in the bottomland hardwood forest. Later, Hurricane Rita's floods carried salt water into the fresh water area. Park Service and other agency personnel from all over the United States helped restore roads and trails. By October, the park was reopened. All the trails except one are available, and from them you might see:

Mammals: Residents include white-tail deer, opossums, raccoons, marsh rabbits, mink, armadillos, gray squirrels, bats, nutria (non-native rodents) and coyotes.

Birds: In Spring and Fall, various birds pass through along the Mississippi Flyway. Look for barred owls, red-shouldered hawks and vultures. Green-backed, tri-colored, little blue and great blue herons, and snowy and great egrets wade the waters. Listen and watch for red-bellied and pile-ated woodpeckers, ibises, cardinals, chickadees, moorhens, a variety of ducks, wrens, and other small birds all year round. Bald eagles nest near the preserve.

Reptiles and Amphibians: Alligators, anole lizards, skinks, a variety of turtles, pig frogs, treefrogs, cricket frogs, and water snakes may be spied from the boardwalks. Young alligators seen along the bayou indicate a nearby nest.

Fish and Water Creatures: The waterways contain fish such as crappie, catfish, spotted and alligator gar, bluegill, and sunfish. Also look for crawfish and their mud chimneys.

Insects and Spiders: Swallowtails, skippers, and fritillary butterflies, as well as beautiful moths, are seen in summer. Watch for large lubber grasshoppers, katydids, dragonflies, and damselflies – and late in the evening, fireflies. Fishing spiders are often spotted sitting on the water's surface, while numerous water insects swim below. You'll be awed by the huge orb webs of golden silk spiders and the black and gold argiopes (orb weaver) with white zigzags in their webs.

Trees, Shrubs and Other Plants: The main swamp trees are cypress, tupelo-gum, red maple, and wax myrtle. At the swamp edges are black willow, hackberry, sweetgum, live oak and water oak. Other hardwood trees live on the higher natural ridges. A walk through the bottomwood forest will reveal persimmons, pecans, wild berries and grapes.

The preserve is painted with color from Spring to early Fall. Along the boardwalks bloom giant blue iris, white swamp lilies, spider lilies, bluish pickerelweed, white popcorn flowers of arrowhead plants, soft pinks of marshmallow plants, yellow bur-marigolds, the buttonbush that attracts butterflies, and many more.

In March and April everything is blooming. In October, experience Fall changes and canoe treks. See the swamps and marsh by the light of the full moon on a ranger-led program in a canoe or on a trail. The Barataria Preserve in every season offers a place to be meditative, listen to the sounds of the swamps or be surprised by a new learning experience.

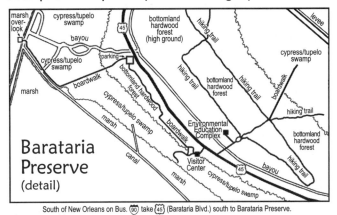

South of New Orleans on Bus. (90) take (45) (Barataria Blvd.) south to Barataria Preserve.

for more information: Jean Lafitte Nat. Historical Park & Preserve ~ 6588 Barataria Blvd. ~ Marrero, LA 70072 ~ 504-589-2330 ~ www.nps.gov/jela/index.htm

The Audubon Center at Beidler Forest west of Charleston, South Carolina

Located in the heart of the South Carolina Low-country between Columbia and Charleston, Four Holes Swamp is a 45,000-acre matrix of blackwater sloughs and lakes, shallow bottomland hardwoods, and deep bald cypress and tupelo gum flats – and a major tributary of the Edisto River. Fifteen thousand of those acres make up what is known as the Francis Beidler Forest.

The Visitor Center, a 1¾ mile boardwalk trail, miles of old logging roads for hiking, and a canoe trail (guided trips only), allow visitors to explore deep into the swamp's interior. Most of the huge bald cypresses in the sanctuary are about 1000 years old, but the oldest is 1500 years old.

Four Holes Swamp is a blackwater cypress/tupelo river swamp. The dark tannin-stained slow-flowing water gives it the "blackwater" portion of the classification. Bald cypress trees and tupelo gum trees predominate in the deepest areas of the swamp. The term "river swamp" refers to the riverine shape of the swamp (60 miles long, by 1½ miles wide in places) and the fact that the water in the swamp is flowing. Water levels vary wildly with the seasons, as the swamp is dependent upon rainfall for its flow. At highest water levels it can be a sheet of water 1½ miles wide. During dry times, it may be bone dry except for pockets of permanent water that are referred to as lakes.

Mammals: White-tailed deer, raccoons, bobcats, otters, gray squirrels, bats (including the rare southeastern big-eared bat), and other mammals roam the swamp.

Birds: Watch for barred owls, red-shouldered hawks, yellow-crowned night herons, flocks of white ibis, seven species of woodpeckers, and many kinds of songbirds. Four Holes Swamp is prothonotary warbler heaven and a good place to see the uncommon Swainson's warbler. The swamp routinely has some of the densest populations of nesting songbirds (for forested habitats) in the country.

Reptiles and Amphibians: Water snakes, greenish rat snakes, and cottonmouth snakes (cottonmouths are the swamp's only venomous species) are often seen from the boardwalk. Alligators and several turtle species love basking on logs in the lake at the boardwalk's end. Anoles and skinks use the boardwalk as a bridge to go from tree to tree. Several species of tree frogs and green frogs are commonly seen and heard throughout the swamp.

Fish and Water Creatures: You may catch glimpses of mudfish, bream, bluegills, crappie, gar, catfish, pickerel, and lots of "food chain fish" like mosquito fish, shiners, chubs and minnows. The swamp is a wonderful habitat for red crayfish, and it seems that just about everything eats them!

Insects and Spiders: Although many spider species live here, the most impressive are the huge fishing spiders (4"+ leg spread) and the golden silk spiders. Water striders and whirligig beetles skim and twirl on the water's surface. Many dragonfly species and the extremely common and beautiful green-tailed damselfly abound.

Trees, Shrubs and Other Plants: In addition to the common bald cypress and tupelo gum, expect to see a variety of mixed hardwoods such as laurel and overcup oaks, red maple, American and water elms, black gum, water locust, and water hickory in the dryer places. Shrubs such as highbush blueberry, Virginia willow, yaupon holly, and American beautyberry can be found throughout the swamp. The swamp's only epiphytic orchid, the greenfly orchid, blooms up in the trees in midsummer. One of the rarest flowers in the state, the dwarf trillium, lives only in Four Holes Swamp. It flowers in early spring along the walk.

Over time, the swamp has served as a source of fresh water, good hunting, and fishing for several Native American tribes. Projectile points and pottery shards dating as far back as 6000 BC have been found on the sanctuary.

In the early 20th century, much of Four Holes Swamp was logged for its biggest and best bald cypress. At that time, Francis Beidler set aside some of his timberlands and did nothing with them. When the Audubon Society and the Nature Conservancy discovered in the 1960s that Francis Beidler's heirs were selling the old growth stand of the Beidler Forest – the last virgin stand of this type of swamp forest – to a timber company, they purchased 3,415 acres of it to create the sanctuary.

Over the years, the Audubon Society and Nature Conservancy have grown the sanctuary to over 15,000 acres, with plans to continue expanding the protected portions of the swamp. Development from the greater Charleston area is spreading rapidly west toward the swamp, and the goal is to protect as much as possible of the swamp and its critical upland edge before that development arrives.

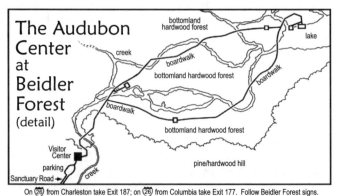

On 26 from Charleston take Exit 187; on 26 from Columbia take Exit 177. Follow Beidler Forest signs.

---

for more information: Beidler Forest Audubon Ctr ~ 336 Sanctuary Rd ~ Harleyville, SC 29448 ~ 843-462-2150 ~ www.beidlerforest.com

Big Thicket National Preserve just north of Beaumont TX

Big Thicket has been called "the biological crossroads of North America" due to the high number of different types of plants and animals found there. In this small area, several major North American biological influences bump up against each other: southeastern swamps, eastern forests, central plains, and southwest deserts. Bogs sit near arid sandhills. Eastern bluebirds nest near roadrunners. There are eighty-five tree species, more than sixty shrub species, and nearly one thousand other flowering plant species. Nearly one hundred and eighty-five kinds of birds live here or migrate through.

At one time, the area known as the Big Thicket covered almost 3.5 million acres. The few human residents were fiercely independent, getting everything they needed from the land. But the abundance of marketable trees eventually caught the attention of the timber industry, and much of the virgin forest was cut down.

Once vast, this combination of pine and cypress forest, hardwood forest, meadow, and blackwater swamp is but a remnant of its former self. Due to its unique biological diversity, nearly a hundred thousand acres of the Big Thicket were designated Big Thicket National Preserve by Congress in 1974 – the nation's first national preserve.

Mammals: White-tail deer, raccoons, bobcats, rabbits, grey squirrels, fox squirrels, opossums, skunks, and even panthers roam the Big Thicket. Non-native feral hogs are also present, and their diggings are uprooting and harming the native vegetation.

Birds: Look for great blue herons, great and snowy egrets, wood ducks, red-shouldered hawks, fish crows, northern cardinals, and belted kingfishers. Many small songbirds migrate through the Big Thicket in spring and autumn. Big Thicket was once home for the ivory-billed woodpecker, which was thought to be extinct for decades. One may have been recently spotted in a swamp in Arkansas, so there might possibly be some left in the less-visited depths of the Big Thicket!

Reptiles and Amphibians: Snakes include water snakes, garter snakes, cottonmouths, rat snakes, copperheads, rattlesnakes, and coral snakes. Tree frogs and spring peepers make up the frog chorus, while dwarf salamanders, skinks, and green anoles scurry around. Mud turtles, sliders, and box turtles may be seen poking along, keeping watch for the few alligators that live here.

Fish and Water Creatures: Watch for minnows, shiners, perch, sunfish, bass and crappies. Crawfish and mosquito-fish swim the shallows, looking for mosquito and other insect larvae. Catfish, eels, and even the rare paddlefish may be seen by the patient observer.

Insects and Spiders: You'll see flies, mosquitoes, butterflies, water striders, water boatmen and many other kinds of insects. Dragonflies and damselflies zoom through the air over wet areas. Golden silk spiders abound – you'll probably see many of their giant webs. Wolf spiders lie in wait for insect prey.

Trees, Shrubs and Other Plants: Big Thicket is home to four of the five carnivorous plants found in the U.S.: sundews, pitcher plants, butterworts, and floating bladderworts. Each has its own unique way of luring prey into its grasp. They all catch insects, generally, but larger plants may capture small frogs, too. They are usually found in bogs and wet prairies.

The cypress sloughs are known for bald cypress, tupelo trees, water elms and water hickories. Beautiful white-flowered swamp lilies are seen at the water's edge, as are the showy pickerelweeds. In spring and summer, a wide variety of wildflowers add a colorful note.

Big Thicket's baygalls are swampy areas that don't drain well and remain wet most of the year. The main trees and shrubs are gallberry hollies, sweetbays, black-gums, and titis, with their hanging clusters of white flowers. Other species may be present as well, such as wax myrtles, white bays, and various ferns and mosses.

What makes Big Thicket so unique is the fact that so many different types of plant communities grow near and even mix with each other. Scientists have noted that the biodiversity of the Big Thicket rivals that of the rain forests. With such an abundance of life, it is fortunate that Big Thicket was added to the National Park Service when it was. Today, park rangers protect Big Thicket National Preserve so that generations from now people can still appreciate this "Biological Crossroads of North America."

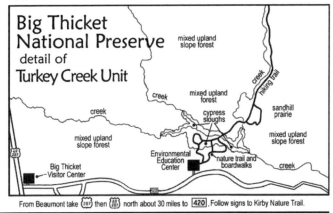

From Beaumont take (287) then (69) (96) north about 30 miles to [420]. Follow signs to Kirby Nature Trail.

for more information: Big Thicket National Preserve ~ 6102 FM 420 Rd ~ Kountze, TX, 77625 ~ 409-951-6725 ~ www.nps.gov/bith

Bluebonnet Swamp in Baton Rouge, Louisiana

Located in Louisiana's capital city, Bluebonnet Swamp is nestled in the heart of Baton Rouge. Tucked away on one hundred acres of natural area, this sixty-five acre wetland transports visitors out of the hustle and bustle of the city into a tranquil, wild cypress-tupelo swamp. With over two miles of walking trails and boardwalks, and an impressive exhibit building that houses many species of native reptiles and amphibians, visitors of all ages can enjoy seeing nature up close.

Bluebonnet Swamp was formed nearly three centuries ago as German farming immigrants moved into the area. In an effort to create easier passage over the mucky floodplain of the Mississippi River, settlers built Highland Road, incidentally blocking the flow of runoff into the river at several low-lying locations. The bottomland hardwood forest in one of these low-lying areas, in the presence of standing water, slowly gave way to the cypress-tupelo forest now known as Bluebonnet Swamp.

This small, isolated swamp remained untouched for more than two centuries, until the city of Baton Rouge expanded southward in the late 1970s and early 1980s and the forgotten swamp was rediscovered and identified as a unique ecological feature worthy of preservation. It was purchased by the Nature Conservancy of Louisiana in the late 1980s. The swamp was transferred to the Parks and Recreation Commission for the Parish of East Baton Rouge (BREC), and with the addition of forty acres of surrounding upland, became Baton Rouge's first nature-based park.

Many plants and animals call Bluebonnet Swamp home. Viewing wild animals in a natural situation requires quiet patience, sometimes difficult for younger visitors to attain. However, volunteer photographers have captured numerous images of the swamp's wildlife, which are regularly updated and on display in the nature center.

Mammals: Visitors with a keen eye and a bit of patience might be able to spot squirrels, raccoons, armadillos, opossums, minks, river otters, swamp rabbits, red foxes, and maybe even white-tailed deer.

Birds: Birds can be seen throughout the year, especially during annual migrations (Baton Rouge is located near the bottom of the Mississippi Flyway, the largest migratory route in North America). While wood ducks, white ibis, and other migratory species are less often seen, visitors might observe blue herons, egrets, owls, hawks, vultures, crows, and many songbirds year round. During migrations, listen for the calls of several species of warblers, and the rare but unmistakable "rain crow" (the yellow-billed cuckoo).

Reptiles and Amphibians: From the safety of the boardwalks, children of all ages will enjoy spotting turtles, snakes, and frogs in the murky swamp water. Most of the commonly seen snakes are harmless water snakes, but sometimes visitors get a chance to view the larger, venomous western cottonmouth. Along the gravel paths, you might see box turtles munching on wild strawberries; lizards and skinks lounging; or a non-venomous rat snake, kingsnake, racer, garter snake, or ribbon snake slipping away. And on the rarest of occasions, a lucky visitor may happen upon a sleek red and black mud snake hunting an amphiuma (a salamander).

Fish and Water Creatures: Sailfin mollies, mosquito fish, crawfish, and even leeches may be seen swimming by.

Insects and Spiders: In warmer months, butterflies and moths, including gulf fritillaries, monarchs, and the very rare Seminole crescent butterflies, delight visitors. They are joined by a variety of dragonflies, beetles, and honeybees. During the summer and fall, you'll be stunned by the size and beauty of the glistening orb webs of the golden silk spiders.

Trees, Shrubs and Other Plants: Bluebonnet Swamp is home to bald cypress, tupelo-gum, and Drummond red maple trees. Growing amidst these stately trees are other plants common to southern swamps – buttonbush, iris, lizard-tail, and swamp lily. In spring and fall, bright goldenrod, Indian pink, cardinal flower, jewelweed, native coneflower, and yellow-top grow in the meadow and along trails and water edges. Less showy flowers such as trillium, green dragon, and jack-in-the-pulpit dwell in the shade of upland hardwood trees such as oak, gum, elm, hickory, pawpaw, beech, and magnolia.

Though Bluebonnet Swamp is relatively young, it has gone through tremendous changes in the last fifty years as a direct result of urban development. Natural drainages leading water out of the swamp have been straightened and lined with concrete, and neighborhoods and businesses surround the swamp where forests and meadows once stood. Pollution, erosion, sedimentation, and altered drainage patterns all threaten the future of Bluebonnet Swamp.

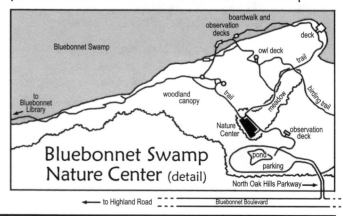

Bluebonnet Swamp Nature Center (detail)

for more information: BREC's Bluebonnet Swamp ~10503 North Oak Hills Parkway ~ Baton Rouge, LA 70810 ~ 225-757-8905 ~ www.brec.org

Bond Swamp National Wildlife Refuge six miles southeast of Macon, GA

Bond Swamp National Wildlife Refuge is a pristine wilderness area, located in central Georgia six miles south of Macon, where the Ocmulgee River flows through low-lying bottomlands butted up against a limestone ridge rich with seashells and marine fossils.

Established in 2000, and made up of more than 4,500 acres of river bottoms periodically flooded by the Ocmulgee River, Bond Swamp is one of Georgia's few remaining bottomland hardwood swamps. It is managed in coordination with Piedmont National Wildlife Refuge, and the adjacent Brown's Mount, which hosts a visitor center and interpretive exhibits. The swampy lowlands, featuring 100-foot-tall trees, extend far beyond the Refuge's borders, covering roughly 12,000 acres. The swamp contains hardwood and pine areas as well as bottomland swamps, beaver swamps and oxbow lakes.

The refuge is open daily all year round from dawn to dusk except during deer and feral hog hunts. Parts of the refuge may be closed during periods of flooding.

Mammals: You may spot white-tailed deer, bobcats, marsh and cottontail rabbits, raccoons, beaver, mink, muskrats, otters, squirrels, black bears, opossums, Seminole bats, armadillos, and even coyotes in and around Bond Swamp. Watch for feral hogs, too, which are wiping out native plants and are dangerous to people and pets. They eat acorns needed by squirrels, deer, bears, and turkeys during the fall and winter, and destroy the eggs of ground-nesting birds.

Birds: Bond Swamp and the wetlands surrounding it contain the highest concentrations of wintering waterfowl in central Georgia. Watch for wood ducks and other waterbirds, shorebirds, and waders such as great blue herons and great egrets. Migrating songbirds include Swainson's warblers, prothonotary warblers, yellow-billed cuckoos, wood thrushes, and Acadian flycatchers. Listen for woodpeckers and turkeys, and watch the sky for hawks, swallowtail kites and the pair of bald eagles, who have a nest in the swamp.

Reptiles and Amphibians: You may see green anoles, 5-lined skinks, river cooters, box turtles, eastern king snakes, snapping turtles, southern fence lizards, cottonmouths, copperheads, rattlesnakes, green treefrogs, spring peepers, and red-spotted newts. Ten-foot alligators have been seen.

Fish and Water Creatures: Look for largemouth and striped bass, white crappie, bluegill and red-eared sunfish, channel and flathead catfish, and shad in the warm swamp waters. In spring, you may also see shortnose and Atlantic sturgeon which migrate annually from coastal saltwater marshes to spawn. Keep an eye out for crawfish, too.

Insects and Spiders: As many as six swallowtail butterfly species, as well as hairstreaks, fritillaries, painted ladies, common buckeyes, admirals, and viceroys, flutter through the Refuge. Be prepared for mosquitoes and gnats. Golden-silk and fishing spiders are also common.

Trees, Shrubs and Other Plants: In these pristine bottomland hardwood swamps you'll find sweetgums, sycamores, black tupelos, longleaf pines, willows, liveoaks and water oaks, redbuds, hickories, tulip poplars and magnolias. You'll even find lowland canebrakes of river cane, a native bamboo, which grows to 30' and which once covered vast areas of Georgia's lowlands and riverbanks. Wildflowers such as Atamasco lilies, southern blue flags, lady's slippers and trumpet vines decorate the moist lowlands with color.

Hardwoods once were common along Georgia's lazy meandering rivers, but most swamps have now been drained, and their trees felled and replaced by farms and pine plantations.

Archaeologists have found flint spearpoints and scrapers in the Ocmulgee River floodplain dating from between 10,000 and 15,000 years ago. Native Americans, from Ice Age hunters to the Muscogees (Creeks) and Seminoles of historic times, relied on this rich region for food, water and shelter.

As Europeans settled and developed the area, they first traded with, then evicted, the original inhabitants who had tried to live peaceably with them. Then they logged the forests and built mills along the Ocmulgee River.

In recent years, the rapidly growing Macon area has begun to threaten the existence of even this last remnant of swamp. To protect and manage the river corridor, concerned citizens, plus local, state and federal government agencies, initiated the Ocmulgee Heritage Greenway effort to preserve what is left. Due to their hard work and persistence, visitors can now hike through more than three miles of nature trails to enjoy and appreciate this marvelous swamp environment.

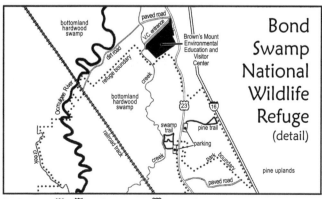

from Macon, take ⑦⑤ to ⑯ E, at Exit 6 go south on ㉓ s. Go 4.2 miles to the Stone Creek entrance on the right.

---

for more information: Bond Swamp NWR ~ c/o Piedmont NWR ~ 718 Juliette Road ~ Hillsboro, GA 31038 ~ 478-986-5441 ~ www.fws.gov/bondswamp

Congaree National Park southeast of Columbia, SC

Congaree National Park lies in the Congaree River floodplain in South Carolina's upper coastal plain. The Park borders the Congaree River for almost thirty miles until its junction with the Wateree River, where together the two rivers form the Upper Santee Swamp.

Some of the park's giant trees grow more than one hundred and fifty feet tall, in one of the tallest temperate forest canopies in the world. The park protects the largest intact remnant of old-growth bottomland forest in the U.S. and has received national and international recognition as a Globally Important Bird Area, an International Biosphere Reserve, and a designated Wilderness Area. Much of Cedar Creek within the park's boundaries is designated Outstanding National Resource Waters.

The Congaree River has run through its floodplain since at least the last ice age, and probably for as long as 60,000 years. The large valley containing the floodplain has many scarps (river cuts) and terraces (old floodplain deposits) dating back to the Pliocene, 3.5 million years ago. This valley has sand and clay deposits left behind by oceans and deltas as far back as the time of dinosaurs, 50-70 million years ago.

Congaree's floodplain forest is typically inundated for brief periods several times annually. The continuous deposition of sand and clay causes the river to change its course, or meander. When a meander in the river is cut off by a flood, an oxbow lake forms. The park features a variety of additional wetland ecosystems: cypress-tupelo sloughs, laurel and overcup oak flats, muck swamps, and streams.

Mammals: White-tailed deer, gray fox, river otter, gray squirrels, raccoons, and other mammals abound on the floodplain. Feral hogs heavily impact the floodplain by rooting in the soils and disturbing plants and other animals.

Birds: Congaree's old-growth forest is well-known for the sheer density of its bird species. Listen and watch for barred owls, red-shouldered hawks, pileated woodpeckers, and white-breasted nuthatches year-round. In the summer you will hear Mississippi kites, yellow-billed cuckoos, blue-gray gnatcatchers, prothonotary warblers, white-eyed vireos, and northern parula warblers. Winter visitors include hermit thrushes, yellow-bellied sapsuckers, ruby-crowned and golden-crowned kinglets, and winter wrens.

Reptiles and Amphibians: In drier spots, watch for eastern box turtles, green anoles, five-lined skinks, and black rat snakes. In and around water, you may see yellow-bellied sliders, river cooters, brown water snakes, red-bellied water snakes, marbled salamanders, barking tree frogs, and green tree frogs.

Aquatic Life: In the water look for bowfin, longnose gar, redfin pickerel, mudminnows, whirligig beetles, and water-striders. You may see crawfish chimneys along the trails.

Insects and Spiders: Tiger beetles patrol the paths, and many butterflies and dragonflies zoom overhead. Black and yellow garden (or writing) spiders and spiny orb weaver spiders spin their webs between trees.

Trees, Shrubs and Other Plants: Giant trees dwarf visitors to Congaree Swamp. Canopy species include bald cypress, loblolly pine, sweetgum, cherrybark oak, swamp chestnut oak, laurel oak, sycamore, water and swamp tupelo, and American elm. Wild grape, poison ivy, climbing hydrangea, supplejack and crossvines snake their way up trees. Red maple and American holly are found in the subcanopy, while ironwood, pawpaw, spicebush and deciduous holly are important understory trees. The forest floor includes switchcane, doghobble, ferns, and sedges; look for the endangered Carolina bogmint in summer.

Native Americans frequented the area as long as 10,000 years ago. Evidence of their passage can be found on bluffs, terraces, natural point bars and man-made mounds along the Congaree River valley. The Congaree River was named for the people whom explorers and settlers encountered.

Because of its fertile floodplain, parts of Congaree were among the first land grants in Richland County in the 1730s and 1740s. Agriculture had to be adapted to frequent flooding by tropical storms in the late summer and early fall and by freshets (sudden surges caused by rain) in the spring.

In the late 1800s, huge tracts of South Carolina's bottomland hardwood forest, including mature 500 to 700-year-old bald cypress, began to fall to the axe. By 1915, much of the old-growth cypress was gone. In the 1950s, writer and outdoorsman Harry Hampton began a long, lonely campaign to protect what was left of the forest. Motivated by renewed old-growth logging in the late 1960s, environmentalists formed the Congaree Swamp National Preserve Association to protect the Congaree floodplain. In 1976, Congress designated 15,000 acres of Congaree Swamp as a National Monument. Eventually expanded to 26,000 acres, the park was redesignated Congaree National Park in 2003, becoming South Carolina's first and only national park.

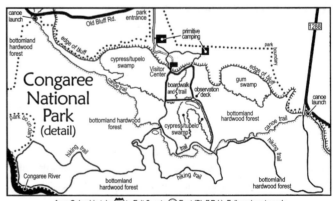

from Columbia take 77 to Exit 5, onto 48 East (Bluff Rd.). Follow signs to park.

---

for more information: Congaree National Park ~ 100 National Park Road ~ Hopkins, SC 29061 ~ 803-776-4396 ~ www.nps.gov/cosw
Friends of Congaree Swamp ~ PO Box 7746 ~ Columbia, SC 29202 ~ 803-783-9270 ~ www.friendsofcongaree.org

Audubon's Corkscrew Swamp Sanctuary near Naples, Florida

Located in extreme southern Florida, Audubon's Corkscrew Swamp has the largest remaining stand of old-growth cypress forest and the largest breeding colony of endangered wood storks in the US. Its warm climate supports a greater variety of plants and animals than may be found in more northerly swamps. Fed by rainwater flowing from Lake Trafford to the northeast, Corkscrew's waters eventually wind their way to the Gulf of Mexico.

A two-mile boardwalk meanders from the Visitor Center through palm and pine uplands, and wet prairie and marsh habitats into an ancient bald cypress forest with trees up to 100 feet tall.

Corkscrew Swamp is wettest during fall and early winter after spring and summer rains flood the sanctuary. Throughout the winter and early spring, water levels recede, the weather is dry and cooler, and visitors can observe migratory bird species as well as nesting raptors and wading birds. When spring and summer rains return, alligators mate and nest, pig frogs chorus in the swamp, and swallow-tailed kites and nesting wood storks soar high above.

Mammals: Endangered Florida panthers, bobcats, bears, white-tail deer, rabbits, raccoons, gray squirrels, river otters, bats, opossums and armadillos roam the sanctuary. Feral pigs dig in the oak hammock – fine food for panthers.

Birds: Nearly 200 bird species visit or live in Corkscrew Swamp. Endangered wood storks nest in the bald cypress trees. Watch for barred owls, red-shouldered hawks, roseate spoonbills, American bitterns, purple gallinules, egrets, ibis, herons, limpkins, anhingas, woodpeckers, and Florida sandhill cranes year round. Sightings vary throughout the year as water levels rise and fall. Seasonal migratory birds include painted buntings, indigo buntings, and pine warblers. Swallow-tailed kites arrive in February from Brazil, then gather for their long return flight in August.

Reptiles and Amphibians: Many reptile and amphibian species swim through the black water and slither through the trees. Alligators, water moccasins, banded water snakes, rough green snakes, peninsula ribbon snakes, red-bellied turtles, peninsula cooters, softshell turtles, mud turtles, Florida snapping turtles, Carolina anoles, leopard frogs, pig frogs, and tree frogs all frequent the cypress swamp. Dusky pigmy rattlesnakes, black racers, rat snakes and oak toads prefer the pine upland areas. The endangered gopher tortoise has recently been sighted at the sanctuary.

Fish and Water Creatures: Gar, catfish, bowfin and bass are among the larger fish species, while sailfin molly, mosquito fish, minnows and flagfish are eaten by smaller swamp predators. Freshwater shrimp and crawfish, along with newts, sirens (amphibians), and apple snails, provide meals for wading birds, young 'gators and small mammals.

Insects and Spiders: Beautiful butterflies – zebras, viceroys, ruddy daggerwings, white peacocks, queens, sulphurs and swallowtails – are frequently sighted. In the water, watch for whirligig beetles, water striders, water scorpions, and fishing spiders. Dragonflies and damselflies are seen in both aquatic larval and colorful adult forms. Young lubber grasshoppers, black with a yellow stripe, quickly molt into gargantuan orange and yellow adults.

Trees, Shrubs and Other Plants: Corkscrew's forests shelter both temperate and tropical plants: Live and laurel oak, myrsine, and wax myrtle thrive in hydric hammocks, hosting butterfly orchids and shoestring ferns. Slash pines, saw palmettos, and sabal palms dominate the pine flatwood habitats. In the swamp, cypress trees, pond apples, strangler figs and swamp bays abound. Pickerelweed, alligator flag, pop ash and red maples all grow in the ancient bald cypress cathedral. Tree limbs are covered with resurrection ferns, lichens and epiphytes, including many orchids. Sunflowers bloom in the fall, blue flag iris in the spring, and scarlet hibiscus during the summer. Swamp lilies bloom year round.

The plume-hunting era of the late 1800s almost wiped out great egrets and other wading birds in the eastern US. Audubon wardens in the early 1900s risked and sometimes lost their lives protecting Audubon rookeries from rifles. Just as bird populations began to recover under the protection of the law, cypress trees, which are water, rot and termite resistant, began to fall to logging company saws.

Corkscrew Swamp Sanctuary was officially established in 1954 to save the old-growth cypress trees. The National Audubon Society protected the cypress swamp and wading bird populations in the majestic sanctuary visitors see today. Continued development, population growth and habitat fragmentation still threaten wildlife all over Florida. Corkscrew Sanctuary, covering more than 12,000 acres, protects an impressive cross-section of truly wild Florida.

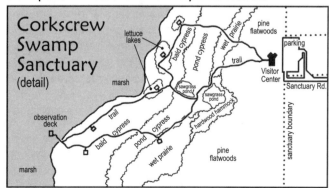

Corkscrew Swamp Sanctuary (detail)

75 to exit 111 (Immokalee Road), then east about 15 miles to Sanctuary Road. Do NOT take Corkscrew Exit.

for more information: Corkscrew Swamp Sanctuary ~ 375 Sanctuary Road West ~ Naples, FL 34120 ~ 239-348-9151 ~ www.corkscrew.audubon.org

Okefenokee Swamp on the borders of SE Georgia and NE Florida near Folkston and Fargo, GA

Okefenokee Swamp is one of the best-preserved freshwater wetlands in the U.S. Extending thirty-eight miles north to south and twenty-five miles east to west, over 90% of the 438,000 acre swamp is protected within the Okefenokee National Wildlife Refuge, which offers access on the eastern side. Stephen C. Foster State Park provides access on the swamp's western boundary.

Okefenokee is a vast bog inside a huge, saucer-shaped depression that was once part of the ocean floor. Peat deposits up to fifteen feet thick cover much of the swamp floor, and some of these deposits rise to the surface and eventually form tree islands, which quiver and shake when stepped upon.

The slow-moving waters of the Okefenokee are tea-colored and acidic due to the tannic acid released from decaying plants. The swamp forms the headwaters for two rivers, the historic Suwannee River, which flows southwest into the Gulf of Mexico, and the St. Mary's River, which flows to the southeast into the Atlantic Ocean.

The swamp's five major habitats – open water, prairie, forested wetlands, scrub-shrub, and upland forest – harbor many species of animals and plants. You might see:

Mammals: White-tail deer, raccoons, fox squirrels, black bear, river otters, bobcats, marsh rabbits, and red foxes inhabit the swamp and surrounding dry edge.

Birds: Great blue herons, green-backed herons, and black-crowned night herons, along with great egrets, cattle egrets, white ibis, wood storks, and sandhill cranes are some of the wading birds which hunt for fish and insects in the swamp. Black vultures and turkey vultures, osprey, red-tailed hawks, and American kestrels hunt from overhead. Wood ducks and owls – Eastern screech, great horned and barred – make their homes in tree cavities above the water. Woodpeckers – red-headed, pileated, and hairy, plus the endangered red-cockaded – inhabit the drier upland forests. Warblers, wrens, thrashers, vireos, finches, cowbirds, sparrows, and robins migrate through or live in the Okefenokee.

Reptiles and Amphibians: American alligators, along with Florida soft-shell turtles, sliders, snappers, and mud turtles, bask in the dark swamp waters. Black, red, gray and yellow rat snakes, kingsnakes, hognose, and the indigo (America's longest snake), are also found in the refuge. Venomous snakes include the Eastern coral, Florida cottonmouth, and three types of rattlesnakes. The calls of pig frogs, spring peepers, and green tree frogs fill the air after a heavy rain.

Fish and Water Creatures: Okefenokee has many kinds of fish: channel catfish, flier, warmouth, bluegill, largemouth bass, bowfin, and Florida gar, plus other common fish species. And, of course, there are plenty of feisty crawfish.

Insects and Spiders: Swallowtail butterflies, dragonflies, damselflies, dung beetles, water striders, golden-silk and diving spiders are just some of the hundreds of insects and spiders that make Okefenokee their home.

Trees, Shrubs and Other Plants: Okefenokee Swamp is covered with cypress, blackgum, and bay forests scattered throughout a flooded prairie featuring grasses, sedges, and various aquatic plants. The surrounding upland and almost seventy islands within the swamp are forested with slash and longleaf pine intermixed with hardwood hammocks. Lakes of varying sizes and depths, and floating sections of peat, are also part of the Okefenokee terrain.

The earliest known inhabitants of the Okefenokee Swamp were tribes of the Depford Culture about 4,500 years ago. The last Native Americans to reside in the swamp, the Seminoles, were forced out in the 1850s. Numerous "swamper" families then settled the area, and operated small homesteads for the next 100 years.

In 1891, the Suwannee Canal Company purchased most of the swamp with the intent to drain it and reclaim the land for agricultural purposes. Their attempt failed, but other companies made fortunes by logging the swamp's virgin pine and cypress forests until 1927. In 1936, most of the swamp was purchased by the federal government to protect it as habitat for migratory birds. Today, Okefenokee and S.C. Foster State Park are managed together as a national wildlife refuge.

to reach S.C. Foster State Park take 177 NE from Fargo 17 miles.

With boardwalks, trails, boat rentals and tours, both the refuge and the state park are well worth visiting.

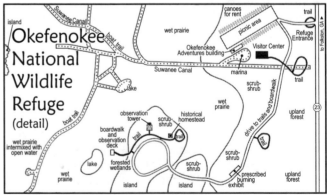

to reach Okefenokee, take 121 23 south from Folkston, GA, 11 miles to Refuge Entrance.

for more information: Okefenokee National Wildlife Refuge ~ Route 2, Box 3330 ~ Folkston, GA 31537 ~ 912-496-7836 ~ www.fws.gov/okefenokee
Stephen C. Foster State Park ~ 17515 Hwy. 177 ~ Fargo, GA 31631 ~ 912-637-5274 ~ http://gastateparks.org/info/scfoster

Weeks Bay Swamp & Pitcher Plant Bog

Located at the extreme southern end of Alabama at Mobile Bay, the Weeks Bay National Estuarine Research Reserve was incorporated in 1986 to help preserve and protect the fragile coastal area from development and pollution. Federal, state, and local communities working hand in hand with The Nature Conservancy have purchased and protected this unique coastal wetland ecosystem. More acreage is added regularly.

Currently covering more than six thousand acres, the Weeks Bay Reserve protects several very different ecosystems: from pine savannah, dry upland forest and lower forested wetland, to a remarkable pitcher plant bog. There are estuarine lowland and freshwater swamps and water bottoms, plus freshwater, brackish and salt marshes – including a sawgrass marsh – marching down to the edges of Weeks Bay, which opens out onto Mobile Bay, a brackish (slightly salty) estuary leading out into the Gulf of Mexico.

Trails and boardwalks allow visitors close-up access to most of these ecosystems from the Visitor Center, but you'll have to take a short drive to the pitcherplant bog, which lies across the Fish River from the Center. Here, carnivorous plants grow right next to the boardwalk for close examination. Widely spaced loblolly pines cast light shade over parts of the bog, and a firebreak surrounds the bog, parts of which are burned off regularly to encourage a natural succession of plants. Since cottonmouth snakes are resident in the Reserve, it isn't wise to step off any paths or boardwalks at any time. Watch for the following wildlife from both sides of the bog boardwalk (and in other parts of the Reserve as well):

Mammals: Marsh rabbits, bobcats, mink, weasels, opossums, gray and red foxes, river otters, and armadillos all find food in the bog.

Birds: Look for sora, king and Virginia rails, marsh wrens, common snipes, and common moorhens lurking in the grasses. Around the bog you may spot downy, red-bellied, red-cockaded, and pileated woodpeckers. Watch overhead for soaring bald eagles, turkey and black vultures, kestrels, red-tailed and red-shouldered hawks, and Mississippi kites. You might see great egrets, cattle egrets, and great blue herons stalking through the low vegetation seeking grasshoppers and other insects. Watch also for smaller birds like sparrows, warblers and eastern kingbirds. As dusk approaches, listen for barred owls and great horned owls.

Reptiles and Amphibians: If you're lucky you may see a gopher tortoise, box turtle or flatwoods salamander, perhaps beneath the boardwalk. Look for such snakes as banded water snakes, coachwhips, gray rat snakes and cottonmouths. Several species of frogs (including bullfrogs), as well as southern toads, can be heard and sometimes seen around the bog.

Fish and Water Creatures: There's seldom any standing water in the bog, so you won't see fish, but watch for crawfish chimneys and their busy builders.

Insects and Spiders: Insects love bogs. You may see buckeyes, monarchs, tiger swallowtails and gulf fritillary butterflies. Look for polka-dot and hummingbird moths. In the taller grasses you're likely to see the huge lubber and other grasshoppers, and the air may be alive with dragonflies, damselflies, bees and wasps, and the funny little connected love-bugs. The lacy dew-spangled webs of golden-silk spiders decorate the bog on damp, cool mornings, and wolf and green lynx spiders stalk their prey through the foliage.

Trees, Shrubs and Other Plants: The bog is mostly populated by small plants, a great many of which are carnivorous since the soil isn't rich enough to keep these highly specialized plants healthy without an occasional addition of insect protein. Watch for white-topped, pale, and crimson pitcher plants, sundews, grass-pink orchids, whitetop sedges, bright orange pine lilies, and rose pogonias. Sphagnum moss may cover the ground between taller plants. Many of the bog plants are rare and protected, so look, but do not touch.

Native Americans once lived a bountiful lifestyle in this area, hunting in the marshes, swamps and forests; crawdadding and netting for fish in the creeks, rivers and the Gulf; and feasting on mussels and other bounty from the ocean beaches. Their burial mounds and shell middens, where they piled shells from the shellfish they ate, are found throughout the Reserve.

Weeks Bay is fairly well protected against damage from humans, but hurricanes can bring devastating winds which break off trees, and high water can flood plants with life-stunting saltwater. Coastal habitats which evolved under such hurricane conditions eventually recover after such catastrophic events, provided human activities haven't seriously overwhelmed the environment. By the way, while you're in the area you might enjoy a visit to Biophilia Nature Center's 10-acre tupelo gum swamp. See their website (at the bottom of this page) for directions.

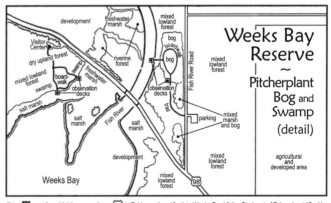

Take 10 east from Mobile, go south on 98 to Fairhope, then 12 mi. to Weeks Bay Visitor Ctr. (west of Foley about 12 mi.)

---

for more information: Weeks Bay Reserve Foundation ~ 11401 US Highway 98 ~ Fairhope, AL 36532 ~ 251-990-5004 ~ www.weeksbay.org
Biophilia Nature Center, Native Plant Nursery & Bookstore (near Fairhope) ~ 12695 C.R. 95 ~ Elberta, AL 36530 ~ 251-987-1200 ~ www.biophilia.net

Index

ern water- 43; venomous- 107; water- 42, 47, 111, 112, 113, 114; water moccasin- 94, 117; yellow rat- 118

snakeskin- 67

snapper. (See turtle, snapping)

snipe; common- 119

soapstone- 41

soil; acid- 11; limestone- 11

songbird- 112

sourgum. (See gum, sour)

sowbug- 66

Spanish moss. (See moss, Spanish)

spatterdock- 10, 34, 35, 103

spawn- 43, 85

spearpoint- 115

specific name. (See scientific name)

spicebush- 116

spider- 72; argiope- 52, 111; black widow- 52; brown recluse- 52; cephalothorax- 20; diagram- 20; diving- 118; fishing- 76, 81, **82, 83,** 92, 93, 111, 112, 115, 117; flower crab- 52; garden- 52; golden-silk- 51, **52, 53,** 111, 112, 113, 114, 115, 118, 119; green lynx- 82, 119; jumping- 11, 19, **20, 21;** palp- 20; spiny-bodied orb- 52, 116; tarantula- 82; web. (See spiderweb) wolf- 82, 113, 119

spiderweb- 52; orb web- 52, 53; silk- 20; dragline- 20, 82; sheet-web- 82; spinnerets- 20, 82;

spiderwort- 6

spiracle- 64

spittlebug- 90, 108

spoonbill; roseate- 117

squealer. (See wood duck)

squirrel- 114, 115; flying- 92, 93; fox- 7, 48, 113, 118; gray- 7, **48, 49,** 51, 111, 112, 113, 116, 117; nest- 48; tracks- 48; skull- 48

staggerbush- 8

starling- 22, 104

Stephen C. Foster State Park- 118

stinkbug. (See bug; stink)

stork; wood- 7, 58, 117, 118

strangler fig- 11

strawberry; wild- 114

strider. (See water strider)

sturgeon; Atlantic- 115; shortnose- 115

sumac; dwarf- 88; shining- 88; winged- 88, 89, 91

sundew- 10, 57, 113, 119; pink- 56; threadleaf- 56

sunflower- 117

sunscreen- 106

sun tea- 24, 108

supplejack- 116

swallow- 99; barn- 100; rough-winged- 100; tree- 99, 100

swamp- 10, 11; beaver- 115; blackwater- 113; black-water cypress/tupelo river- 112; bottomland hardwood- 115; cypress-tupelo- 114; estuarine low-land-119; mangrove, 11; muck- 116; tupelo-cypress- 111

swan- 58

sweetbay. (See magnolia, sweetbay)

sweetgum- 6, 27, 49, 61, 111, 115, 116

sweetspire- 92, 93

swift- 40, 99; chimney- 100

swimmerets- 38, 39

switchcane. (See cane)

sycamore- 6, 49, 115, 116

T

tadpole. (See frog)

talons- 16, 46

tannin- 10, 112

tarflower- 8

termite- 50; Formosan subterranean- 104

terrace- 116

territorial- 56

territory- 61

thermal- 98

thrasher- 50, 118

thrush; hermit- 116; wood- 115

tick- 20, 106; black-legged- 62; removing- 106

titi- 113

titmouse- 66

toad- 14, 102; cane- 104; oak- 117; southern- 97, 119

tortoise; gopher- 80, 117, 119

toxin- 21

tracks- 108

trail- 114, 118, 119

treefrog- 11, 66, 111, 112, 113, 117; Cuban- 104; green- 17, 101, **102, 103,** 115, 116, 118; squirrel- 102

trillium- 114; dwarf- 112

tropics- 54

tulip tree- 6, 98, 99; tulip poplar- 115; yellow poplar; 98

tupelo- 10, 22, 23, 27, 112, 113; black- 115; swamp- 116; tupelo-gum- 111, 114; water- 116

turkey- 115

turtle- 35, 111; box- 80, 113, 114, 115, 116, 119; carapace- 76; chicken- 79, **80, 81;** cooter- 80, 81; peninsula-117; river- 115, 116; eggs- 80, 81; Florida soft-shell- 118; mud- 80, 81, 113, 117, 118; plastron- 76, 80; red-bellied slider- 117; slider- 79, 81, 113, 118; yellow-bellied slider- 80, 116; snapping- 11, 14, 25, **76, 77,** 79, 115, 118; alligator snapping- 76; softshell- 80, 81, 117; stinkpot- 35, 79, 80, 81; yolk sac- 80

U

ultraviolet- 102

upland- 6; hardwood- 114; palm- 117; pine- 117

Upper Santee Swamp- 116

V

V-formation- 58

Velociraptor- 66

venom- 94

viburnum- 6

vine; pepper- 6; rattan- 6; trumpet- 6, 10, 115

viper; pit- 94, diagram- 94; facial pits- 94; eggs- 94

vireo- 118; white-eyed- 116

Virginia creeper- 6, 94

Virginia willow- 92

vision; binocular- 16; color- 90

Vitamin D- 106

vulture- 26, 31, 111, 114; black- 46, **98, 99,** 118, 119; chick- 98; soaring- 98, 99; turkey- 40, 46, 98, 99, 118, 119

W

walking stick; make one- 108

warbler- 118; northern parula- 116; pine- 117; prothonotary- 46, 112, 115, 116; Swainson's- 112, 115

warmouth- 118

wasp- 119; hunting- 82, 83; ichneumon- 100, 101; paper- 52, 53; yellow jacket- 52

waterlily- 10, 71, 75, 77, 81, 103; white- 82

waterlily, yellow. (See spatterdock)

water boatman- 72, 113

waterbug, giant- 72

water hyacinth- 10, 104

water scorpion- 117

water spangles- 15, 44

water strider- 71, **72, 73,** 75, 83, 112, 113, 116, 117, 118; pond skater- 72; skipper- 72

wax myrtle- 6, 8, 26, 37, 51, 111, 113, 117

weasel- 119; long-tailed- 56, **68, 69**

web. (See spiderweb)

Weeks Bay National Estuarine Research Reserve- 119

Weeks Bay Swamp & Pitcher Plant Bog- 119

weevil; acorn- 18

West Nile virus- 106

wetland- 9, 10, 11, 56, 58; draining- 86; forested- 118, 119

wet prairie- 10, 58, 113, 117

whip-poor-will- 32, 102

whistler. (See wood duck)

wild boar. (See hog, feral)

Wilderness Area- 116

willow- 26, 27, 57, 93, 115; black- 10, 111; Virginia- 10, 112

wing- 46, 66

wiregrass- 8

witch hazel- 6

woodpecker- 99, 112, 117; downy- 119; flicker- 30; hairy- 118; ivory-billed- 30, 113; pileated- 30, 31, 111, 116, 118, 119; red-bellied- **30, 31,** 111, 119; red-cockaded- 30, 118, 119; red-headed- 118; skull- 30; tongue- 30; yellow-bellied sapsucker- 30

woody. (See wood duck)

wren- 40, 118; Bewick's- 66; Carolina- 65, **66, 67,** 69; marsh- 66, 119; winter- 116

Y

yellow-belly.(See turtle, yellow-bellied)

yellow-top- 114

yellow poplar. (See tulip tree)

Z

zapper; bug- 106

zooplankton- 84